Constitutional Environmental Rights

Constitutional Environmental Rights

Tim Hayward

OXFORD
UNIVERSITY PRESS

OXFORD

UNIVERSITY PRESS

Great Clarendon Street, Oxford OX2 6DP

Oxford University Press is a department of the University of Oxford.
It furthers the University's objective of excellence in research, scholarship,
and education by publishing worldwide in

Oxford New York

Auckland Cape Town Dar es Salaam Hong Kong Karachi Kuala Lumpur
Madrid Melbourne Mexico City Nairobi New Delhi Shanghai Taipei Toronto

With offices in

Argentina Austria Brazil Chile Czech Republic France Greece
Guatemala Hungary Italy Japan South Korea Poland Portugal
Singapore Switzerland Thailand Turkey Ukraine Vietnam

Oxford is a registered trade mark of Oxford University Press
in the UK and in certain other countries

Published in the United States
by Oxford University Press Inc., New York

British Library Cataloguing in Publication Data

Data available

Library of Congress Cataloging in Publication Data

Hayward, Tim.
        Constitutional environmental rights / Tim Hayward.
        p.cm.
        Includes bibliographical references.
        ISBN 0-19-927867-9 (alk. paper) - ISBN 0-19-927868-7 (alk. paper)
        1. Environmental justice - Political aspects. I. Title.
        GE220.H39 2005
363.7-dc22   2004023817

ISBN 0-19-927867-9 (hbk)
ISBN 0-19-927868-7 (pbk)

3 5 7 9 10 8 6 4 2

Typeset by Newgen Imaging Systems (P) Ltd., Chennai, India
Printed in Great Britain
on acid-free paper by
Biddles Ltd., King's Lynn, Norfolk

For David and Holly

Contents

Acknowledgements

Work on this book was initially stimulated through conversations with several friends and colleagues. For their encouragement, and for their guidance on legal aspects of the inquiry, thanks go to Michael Anderson, Alan Boyle, Christine Boch, Chris Himsworth, Antonia Layard, and Leonor Moral Soriano. Drafts of the work in progress benefited from discussions at various seminars, conferences, and workshops, and I would like to thank everyone who has contributed to its development at these events and in personal conversation, in particular Brian Barry, John Barry, Avner De-Shalit, Andrew Dobson, Andrew Light, David Miller, John O'Neill, Graham Smith, and Susan Stephenson.

A substantial portion of the initial research was made possible by ESRC grant R000222269 and this is gratefully acknowledged. Part of the research was conducted during a visiting fellowship at the Oxford Centre for Ethics, Environment and Society (OCEES), Hilary Term 1998, for which I warmly thank my hosts at Mansfield College. The rest of the work was carried out at the University of Edinburgh where I have enjoyed the support of excellent colleagues and the additional freedom to write afforded by a couple of terms' sabbatical leave. The University also supported the 1998 public seminar 'Constitutional Environmental Rights for Scotland?', whose assembled panel of lawyers, campaigners, and politicians helped simultaneously to broaden and to focus the perspectives that have come to inform this work, and I would particularly like to thank, in addition to people named elsewhere, Sarah Boyack and Andy Myles. I am also indebted to Eurig Scandrett and Friends of the Earth Scotland for the insights yielded by several seminars they have sponsored on environmental justice.

Special thanks go to my colleagues Russell Keat and Lynn Dobson for reading all of the chapters at critical stages in their development and making numerous constructive suggestions for improvements. In my final push to get the book completed, too, they were generous in their assistance. For comments on individual chapters I am also very grateful to Elizabeth Bomberg, Sara Rich Dorman, Robyn Eckersley, Cecile Fabre, Elizabeth Fisher, Kimberly Hutchings, Ben Minteer, and Bob Pepperman Taylor.

It goes without saying that no one other than the author can be held responsible for errors or omissions, but particularly with regard to questions of law, on which I am no expert, I emphasize that any mistakes will be my own, and that the good advice of those I here thank certainly saved me from making others.

Chapter 4 is a lightly revised version of a chapter that appeared in Ben A. Minteer and Bob Pepperman Taylor (eds.) *Democracy and the Claims of Nature* (Lanham, MD and Oxford: Rowman & Littlefield, 2002), and I thank the publishers for their permission to reproduce the material here.

Introduction

The central claim of this book is that a right of every individual to an environment adequate for their health and well-being should receive express provision in the constitution of any modern democratic state. This claim is to be defended against six general lines of criticism which will be outlined in the latter part of this Introduction. First, though, the general background and rationale for the claim will be sketched out.

1 Background

The argument of this book has developed out of research guided by the initial, tentatively formulated question, 'would constitutional environmental rights be a good idea?' The question arose on the basis of two quite general thoughts: first, that environmental protection is sufficiently important to warrant the provision of guarantees for it at the highest political level, which for practical purposes means the constitutional; second, that because environmental protection is equally important for everyone, and for reasons which transcend the particular terms of any actual political association, it ought to be considered a human right. Combining these thoughts suggests a general case in favour of constitutional recognition of a fundamental right to an adequate environment. As I shall shortly explain, though, there are significant differences between suggesting there is a case and actually explicating and defending such a case.

While still formulating a research plan, I scoured the literature of political theory—both 'green' and mainstream—to find how the case had been treated to date. But the main finding was that it had not been considered at all. Some political philosophers had lent theoretical support for the principle articulated in the 1987 Brundtland Report of a fundamental human right of everyone to an environment adequate for their health and well-being, and some 'green' theorists had considered the general merits of such a right in relation to environmental goals. Yet, if a human right to an adequate environment were to be effectively implemented, it would need to be recognized in states' constitutions alongside the established rights of constitutional democracies, and the question whether it could or should be I did not find addressed anywhere. Nor did I find any political theory discussions of constitutional approaches to environmental protection more generally.

Yet if political theorists had not attended to the hypothetical question of whether constitutional environmental rights would be a good idea, it was all the more significant to discover that as a matter of fact, at the time in question, around 1997, there were already some thirty states, constitutions in the world that provided express environmental rights. Reflecting on this fact was an extensive literature of legal theory which has continued to develop, and has provided the greater part of the material examined in the subsequent research and presented in this book. This meant that the question need not be treated as a purely hypothetical one: the framers of some thirty constitutions, at least, had already thought the idea a good one. The question now became that of whether the reasons in favour of the idea were of more general applicability. It has also been tempting to ask whether this indicates a trend pointing in the direction of an eventually universal recognition of environmental rights as an integral and standard part of the constitutional commitments of a modern state. In the course of the research for this book I have uncovered many good reasons to think that it might. What the research has also uncovered, though, are equally many counterarguments.

The question whether a growing number of states *will* constitutionalize environmental rights is a matter of empirical prediction on which I would not directly venture comment; the question of concern here is whether any given state, or at least any state with the features of a modern constitutional democracy, *ought* to do so. This question, then, is of a general form: it is not asking whether any particular state might, for reasons that could be quite specific to its own political culture, decide it ought to provide such rights; it is asking whether there are reasons applying with similar normative force to any constitutional democracy at all. If there are such general reasons they must, or so I shall argue, presuppose that there is a fundamental human right to environmental protection which is a genuinely universal right in as robust a sense as those already recognized as such. At the heart of the affirmative answer to the question which I have eventually come to formulate there is thus the following basic argument. The right of every individual to an environment adequate for their health and well-being is a fundamental human right; every constitutional democracy ought (among other things) to guarantee fundamental human rights as fundamental rights in its constitution; therefore every constitutional democracy ought to guarantee this right as a fundamental right in its constitution.

Now while there is widespread evidence that such an argument has the plausibility to make the question ripe for discussion, that evidence should by no means be taken to imply that the argument has already won the day. There will certainly be people who would readily assent to it, and many who campaign on the basis of it, and, as has been noted, in some states they have even met with success. Against this, however, have to be set some significant countervailing considerations. To begin with, if a number of states—and on a recent reckoning it is around fifty[1]—have constitutional environmental rights, that still means the majority of states, including the preponderance of the wealthiest and most powerful states, do not; of those that do, a closer inspection of the force and status of the rights provided reveals that they are not always considered to be on a par with the more established rights; also, among the states that provide them are a number which cannot be said to have an especially impressive record in practice of either environmental or human rights protection. Indeed, some of the states with much better records on those scores have set themselves in principled opposition against constitutionalizing the right. Finally, despite the various references to such a right that can be found in international law (see Chapter 1, Section 1.4), there has been no binding statement or authoritative declaration of the 'existence' of that right such as could be taken to provide definitive normative direction to constitution framers.

Where there is little significant disagreement, though, is about the importance of making some form of provision for environmental protection at the constitutional level, even if in the form of a state duty or objective rather than necessarily as a fundamental individual right. This is now indeed widely recognized. Globally, more than a hundred countries have constitutional environmental provisions of some kind; no recently promulgated constitution omits these, and many older constitutions are being amended to include them.[2] Where there is also little significant disagreement—as I shall shortly show—is about the existence of practical connections between the pursuit of environmental aims and the protection of human rights. Taken together, these two broad areas of agreement allow the main substantial elements of the rationale for constitutional environmental rights to be made evident. However, it has also to be stressed that they are not, even in conjunction, sufficient to establish the case.

In the section that follows, therefore, I shall briefly explain why agreement on the desirability of constitutional provisions for environmental protection and agreement on the existence of significant linkages between environmental and human rights aims are based on considerations about the world that amount to necessary, yet not sufficient, conditions for claiming that there is a fundamental right to an adequate environment that ought to be constitutionalized.

2 Rationale

The challenge for this book is not to show that constitutions should say *something* about the environment, as there is little controversy about this; rather, it is to show that the constitutional commitment should be to provide for its protection as a *fundamental right*. That is to say, the provision should not take the form of some less binding constitutional commitment such as a statement of social policy; it should not be classed merely among 'social rights' as such a category is sometimes distinguished from fundamental rights proper; and it should not provide solely procedural rights (such as rights to information, access to justice, and to environmental decision-making). In what follows I shall first show why the rationale for constitutional environmental protection suggests but does not strictly entail a case for constitutional environmental rights; I shall then show why the evident linkages between environmental protection and human rights suggest, but do not strictly entail, a case for considering environmental protection itself to be a fundamental right such as should be constitutionally entrenched.

2.1 The rationale for a constitutional approach to environmental protection

Environmental problems today are ubiquitous, and they threaten potentially everybody, relatively indiscriminately;[3] they can be serious enough to present a threat to states' security and to create new sources of interstate tension. The most general rationale for taking a constitutional approach to environmental protection, therefore, is that the seriousness, extensiveness, and complexity of environmental problems are such as to prompt a need for concerted, coordinated political action aimed at protecting all members of populations on an enduring basis.

Constitutional level provision for environmental protection has the potential to meet these needs in a number of ways.

First, and most generally, it enshrines a recognition of the importance a society attaches to environmental protection. Constitutional provisions 'achieve the highest rank among legal norms, a level at which a given value trumps every statute, administrative rule, or court decision' (Brandl and Bungert 1992: 4); 'laws below the constitutional level have a weaker position than constitutional laws because ordinary legislation may be easily amended, overruled or altogether nullified' (Witzsch 1992: 10).

Secondly, constitutional provisions can promote the coordination of environmental protection measures within a jurisdiction. In most jurisdictions environmental laws and regulations have developed in a disparate piecemeal fashion. While this is to some extent unavoidable—given the complex, multifaceted, and unpredictable character of environmental phenomena, and how these bear on various social and legal matters in various different ways—many commentators nevertheless stress the need for a unifying basis for the integration of various laws.[4] Indeed, since environmental law is not a strictly defined area of law, but one whose provisions overlap criminal, property, construction, and water law, an advantage of constitutionalizing environmental goals is that it provides an overarching legal-normative framework for directing environmental policy.

Thirdly, it can also serve to promote the coordination of environmental protection measures between states. Many environmental problems transcend national state boundaries, and so the principled and effective harmonization of legislation to address them is likely in the long run to depend on stable and strongly legitimated principles. It is worth noting the increasing interdependence of state constitutional law and international law, whereby few states would enshrine constitutional laws at odds with international law principles. It is also noteworthy that many constitutions, as drafted or revised these days, especially in relation to rights, have very similar provisions.

A fourth advantage that follows from addressing environmental concerns at the constitutional level is that environmental protection need not depend on narrow majorities in legislative bodies.

This is an important consideration, especially in liberal democracies, since if environmental protection measures may be costly or unpopular in the short term, then governments whose eye is on the next election have an incentive to cut back on them.

Finally, it can help foster citizen involvement in environmental protection measures. Although constitutional provisions are normally immune to routine political revision, there are ways in which they can serve to enhance a democratic culture, in particular by allowing and encouraging greater citizen participation in environmental decision-making processes. This is partly because they can underpin rights of participation and information, and also because they can play a broader cultural and educational role in motivating that participation. The extent of this latter advantage may depend on the regard in which their constitution is held by the people, but to some degree it is likely to be generally true, as Brandl and Bungert suggest, that 'as the supreme law of the land, constitutional provisions promote a model character for the citizenry to follow, and they influence and guide public discourse and behaviour' (Brandl and Bungert 1992: 4–5).

In sum, providing for environmental protection at the constitutional level has a number of potential advantages: it entrenches a recognition of the importance of environmental protection; it offers the possibility of unifying principles for legislation and regulation; it secures these principles against the vicissitudes of routine politics, while at the same time enhancing possibilities of democratic participation in environmental decision-making processes.

The question then is whether the rationale for making some form of constitutional provision for environmental protection necessarily extends to supporting a requirement that the provision should have the form of a right as opposed to a more general statement of policy objectives. Certainly, there are reasons to think that the advantages mentioned are likely to be more fully and firmly secured if constitutional provision for environmental protection has the form of a right. Rights in principle correspond to the most stringent form of constitutional imperative, and can thus best embody the *importance* of environmental protection: a substantive environmental right would mark the seriousness of environmental concern, giving environmental quality comparable status to other economic and social rights, with some priority over non-rights-based objectives (Boyle 1996: 49), thus also giving it some immunity from the lobbying and trade-offs that characterize decision-making processes that embody a presumption in favour of more immediate economic interests. In signalling the 'trumping' status of environmental concern in relation to lesser obligations of the state, rights provide means for citizens and their associations to challenge the state when it fails to meet its obligations. Giving constitutional force to a right of environmental protection can give this a due weight in the balance with other social values which already have the status of rights, particularly those associated with economic development, rather than being seen as a partisan cause.

Nevertheless, the rationale for constitutional protection of the environment does not strictly imply a case for rights rather than simply for a statement of policy principles. Compared to policy statements, rights introduce a more individualistic dimension and more stringent requirements, both of which require further justification. On the basis of the rationale so far considered alone, it can be argued that such justification is lacking, and it can therefore be questioned whether a right to an adequate environment is really on a par with established fundamental human rights that constitutions should provide.

So the rationale for making constitutional provision for environmental protection includes persuasive, but not sufficient, reasons in support of the claim that a right to an adequate environment ought to be included as a fundamental right in the constitution of any modern democratic state. That claim would be undermined if it could convincingly be argued that environmental protection, however important as a general social objective, was nonetheless not properly to be considered a human rights issue at all.

2.2 *The rationale for taking environmental protection to be a human rights issue*

The general proposition that environmental protection should be regarded as a human rights issue can in fact be supported in a number of ways. The critical question will be whether such support extends more specifically to a *sui generis* human right to environmental protection.

To begin with, it may be noted that there are evident practical linkages between the respective causes of human rights and environmental protection since environmental harms and human rights abuses often go together. The flagrant cases where environmental campaigners themselves become victims of human rights violations—and as Anderson observes 'serious damage to the physical environment is frequently accompanied by repression of activists and denial of access to information' (Anderson 1996a: 4–5)—are symptomatic of the more general point that under certain political and socioeconomic circumstances—which in some parts of the world are quite prevalent—both the environment and human rights come under threat together. Moreover, threats to the environment can themselves directly constitute threats to lives and livelihoods, health, and well-being. A corollary is that those concerned with the protection and promotion of environmental quality may often have reason to make common cause with defenders and promoters of human rights. Thus, in practice, environmentalists and human rights workers have often joined, for instance, in local struggles over land and water rights, toxic dumping, and disruptive construction projects. Particularly over such issues as environmental health hazards and threats to indigenous peoples' resource bases, the linkage has been a very practical one. 'Most mass movements at the grassroots are not just human rights, nor just environmental, but inevitably both. They have to be, if they are conscious of the role of natural resources in their lives, and of the dominant forces exploiting those resources' (Ashish Kothari quoted in Sachs

1995: 9). Also at the international level there is an increasing tendency for environmentalists and human rights activists to work
together toward common goals. Michael Anderson sees a natural
affinity between organizations such as Greenpeace and Amnesty
International, for instance, since both aim to reduce the reserved
domain of domestic jurisdiction protected under Article 2(7) of
the United Nations Charter and to restrain the exercise of unaccountable power by governments and private actors (Anderson
1996a: 2–3).

Nevertheless, the aims of human rights do not always coincide
with those of environmental protection, and even when there
are linkages between them, they can still be conceived of as quite
distinct. Thus even though proponents of human rights and the
environment can sometimes make common cause in the face of
common threats, their aims and priorities are not always or necessarily the same. In fact, alliances between respective defenders of
human rights and of the environment are often based on considerations of a pragmatic kind rather than of fundamental principle
that would favour a new and distinctive human right to an adequate environment. The reasons environmental campaigners
have to favour a human rights approach to environmental protection (see, for example, Aiken 1992; Nickel 1983) are that it
allows them 'to appeal to traditional human rights norms and to
use the institutions and mechanisms developed to promote and
implement human rights at the international level. The human
rights movement has strong international recognition, support,
and institutions and thus has valuable resources to offer environmentalism' (Nickel 1983: 283). Human rights proponents, for
their part, may see environmental protection as a means to the
end of fulfilling human rights standards. 'Since degraded environ-
ments contribute directly to infringements of the human rights
to life, health, and livelihood, acts leading to environmental
degradation may constitute an immediate violation of internationally recognized human rights' (Anderson 1996a: 3). Yet this
does not mean there is any internal normative connection
between the justificatory rationale of those recognized rights and

environmental protection. Thus, as Günther Handl observes, '[w]hile it should be self-evident that there is a direct functional relationship between protection of the environment and the promotion of human rights, it is much less obvious that environmental protection ought to be conceptualized in terms of a generic human right' (Handl 1992: 119).

As a matter of principle, though, for some it is self-evident that there is a human right to an adequate environment. Their intuition is that an adequate environment is as basic a condition of human flourishing as any of those that are already protected as human rights. Yet, this intuition alone does not suffice to make the case. Consider, for example, the human need for sleep, something which is also a basic condition of their flourishing but which one seldom hears of being proposed as a human right. The reason is not that sleep is unimportant, but that those circumstances which can give rise to sleep deprivation of a severity sufficient to put it on a par with other human rights abuses would invariably be circumstances which themselves already involved the violation of existing recognized human rights: at an extreme, forceful sleep deprivation is a means of intentional torture, and hence a violation of the right not to be tortured; less extreme circumstances of sleep deprivation may be a result, say, of aircraft noise in the immediate flight path of a major airport which would qualify, if severe enough, as a violation of a right to the quiet enjoyment of one's home and family life. The proposition that there is a human right to an adequate environment could be responded to with an equivalent line of reasoning: humans' need for an environment adequate for their health and well-being may be threatened by a range of specific environmental problems, and if any of these is severe enough in its effects on human health and well-being to be considered a human rights issue, then it will be such in relation to human rights that are already recognized. Certainly, claims of a right to an adequate enivironment have been mobilized politically in a way that suggests it is a distinct human rights issue in a way that a right to sleep is not. Yet, environmental protection can be considered a human rights issue without that necessarily implying that there is a human right to an adequate environment.

Thus, as is shown by a number of contributors to the volume edited by Boyle and Anderson (1996), for instance, a human rights approach to environmental protection may be commended without implying that there is a distinct *sui generis* human right to an adequate environment: human rights norms which are already protected under international instruments and domestic constitutions can play an important role in environmental protection. As noted in that volume's introduction,

the importance of civil and political rights lies in their ability to foster an environmentally-friendly political order. The realisation of such rights—including the rights to life, association, expression, political participation, personal liberty, equality, and legal redress—goes a long way toward enabling concerned groups to voice their objection to environmental damage. These guarantees are necessary preconditions for mobilising around environmental issues and making effective claims to environmental protection.   (Anderson 1996a: 5)

Nevertheless, in practice, attempts to invoke civil and political rights directly in the pursuit of environmental claims have been few, and, as Churchill (1996) and Douglas-Scott (1996) note, even these have met with mixed success. Social and economic rights may be thought to have a more immediate connection with environmental protection because such rights are related directly to human well-being and capacity-building, rather than simply the character of the political order. Thus, the right to health, for instance, 'if approached rigorously, requires the state to take steps to protect its citizens from a poisonous environment and to provide environmental goods conducive to physical and mental well-being' (Anderson 1996a: 5–6). Moreover, there are human rights lawyers broadly favourable to this approach who suggest that even if established human rights may not necessarily provide adequate environmental protection, they could be mobilized to do so. Nevertheless, the existing systems for implementing and monitoring social and economic rights construe these rights rather narrowly, and continue to approach environmental questions only indirectly. Thus Anderson, for instance, suggests that there are good reasons to suspect that the mere mobilization of existing rights norms would not be a satisfactory substitute for a dedicated right to an adequate environment.

One other possibility, though, is that existing substantive rights can 'be reinterpreted with imagination and rigour in the context of environmental concerns which were not prevalent at the time existing rights were first formulated' (Anderson 1996a: 7). Boyle and Anderson point out that many of the Ksentini Report's draft Principles on Human Rights and the Environment (see pp. 29–31 below) reformulate existing rights such as life and health so as to develop their environmental dimensions. However, examples of courts that have inferred or derived environmental rights from non-environmental rights provisions reveal that—since environmental protection is not the intended aim of the rights in question —the inference typically depends on a degree of judicial activism that would not be acceptable as a generalizable principle in constitutional democratic states since it cuts against the principle of the separation of powers, a matter that is discussed more fully in Chapter 4. The suggestion that an express environmental right is not necessary because remedies can be deduced from existing rights of life, health, and so on, is ultimately then not very credible, since environmental protection is not a primary aim of these rights and may not even always be a derivative aim, or not one strongly enough established to support claims in courts. If what is derived is in effect a substantive environmental right, then it would be rational, and more legitimate, for this to be declared as such.

2.3 Section conclusion

We have seen, then, that the case for a human right to an adequate environment can be strongly motivated from both the environmental and the human rights side, and that there is a role for such a right; we also saw that the case for constitutional protection of the environment can generate a presumptive case for a constitutional environmental right. The arguments so far considered, though, while motivating the case for it, do not supply adequate grounds to establish that there is a human right to an adequate environment that ought to be constitutionalized—hence the aim of this book.

3 Overview of the arguments of the book

The central claim of this book, that every constitutional democracy ought to guarantee a fundamental right to an adequate environment in its constitution, rests on the premise that this is a human right. The first challenge, then, is to show why the right to an adequate environment can be considered a genuine human right, and thus has the requisite normative force to motivate its constitutionalization. As will be shown in Chapter 1, there is some evidence that the right is in the process of attaining the status of a genuine human right in international law; but this evidence is not conclusive, and anyway, independently of this, it is important to establish that the right has a normative underpinning comparable to that of established human rights. The main purpose of the first chapter is therefore to set out the normative case for it as a human right. After entering some initial observations about the scope and formulation of the right, and clarifying that it is not proposed as a panacea for every environmental problem, I examine the case in the light of the criteria that a genuine human right can reasonably be required to fulfil. I show that the critical aspect of this case is not so much to establish the normative importance of environmental protection or its universality, since the right demonstrably corresponds to a human interest as significant and general as others that are already protected as human rights; it has rather to do with identifying and justifying the duties which correlate with the right. What I show, though, is that this does not pose any special problems that do not apply also to established human rights. My presentation of the case takes the form of an argument that if there are any genuine human rights at all, then the right to an adequate environment can and should be counted among them. I demonstrate that the environmental right does not fail any reasonable test of genuineness that would not also be failed by those human rights which are already firmly established in international law and in the constitutional order of modern democratic states.

Chapter 2 takes on the challenge to show why, even if the right is a genuinely universal moral right, it should necessarily be enshrined as a fundamental right in a state's constitution. For it has to be recognized that not all and not only human rights are constitutional rights: on the one hand, given that the discourse and institutions of human rights are in a state of constant evolution, there is not a uniquely definitive catalogue of human rights that each state could even in principle be taken to be bound to; on the other, given that different states will have different traditions, values, and practical exigencies, they will not only interpret (and to some extent select) human rights according to their own lights, but may also include rights that respond to specific exigencies of their own political, legal, social, cultural, and economic context. It has, therefore, to be recognized that the reasons for entrenching rights in a constitution are not necessarily reducible to a normative argument for the right as a human right, and that there may be specific reasons why a human right to an adequate environment might not appropriately be constitutionalized as a constitutional right. Chapter 2 considers the alternatives. As was noted earlier in this Introduction, there is no serious disagreement that mention of principles of environmental protection now belongs in states' constitutions, but some people argue that this would appropriately take the form of a statement of policy rather than a right; others argue that even if environmental protection is provided as a right, it should be classed as a social right, a category subordinate to and less binding than the fundamental rights of a constitution; still others argue that to the extent that environmental protection is the substance of fundamental rights, these rights should be procedural rights only. In response I explain why, while none of these alternatives should be ruled out as supplementary provisions for environmental protection, none of them ought to be substituted for a fundamental substantive right.

Thus while not relying, as a premise, on a claim that *all* human rights, without any kind of qualification, ought to be provided as fundamental rights in the constitution of a modern democratic state, what I do show in Chapter 2 is that if it is accepted that *any* human rights ought to be constitutionalized as fundamental rights, then it must be accepted that the right to an adequate environment ought to be among them.

At this point in the book, having set out the basic statement of its argument, I turn to address some questions regarding its practical significance. The argument up to this point could be said to have established nothing more than that constitutional documents ought to include a certain form of words. Yet even assuming that constitutional words do have real normative significance for the legal and political practices of a state, it does not necessarily follow that what a constitutional right can achieve in practice corresponds to what one might suppose it should; and when it comes to the right to an adequate environment in particular, there are various reasons to doubt that it would. Chapter 3 thus turns to consider, as reasons for resisting the constitutionalization of the environmental right, some critical arguments intended to show that it might not be *effective* if constitutionalized. To be sure, there are real difficulties which bear on the effectiveness of environmental rights. However, I argue that the problems jurists identify in trying to make a right to an adequate environment justiciable are not insurmountable, and that the obstacles to success in environmental cases do not so much show up problems that would make the right unworkable as ones it could help alleviate. Nevertheless, a consequent objection is that the measures necessary for effective enforcement of environmental rights would require courts do to things which they cannot and should not do. In response to this I point out that courts *can* deal with the complex issues involved in environmental cases since this is shown by the experience of specialist environmental courts. It is therefore not so much their technical competence as their *constitutional* competence that it is at issue. With regard to this I argue that the kind of jurisprudence that has to be deployed by courts in dealing with environmental cases is in the most important respects the same as that required for human rights cases more generally. This means that there is no deep objection to the constitutional legitimacy of courts ruling on the right to an adequate environment which would not also be an objection to their ruling on established human rights. Chapter 3 thus shows that the practical difficulties for the implementation and enforcement of a right to an adequate environment are not insurmountable. Rather it is ultimately a question of political will and a political conception of the purposes of a constitution. To suppose that the obstacles are insurmountable is to take a view of the political process as unamenable to change or rational normative persuasion.

At this point, however, an issue to deal with is that the entrenching of rights in a constitution precisely insulates them from the normal political process. When a constitutional provision is entrenched in the form of a right, it is presumed to have a 'trumping' force with respect to other social values and policies if these conflict with it. Thus there is the question of the democratic legitimacy of constitutional rights which thereby set certain substantive values beyond the reach of routine political revision and have the effect of pre-empting decisions that might otherwise be arrived at through democratic procedures. To the extent that the right to an adequate environment can be taken to embody substantive value commitments it would appear to be vulnerable to the criticism that its constitutional entrenchment is undemocratic. It is to this criticism that Chapter 4 seeks to develop an answer. I suggest that the criticism cannot be applied with much force to *procedural* environmental rights, since these can be construed as rights of democratic participation. The crucial question is how substantive environmental rights might be defended. One line of defence I investigate is how arguments for the democratic

legitimacy of social rights might be applied in suppot of environmental rights. I suggest, though, that because such arguments are
somewhat problematic in their own terms and because, more
crucially, there are also important differences between environmental and social rights, a separate line of defence could be more
appropriate. Thus I seek to show how substantive environmental
rights, in common with some existing and far less controversial
rights, can in fact be justified, not simply indirectly by reference
to the material preconditions of democracy, but on the very
grounds upon which democracy itself is justified. Such rights
would have a very strong democratic legitimation which could
undercut the main criticism altogether and thus meet the challenge addressed in this chapter.

The arguments developed to this point depend to a significant
degree on assumptions about states' existing commitments to
environmental protection and human rights. A question that
has to be asked, therefore, is whether, to the extent that the aims
of constitutional environmental rights are justified, they are not
already covered by existing commitments. If they are, then the
argument is vulnerable to the objection that a constitutional right
to an adequate environment would be redundant. Earlier, in
Section 2.1 of this Introduction, it was argued that a distinct *human*
right to an adequate environment would not be redundant in the
light of coverage currently provided by human rights, but this does
not rule out the possibility that a given state's constitutional provision for rights, combined with its environmental laws, could
meet the substantive requirements of the right. In one respect,
this possibility does not pose any real problem for the argument
of this book: if there is a state which in practice guarantees everything sought by the right to an adequate environment, then that
state would have no reason to refrain from express constitutional
affirmation that it does, and would indeed have some reason to
vaunt the fact. Moreover, states do not generally eliminate formal
constitutional reference to a right because they fulfil the substance
of that right. In another respect, though, the possibility does
represent a problem in that it bears on the question of whether

pursuing the constitutionalization of a right to an adequate environment is really a worthwhile strategy.

Now this question, which is addressed in Chapter 5, cannot be treated purely as a theoretical one, since it depends in crucial ways on how any given state's commitments are interpreted and implemented in practice. Because the effectiveness of constitutional environmental rights depends on how a state implements and enforces its constitutional commitments, which no two states do in an identical manner, this presents a problem for any attempt to attain an answer to the question with any significant degree of generalizability. It is with regard to this problem that there are distinct advantages in considering the question in the context of states which are members of the European Union (EU). As states which are bound by law to fundamental norms which are not necessarily of their own making, the specificities of the individual states' constitutional culture, environmental policies, rights enforcement mechanisms, and so on, can to a certain degree be bracketed out in order to focus on the question whether provision of a substantive environmental right with constitutional force has the potential to add anything to the environmental and human rights provisions that already bind them. Accordingly, I go on in this chapter to seek to identify the main environmental rights currently enjoyed by citizens of states within the EU, and to assess whether these could be significantly enhanced by the provision of a fundamental substantive right to an adequate environment, entrenched or binding at the 'constitutional' level of the EU. I consider the environmental provisions of foundational treaties and European Community Law relating to the environment, and show that while some policy principles and directives may under certain circumstances issue in environmental rights for citizens, the protections they offer nevertheless fall short of what might be expected of a substantive environmental right with constitutional force. The environmental protections afforded by human rights law are also considered, but here too it is shown that while there is some scope for invoking non-environmental human rights for environmental ends, and also the potential for citizens to exercise procedural rights to these ends, it is not so great as to render nugatory a substantive environmental right with constitutional force.

Although Chapter 5 focuses on the specific context of states within the EU, this context also captures significant aspects of broader global trends. It is increasingly the case that the continued pre-eminence of the nation-state as sole authorized administrative agency for a territory is not equally matched by its having sole sovereignty with regard to the norms it has to administer. Pressures for constitutional environmental rights thus come not only from within states, in particular from agents of civil society, but also from without, from the influence and precedents of international agreements and treaties. Thus important aspects of the argument developed are generalizable to non-European democratic states to the extent that they have comparable development, rights, and environmental records. Nevertheless, the situation of European states is not directly comparable with that of all states throughout the world, especially poorer ones, not only because of the *sui generis* nature of the Union, but also because its member states have already attained a certain level of development, rights protection, and environmental protection, which are not equally matched by all states.

This brings us to the final challenge to the book's line of argument. Many of the most serious environmental threats transcend the territorial boundaries of nation-states, and the focus on states' constitutions as the locus for securing environmental rights might therefore be considered not only inappropriately parochial, but even counterproductive in that a state may pursue an environmental national interest at the expense of environmental interests of others. A disadvantaged state might have relatively little capacity to protect its citizens' environmental rights against environmental threats even when these are domestically generated, while more powerful states may be able to enhance their citizens' environmental rights by effectively exporting environmental problems to poorer countries.

In Chapter 6, accordingly, the following two questions are addressed: whether the focus on *constitutional* environmental rights tends generally to perpetuate an inappropriately state-centric approach to environmental problems; and whether this approach specifically tends to reinforce the environmental rights of citizens of rich and powerful states at the expense of those of poorer nations. I show to begin with that the focus on environmental rights at the level of states is justified for both practical and principled reasons: practically, states remain the key sites of legitimate political power; and notwithstanding tensions between the normative principles of human rights and state sovereignty, some aspects of global justice, including environmental justice, depend on reaffirming sovereign rights, particularly of poorer states, to protect their peoples' interests against the forces of economic globalization. Also, because the constitutional rights provided by states fulfil an important role in developing international law relating to human rights in general and environmental rights in particular, the recognition of environmental rights even in richer states can contribute to the development of international norms that would require respect for the environmental rights of people globally. This leaves the issue of whether the constitutional enhancement of citizens' environmental rights in richer and more powerful states might nevertheless meanwhile exacerbate the environmental problems of poorer nations. In response I point out that there is already a massive 'exportation' of environmental problems from richer to poorer countries, and that if the environmental interests of the rich are better protected than those of the poor this is because the economically disadvantaged have less power to resist the imposition of threats to them. The existing global distribution of environmental harms, as well as of the benefits derived from environmental services and natural resources generally, is largely a result of market forces operating under a regime of rights that is in principle opposed by the right to an adequate environment. I therefore argue the interests of poorer countries should not be assumed to oppose the development of constitutional environmental rights in richer countries. Rather, their interest is to bring about conditions that would make it possible to secure those same rights for themselves. Indeed, as an

indication that in poorer states there is a recognition of the importance of constitutional environmental rights, it is noted that some
of the most important precedents in this field have been set in
such states. I thus conclude that the constitutionalizing of environmental rights can be expected to contribute to rather than
detract from the process of building environmental justice, not
only domestically but also globally.

Notes

1. This is the estimate of Dinah Shelton (2000: 22). The exact number is
   somewhat difficult to determine, partly for the reason—discussed
   below in the text—that the language, positioning, and framing of constitutional provisions can sometimes leave uncertainty as to their
   intended status or force; also, at any given time there are always some
   constitutions which are undergoing amendment. It is clear, though,
   that the number has been steadily increasing over the past fifteen
   years. For an extensive, if not quite exhaustive or completely up to
   date, list quoting the relevant portions of the constitutions see Anton
   (1998).
       While constitutional environmental rights are found in states'
   constitutions on all continents, and in states with a variety of legal traditions (Bruch, Coker, and VanArsdale 2000: 63), it is noteworthy that
   among the states without them are Japan, the United Kingdom,
   Germany, France, Italy, Australia, Canada, and China. Nor are they provided in the federal constitution of the United States, although the
   state constitutions of Alaska, Hawaii, Illinois, Massachusetts, Montana,
   Rhode Island, and Texas, as well as Puerto Rico, do include express
   environmental rights (Tucker 2000; Popović 1996b).
2. Lorenzen (2000) lists 109 states with constitutional provisions relating
   to the environment.
3. The qualification 'relatively' is important in relation to questions of
   environmental justice—something highlighted in Hayward (1995) see
   also the final chapter of this book.
4. Lord Woolf (1995) has spoken of a need to overcome fragmentation
   and Miller (1998: 9) of a lack of coherence among environmental laws
   and principles in the UK. Glasewski (1996) notes that the constitutionalizing of an environmental right in South Africa was the outcome of a

search for a comprehensive environmental norm; and Anderson considers the fundamental right to environmental protection as 'a general remedy with enough flexibility to fill gaps in statutory regulation'. (Anderson 1996b: 224–5). Bruch, Coker, and VanArsdale (2000: 1) find that 'the frequently incomplete nature of environmental legislative and regulatory regimes' means that constitutional environmental provisions 'can provide a "safety net" for resolving environmental problems that existing legislative and regulatory frameworks do not address'.

The Case for a Human Right to an Adequate Environment

This chapter presents the case for the proposition that a right to an adequate environment is a genuine human right. The main burden of argument is to defend this proposition against sceptical counterarguments to the effect that the human rights discourse should not be expanded to include environmental rights, since this would overextend it and thereby weaken its normative force. However, the proposition can also be questioned from an environmentalist perspective: here the challenge is to defend the apparent reduction of environmental concern to a concern with human interests in it, and indeed to meet the potentially more damaging criticism that this is even counterproductive to some important aims of environmental concern.

The first section, accordingly, establishes why the right to an adequate environment is something which environmentalists—notwithstanding their reservations—have good reasons by and large to support. I begin with an explanation for the particular formulation of the right I am focusing on, and offer some remarks about the scope and potential applications of the right. I then respond to criticisms that the scope is not only inadequate for, but can even run contrary to, important environmental aims. The main response is that the right is not proposed as a panacea for every environmental problem but that it nonetheless has a significant and distinctive role to play.

Having thus defended in principle the desirability of pursuing environmental protection as a human right, I then turn to consider the grounds for claiming that it actually has the status of a genuine human right. Different criteria have been proposed for determining the genuineness or otherwise of any putative human right, and the criteria which are most crucial and least controversial can be grouped into two kinds: those that would be satisfied in establishing a moral case for the right in question as a human right, and those on the basis of which recognition of the right in international law would be established. In Section 1.2 I explain why both kinds of criteria are relevant and how they are linked in the very concept of a human right.

Regarding the moral case, to be discussed in Section 1.3, I do not propose to dwell at length on the ultimate moral grounds for establishing human rights in general or the environmental right in particular. Rather, the question of how we can say the right to an adequate environment is a human right is posed in the light of reasons to doubt or deny that it is. The background assumption is that there *are* human rights that are recognized as such (internationally, by states, and by citizens), and about which such doubts do not apply, and that these meet the relevant moral criteria of genuineness. So the question is whether the right to an adequate environment meets each test of genuineness that can reasonably be proposed. Thus the form of the claim to be tested is that if there are any human rights, then a right to an adequate environment is one of them. It thus assumes that traditional liberal civil and political liberties have the status of human rights and that any objection to the environmental right which would also count as an objection to those rights cannot serve to refute the claim.

Regarding the question of the status of a right to an adequate environment in positive, particularly international, law, there is, as I explain in Section 1.4, reasonable disagreement about what actually counts as international recognition, as well as, in the case of at least some of the criteria proposed, whether the right meets them. Nevertheless, on the basis of the precedents surveyed, I suggest there is sufficient evidence to claim that the right is at least in the process of emergence internationally, and the fact that it is already recognized in certain countries and global regions lends support to the view that its consolidation internationally can reasonably be expected.

1.1 The case for pursuing environmental ends by means of human rights

The challenge of this section is to defend an approach to environmental protection which takes this to be a matter of *human* rights. There are influential currents of environmental thought which in fact take the fundamental problem environmentalism has to address as lying in humans' pursuit of their own interests to the exclusion, or disadvantage, of the good of other inhabitants and constituents of this planet. Such thinking would have it that enhancing human rights in relation to the environment could represent a further entrenching of such problems rather than a solution to them. I shall not claim that the approach defended here represents a comprehensive solution, but I shall show why there is reason to think it is part of a solution; I shall also point up problems in the radical environmentalist critique itself. To begin with, though, I shall briefly explain the reasons for focusing on the formulation of the right as that of every human to an environment adequate for their health and well-being. I shall also indicate what intermediate objectives, suitable for constitutional implementation, it can be expected to aim at under interpretations that can reasonably be expected to apply.

1.1.1 The scope of an environmental human right

The growing numbers of authoritative and binding instruments providing environmental rights deploy a variety of wordings to describe the substance of the right. A survey of around fifty examples of an expressly formulated substantive constitutional environmental right shows that by far the commonest formulation is a right to a clean or healthy environment (Anton 1998).

Quite distinct formulations of environmental rights are also to be found, though: some constitutional rights also make reference to ecological equilibrium or balance (e.g. Brazil, Cape Verde, Costa Rica, Mongolia, Mozambique, Paraguay, the Philippines, Portugal, Seychelles), and some (e.g. Hawaii) to sustainable development (although more often, and more appropriately, this is included as a state objective rather than as the substance of a right); reference is also made to an environment 'suitable for development of the person' (e.g. Spain); some US state constitutions mention the aesthetic aspect of environmental quality (e.g. Pennsylvania, Massachusetts). When examining the general case for a fundamental human environmental right, though, there is good reason to focus on the more prevalent formulation, the model for which is provided in the Brundtland definition of a right to an environment adequate for health and well-being. This focus is adopted because the other formulations either introduce more ambitious and potentially problematic aspirations or else can actually be subsumed under the Brundtland definition.

To refer to 'ecological equilibrium', for instance, is to introduce problems of interpretation which are possibly insurmountable, and certainly likely to generate interminable contestation: for what exactly it means for an ecosystem to be 'in equilibrium' (and whether that is a good thing anyway), and what makes one equilibrium 'better' than another, are questions about which there is both uncertainty and disagreement among ecologists. The most obvious way to reduce disagreement, if not uncertainty, is to take the yardstick for a favourable ecological equilibrium to be its conduciveness to human flourishing: but this is, in effect, to treat the objective as that of securing an environment adequate for health and well-being.[1]

Reference to sustainable development introduces considerations that go beyond environmental concerns, and also beyond feasibly justiciable individual rights: the idea of sustainable development, on Brundtland's formulation, comprises the environmental right as just one of three main components—the other two being rights of equity or social justice, and rights of future generations—and these would require to be separately stated. The idea of sustainable development is, of course, also richly contested, in both its parts and its whole, and that in itself makes it an unpromising objective of enforceable rights. The idea of sustainable development represents something that states may strive to realize, but when, and to the extent that, they fail to realize that ideal, it is far from clear against whom, or on what basis, any individual could make any rights claim.

References to an environment 'suitable for the development of the person', or conducive to a 'life of dignity', can be understood as ways of fleshing out the idea of an environment adequate for human well-being, and so are variations on the main theme rather than alternatives to it. Similarly, reference to the aesthetic, spiritual, or other cultural values attaching to the environment can be taken as fleshing out (culturally specific) conceptions of what human well-being entails.

For these reasons, I shall in this work be focusing primarily on a 'right to an environment adequate for (human) health and well-being', a substantive environmental right which involves the promotion of a certain level of environmental quality, and it is this that is to be understood by reference to a substantive environmental right, unless otherwise stated. In its actual implementation, the right can be cashed out to cover a wide range of environmental issues. Such a right is broadly conceived in the draft principles of the UN Sub-Commission on Human Rights and the Environment, and includes a number of interpretative elements, the extent and mix of which could best be determined at the stage of deciding on actual instruments of implementation. Among these elements are rights of all persons to

—freedom from pollution, environmental degradation and activities that adversely affect the environment, or threaten life, health, livelihood, well-being or sustainable development;
—protection and preservation of the air, soil, water, sea-ice, flora and fauna, and the essential processes and areas necessary to maintain biological diversity and ecosystems;
—the highest attainable standard of health free from environmental harm;

—safe and healthy food and water adequate to their well-being;

—a safe and healthy working environment;

—adequate housing, land tenure and living conditions in a secure, healthy and ecologically sound environment;

—not to be evicted from their homes or land for the purpose of, or as a consequence of, decisions or actions affecting the environment, except in emergencies or due to a compelling purpose benefiting society as a whole and not attainable by other means;

—timely assistance in the event of natural or technological or other human-caused catastrophes;

—benefit equitably from the conservation and sustainable use of nature and natural resources for cultural, ecological, educational, health, livelihood, recreational, spiritual or other purposes. This includes ecologically sound access to nature;

—preservation of unique sites, consistent with the fundamental rights of persons or groups living in the area. (Ksentini 1994: articles 5–13)

As well as these rights which would be held by 'all persons', the draft declaration also mentions, following on from the qualification made with regard to the last of them, group rights of indigenous peoples[2]

—to control their lands, territories and natural resources and to maintain their traditional way of life. This includes the right to security in the enjoyment of their means of subsistence.

—to protection against any action or course of conduct that may result in the destruction or degradation of their territories, including land, air, water, sea-ice, wildlife or other resources.

The importance of procedural rights is also separately noted. These include, in particular, rights of all persons to

—information concerning the environment. This includes information, howsoever compiled, on actions and courses of conduct that may affect the environment and information necessary to enable effective public participation in environmental decision-making. The information shall be timely, clear, understandable and available without undue financial burden to the applicant.

—active, free, and meaningful participation in planning and decision-making activities and processes that may have an impact on the environment and development. This includes the right to a prior assessment of the environmental, developmental and human rights consequences of proposed actions.

—effective remedies and redress in administrative or judicial proceedings for environmental harm or the threat of such harm.

The above lists are provided only for illustrative purposes, however. In this book I shall not be assuming or advancing any detailed stipulations about how exactly the right to an 'environment adequate for health and well-being' might or ought to be interpreted in specific contexts. Such stipulations would not only need to be sensitive to context, but would also depend on relevantly authoritative understandings of how they should be interpreted and applied. There is inevitably scope for contestation about each of the terms in which the content of the right is expressed, but in this respect the right does not differ from any other human right in its declaratory formulation.

1.1.2 Addressing doubts from an environmental perspective

When considering the scope of the right from an environmental perspective, however, it is to be observed that in making the criterion of environmental protection its adequacy for human health and well-being, whatever way this is interpreted, it does not necessarily capture all aspects of environmental concern. Its most obvious application would be with respect to pollution, waste disposal, and other sorts of toxic contamination, since the most immediate threats to health and well-being concern contamination of air, water, and food. To be sure, depending on how health and, particularly, well-being are construed, many other issues could ultimately be brought under this rubric, including, as was noted in the indicative list of interpretative elements above, aspects of environmental concern that touch on the quality of life in aesthetic, cultural, and spiritual terms. Still, the right is not proposed as a panacea for all of the problems arising from our interactions with nonhuman nature, but as just one, albeit significant, approach to dealing with them—as what Nickel calls 'one useful part of the normative repertory of environmentalism' (Nickel 1983: 283).

A critical question from an environmental perspective, though, is whether the environment is really very well served by enhancing the rights of *humans*, particularly in view of how it often seems to be precisely the human pursuit of their rights-protected interests which are causing environmental harm in the first place. If the human environmental right in question continues to imply that the environment is nothing more or other than a resource for human benefit, it is vulnerable to the criticism that it is 'anthropocentric'. A human right to an adequate environment is, in an obvious sense, a human-centred right: it considers the environment only under the aspect of its contribution to *human* health and well-being; no provision is explicitly sought for the nonhuman beings that coexist within our environment; and no mention at all is made of the environment 'for its own sake'. Does this constitute an objection to it from an environmental perspective?

The first point to note in answer to this question is that there is in fact a wide variety of environmental perspectives, many of which are also anthropocentric in the same general sense of being concerned with harm to the environment because, and inasmuch as, it affects humans too. From such perspectives, anthropocentrism is not necessarily taken to be unproblematic, but it is considered to be in some ways unavoidable, and in some ways even desirable: for ethics—environmental or otherwise—is inherently concerned with the well-being of humans, and it is right and proper that it should be. The problematic aspect of anthropocentrism has to do with whether this concern should be developed to the exclusion of or at the expense of the nonhuman constituents of the planet. With respect to this point a distinction is sometimes drawn in environmental ethics between 'strong' and 'weak' anthropocentrism.[3] From the standpoint of 'strong' anthropocentrism, it is justified to have an *exclusive* concern with human interests, and a complete disregard for the good of nonhumans or of the environment considered as anything other than humans' 'life-support system'. In 'weaker' versions, however, anthropocentrism is not exclusivist in this way: even if the primary focus is on human interests, and even if—other things being equal—these are accorded priority over nonhuman interests, this does not mean that no account at all is taken of the latter or that priority is necessarily given to human interests when other things are not equal—so that, for instance, when relatively trivial human interests conflict with vital interests of nonhumans the former may not be accorded priority. Moreover, 'weak' anthropocentrists generally recognize that human interests are inseparable from the good of the nonhuman constituents of the environment in many ways, some of which we may not yet be aware of, so that a reasonable working presumption (which is absent from 'strong' anthropocentrism) is that where there is not a serious cost in human terms there is a positive reason actively to show concern for features and constituents of the nonhuman environment, regardless of whether humans stand to derive any immediate benefit.[4] Accepting that not every problem can be avoided in relation to the environment, any more than ethical dilemmas can be effaced from relations among humans, 'weak' anthropocentrism is thus taken to be a defensible stance by many environmental ethicists (Aiken 1992: 196; Hayward 1995: 58–62).

In which of the senses distinguished, then, is the human right to an adequate environment anthropocentric? The right could be taken as formally neutral between stronger and weaker versions since on its face it neither commends nor condemns a disregard for the good of the nonhuman constituents of the natural world. Materially, though, and in its applications, the right cannot be conceived as implying or condoning indifference towards the nonhuman world since in requiring that the nonhuman environment should be preserved in a condition that is adequate for human health and well-being it implies—especially in a world as disrupted by anthropegenic environmental harms as this one now is—rather stringent demands of environmental protection. Moreover, part of its core rationale is to oppose the unbridled pursuit of those rights that do manifest the most 'strongly' anthropocentric tendencies

(i.e. those which favour the blind pursuit of economic development without regard to its environmental impacts). It is hard to
conceive that in its implementation the right could be anthropocentric in the strong sense, and there are good reasons to think
it would not be. At the very least we might anticipate what
Redgwell refers to as a 'fortuitous spill-over effect to non-humans
in the recognition of such an environmental right' (Redgwell
1996: 87). Beyond that, it is reasonable to suppose that the more
that humans come to understand about the interconnectedness
of their health and well-being with that of nonhuman nature, the
more inseparable appear their interests with the 'good' of nature.

Of course, it remains the case that, even if weakly, the right is
nonetheless anthropocentric, and in the event that human interests do not coincide with nonhuman interests, as they cannot
always be expected to do, then other things being equal, the
human interests will prevail. Is this objectionable? Here, I would
observe that not all human interests are the same (which is a reason why ethical conflicts and dilemmas in general can arise), and,
more pointedly, that not all anti-anthropocentric positions are
the same: so it is to be expected that some human interests coincide with some nonhuman interests while not all nonhuman interests coincide either with all human interests or all other nonhuman
interests. Hence, it is to be observed that actual policy prescriptions
do not necessarily differ according to whether they are argued for
on 'anthropocentric' or allegedly 'non-anthropocentric' grounds
(Norton 1991; Light and Katz 1996; de-Shalit 2000).

Furthermore, 'non-anthropocentric' grounds can issue in conflicting guidance to action; and this is because their own values
conflict. The proposition that anthropocentrism (in ethics) is
objectionable is a normative judgement which presupposes a normative standpoint. The use of 'anthropocentrism' as a term of
criticism originally presupposed a theistic standpoint whereby
'human-centredness' was seen as a vain alternative to a 'God-
centred' view of the world (Hayward 1998b). The accusation as
levelled in the context of environmental values, however, does
not (normally) presuppose a 'God-centred' view of the world, and

in fact a variety of standpoints can be found in the literature of environmental philosophy, including ecocentrism, biocentrism, sentientism, and deep ecology. Depending on which alternative is chosen, and how it is interpreted, various value deliverances are possible, and these can conflict with one another: to take an obvious example, protection of individual members of a species can be incompatible with protecting the flourishing of the community or ecosystem in which they live (Callicott 1980). Thus an evident problem with the rather diffuse range of possible criticisms of anthropocentrism is that there is no way, consistent with them all, of non-arbitrarily selecting one basis (e.g. sentience, biocentrism, ecocentrism, etc.) rather than another from which to develop a coherent and compelling alternative.

There is thus no single version of the anthropocentrism objection that is simultaneously well founded and decisive as an objection to environmental human rights. Furthermore, any one of them would only be decisive as a reason for its adherents to reject that right on assumptions that would also require all other human rights to be rejected on the same grounds. I do not stray further into debate of this issue, since this book takes as its premise that human rights have a justification and legitimacy which precludes their being rejected.

A human rights approach provides a link to interests and motivations, and thus to actual practices, in a way that more abstract notions of a 'right *of* environment' or of 'nature's intrinsic value' do not. A human right to an adequate environment does not preclude the taking of other, complementary, approaches to environmental and ecological problems. It might also serve in many ways to support them and to enhance their potentiality for success. It should not be forgotten, after all, that even when environmental concern focuses on the good of nonhumans, its success depends on the political, economic, and legal resources available to the humans pressing the case: these resources, I believe, are on the whole more likely to be enhanced than hindered by certain entrenched rights which can be mobilized for that very purpose. Furthermore, there is good reason to believe that once a basic right is established, practical jurisprudence and wider social norms will develop progressively to support more ambitious, less immediately anthropocentric, aims. In short, it could be seen as an important first step that might lead to further steps in the future.

The main argument of this book is addressed to critical questions of a quite contrasting sort. These stem from doubts, arising from the perspective of human rights concern, that the right in question might already overextend the rights discourse.

1.2 A genuine human right?

We turn now to the question of whether a right to an adequate environment has the status of a genuine human right. The answer depends on what criteria of genuineness it is held that a genuine human right must fulfil; and the selection of appropriate criteria in turn depends on the theoretical stance adopted regarding the question of when it can be true to say of a right that it exists.

Traditionally, two opposing stances have been taken by theorists of rights with regard to this general question. On the one hand, those who emphasize that human rights are rights humans hold 'simply in virtue of being human' take the view that human rights are essentially moral rights. Statements about the existence of human rights on this view would be true even in the event that no regime in the world actually recognized them as existing. For moral truths do not depend on the contingencies of human conventions, or therefore on whether the right in question happens to be implemented in any actual political and legal system. Part of the very point of human rights, on this view, is to provide a standard by which the justice and humanity of actual state norms can be judged. On the other hand, a contrary view is that there are and can be no genuine sources of moral norms outside the actual human social practices and institutions within which concrete norms have developed over the course of history. On such a view, real human rights, as opposed to merely rhetorical ones, are those which are declared as such in actual treaties binding on the states signatory to them, and are actually implemented and enforced within specific jurisdictions. Human rights do not 'exist' in a realm of pure morality or natural law, but emerge into existence with the concrete recognition of them in real institutional practices as having binding normative force.

Now the view I propose holds that, in order to answer the question whether the right to an adequate environment is a genuine human right, it is not a matter of choosing between these competing theoretical stances but of accepting that both provide criteria that have to be met. I shall therefore briefly state why neither the moral argument nor legal evidence is on its own sufficient for establishing the genuineness of a human right. I shall then indicate how they are conceptually linked.

The case for thinking of genuine human rights as moral rights has its roots in a venerable tradition of political thought but it has been given a recent restatement by Thomas Pogge, a political philosopher who is highly alert to the altered political circumstances that characterize the contemporary world. Pogge distinguishes 'moral human rights' from 'legal human rights' and holds that the existence of the former does not depend on the existence of the latter. Now in one respect, this is to articulate an uncontroversial aspect of the understanding of human rights: their existence as moral norms does not depend on their being recognized by any given legal order, and is not negated by a regime that denies and violates them. In another respect, though, Pogge's understanding is not so uncontroversial:[5] for he denies not only any necessary practical linkage between 'moral human rights' and 'legal human rights' but even 'any conceptual connection of human rights with legal rights' (Pogge 2002: 46).

We should thus consider the question of what exactly a moral human right is, in order to understand under what conditions it exists or can be said to be genuine. I propose to begin by considering the two most familiar ways in which the concept of a moral right can be made intelligible. In each of these ways, a conceptual linkage to legal rights is a constitutive aspect of the characterization.

(i) A moral right can be so understood as having the formal structure of a legal right—a legal 'claim-right' in Hohfeld's (1918) terminology—insofar as asserting that a moral right exists entails the claim that a correlative moral duty exists. For example, asserting that '*A* has a moral right that *B* tell her the truth' entails that '*B* has a moral duty to tell *A* the truth'. The only essential difference between a moral right thus understood and a legal right of the equivalent form is that whereas a legal right derives its normative direction and force from the law, the moral right derives its normative direction and force from morality. The morality in question needs only be such that parties *A* and *B* are taken to be bound by its principles or rules in order for such statements to have truth within that morality. There can be any number of moralities within which such propositions are capable of having meaning and truth. Many moral rights, so understood, would not therefore be candidates for being considered human rights: the assertion of a human right implies that the moral horizon it draws its justification from is not one of a plurality of moralities, but a morality that applies to everyone everywhere; it also implies a certain weightiness of the moral values at issue. On this conception, then, a 'moral human right' would belong to a subset of all possible moral rights; it would be a moral right of each human corresponding to a moral duty of each human—or at least some humans (see below)—with regard to some X that is deemed to have a certain weightiness in the scheme of morality that is deemed to bind all humans into a moral community.

(ii) The assertion of a moral right can alternatively be so understood that it does not itself necessarily or directly entail a determinate corresponding moral duty; rather, it is an assertion that a particular moral desideratum ought to receive practical recognition as a legally enforceable or constitutional right (whereby corresponding duties are created by the law). Here, the conceptual linkage to legal rights does not (necessarily) lie in the form of the asserted moral right; rather, what makes this a moral *right* is the demand the assertion represents, on moral grounds, for the creation of a legally enforced right which would protect or fulfil the moral desideratum. Such a moral right thus has a dual

normativity: the normativity which generates the moral desideratum; and the normativity that generates the claim that the
desideratum ought to have a determinate status in the actual legal
and political affairs of humans (which includes the implication
that it should be backed up by force, the force underpinning the
rule of law).[6] A 'moral right' which has this kind of normative
force would normally be considered a moral human right.

Thus although understandings (i) and (ii) are distinct, in each
in its way the notion of a moral right depends for its intelligibility
on the concept of a legal right. It may also be noted that (i) and
(ii) are not mutually exclusive, and a moral right, especially if it is
a moral *human* right, could be understood in such a way as to
combine the two senses so that the right–duty relation posited in
morality (as in (i)) is demanded or required to be preserved in a
legal right–duty relation (as in (ii)).

In what sense then are 'human moral rights' to be understood
on Pogge's view? Since he thinks they have not even a conceptual
connection with legal rights it is not surprising that he in fact
understands them in neither of these ways. He rejects the understanding of moral rights (i) insofar as this corresponds to an
'interactional' conception in contrast to an 'institutional' conception, which he favours. On the interactional view, rights–duties
relations exist between individuals, thereby imposing constraints
on individual conduct, but these are 'constraints that do not presuppose the existence of social institutions' (Pogge 2002: 45). On
the institutional view, by contrast, human rights 'impose constraints, in the first instance, upon shared practices' (Pogge 2002:
170). Pogge explains the different implications of this alternative
view by reference to a human right not to be enslaved:

On an interactional view, this right would constrain persons, who must
not enslave one another. On an institutional view, the right would constrain legal and economic institutions: ownership rights in persons must
not be recognized or enforced. This leads to an important difference
regarding the moral role of those who are neither slaves nor slaveholders.
On the interactional view, such third parties have no responsibility

toward existing slaves, unless the human right in question involved, besides the negative duty not to enslave, also a positive duty to protect or rescue others from enslavement. Such positive duties have been notoriously controversial. On the institutional view, by contrast, those involved in upholding an institutional order that authorizes and enforces slavery—even those who own no slaves themselves—count as cooperating in the enslavement, in violation of a *negative* duty, unless they make reasonable efforts toward protecting slaves or promoting institutional reform.   (Pogge 2002: 171–2)

I believe Pogge is right to favour an institutional understanding of human rights, for reasons I further elaborate upon below (when discussing Cranston's interactional view). However, the most familiar institutional understanding, which assumes a conception of the moral aspect of human rights conforming to (ii) discussed above, is expressly rejected by Pogge too.

On the familiar institutional understanding of human rights, which presupposes social relations that require governance under the rule of law, if a moral right to X is to be understood as a *human* right to X this implies as an intrinsic part of the understanding that the right ought to be recognized constitutionally and accorded legal protection. 'So understood, human rights require their own juridification. Each society's government and citizens ought to ensure that all human rights are incorporated into its fundamental legal texts and are, within its jurisdiction, observed and enforced through an effective judicial system.' (Pogge 2002: 45). This view, which I broadly subscribe to, Pogge finds also in Jürgen Habermas: '"The concept of human rights is not of moral origin, but . . . *by nature* juridical." Human rights "belong, through their structure, to a scheme of positive and coercive law which supports justiciable individual right claims. Hence, it belongs to the meaning of human rights that they demand for themselves the status of constitutional rights"' (Pogge 2002: 223, n. 72). However, Pogge rejects this understanding and claims that their juridification is neither sufficient nor necessary for the real enjoyment of the substance of human rights. I certainly agree that it is not sufficient, but I would question why Pogge considers it not to be necessary. Pogge's view is that where there is secure access to the object of a human right, there is no need for its juridification. In reply to this, however, one is bound to ask what may make the access 'secure' if not the background assumption that should circumstances change and a threat to the enjoyment arise then there would be an enforceable—*juridified*—right to appeal to. I would suggest that in any society governed by the rule of law—and that is the context presupposed in the present discussion—it is law which ultimately guarantees that security. Certainly, if a human right is to 'constrain legal and economic institutions', as Pogge envisages, it is hard to see how it will unless it has some constitutional force that can be applied, as necessary, through law.

Yet, it is not this practical issue alone that raises questions about Pogge's position, for there is also, and inseparable from it, an important question of principle. Pogge sees human rights as 'moral claims on the organization of one's society' (p. 64), claims which consist in the 'demand' that 'coercive social institutions be so designed that all human beings affected by them have secure access to X [the object of the right]' (p. 46). Yet what makes a moral claim or a demand into a right is some *justification*. In particular, since the demand implies an obligation on the part of others, and an obligation represents a limitation on their freedom, this limitation on their freedom requires justification (Hart 1984). Here is the question of the 'second source of normativity' mentioned in explication of moral rights (ii), that which makes of the moral desideratum, as initially presented in the form of a *good*, into a claim of *right*. Moral demands which are advanced in terms of an avowedly juridified conception of human rights allow the posing of the question of their justification because they can be assessed in relation to the criteria which already give coherence and legitimacy to an existing system of rights within the rule of law. On the Habermasian view, for instance, they would be validated by testing whether the demands satisfy the discourse principle:[7] 'the only law that counts as legitimate is one that could be rationally accepted by all citizens in a discursive process of opinion- and will-formation' (Habermas 1997: 135). The claims that any moral discourse is keying into, by referring to its goals in terms of human rights, are already claims relating to the legitimate scope of states' powers. New moral claims may justifiably be viewed as partisan, and thus not as appropriately the subject of coercion, unless they can in principle pass tests of more general validity. In order even to be subject to such tests, they must be presented as claims to recognition within the broader scheme of rights which are already recognized as genuine human rights.

On Pogge's conception of moral human rights, their claims and demands do not need to conform to the standards of legitimacy of legally recognized human rights. The positing of a dichotomy between 'moral human rights' and 'legal human rights', however, severs the conceptual linkage between morality and law which is integral to the very notion of a human right—and, what matters in the context of the present chapter—to the possibility of justifying the claim regarding any particular putative human right that it is a genuine one.

Returning to the specific human right which is the topic of this book, then, the point can be applied. It would be possible to mount an argument for the right to an adequate environment as a moral human right and then insist that individuals and states that do not recognize it just need to get their moral views in better order. But in the face of the predictable counterargument that it depends on, say, a comprehensive doctrine of the good that as a matter of fact is not shared across any given society, or the globe, one would be left in the position of proselyte. One would of course still be able to claim it *ought* to be a human right, and yet that claim alone would not *make* it one for anybody who is not already a convert to the cause. By saying this, I am not at all seeking to detract from the worth of the moral persuasion approach, only saying that in the final analysis it is not sufficient to establish that a contested human right ought to be considered a genuine one.

The concept of a moral right then is *formally* a derivative of the concept of a legal right. This by no means implies, however, that the substantive normative content of any right as argued for morally derives from the content of positive law; on the contrary, particularly when it comes to human rights, it is morality that supplies the substantive normative standard. Enacted law is not taken as its own standard of legitimacy. Human rights in fact provide a standard of legitimacy by which the principles and applications of law are to be judged. What makes this possible is not simply the moral content and the rights form, but also the determinate sociohistorical meaning of human rights. Thus whereas Pogge appears to view law as pure positivity, sets aside questions of its internal normative justifications, and thus posits morality as applying outside the law, the view I take is closer to that of Habermas: 'The law receives its full normative sense neither through its legal form per se, nor through an a priori moral content, but through a procedure of law-making that begets legitimacy' (Habermas 1997: 135). Habermas observes:

Human rights are Janus-faced, looking simultaneously toward morality and the law. Their moral content notwithstanding, they have the form of legal rights. *Like* moral norms, they refer to every creature 'that bears a human countenance', but *as* legal norms they protect individual persons only insofar as the latter belong to a particular legal community—normally the citizens of a nation-state.   (Habermas 1998: 161)

Habermas's view is that 'human rights are not pre-given moral truths to be *discovered* but rather are *constructions*', and they 'have an inherently juridical nature, and are conceptually oriented toward positive enactment by legislative bodies' (Habermas 1998: 164).

We have, then, to reckon with the fact that there are some human rights recognized to have a definite status as such in law, and we should therefore assume that it is to this status that any putative human right aspires. Moral argument at least has to show why a putative human right—such as that to an adequate environment—ought to have a similar status. So if an account cannot be provided of what it is to have that status, then the argument cannot be properly developed. A genuine human right has to meet the standards that any right recognized legally as a human right has to meet.

This is not to say, though, that the genuineness of a human right depends on its existing in a sense that would satisfy a legal positivist. So here I would just make explicit why legal evidence is not sufficient for establishing the genuineness of a human right and why the moral case therefore cannot be considered irrelevant or unnecessary. Indeed, I think it would be absurd to suppose that a reasonable moral argument for the genuineness of a new human right could be dismissed simply on the ground that the right was not (yet—at the moment of its formulation) implemented or enforced, for if a *human* right is to be implemented it will first have been conceived as an ideal. It may for a time 'exist' as a pure moral ideal and only later be institutionalized. Furthermore, it is a feature of the normative force and very *raison d'être* of human rights that they are conceived to rectify harms and wrongs of an imperfect world, and so it is no objection to them simply to assert that the world is not perfect in the way the right normatively aims for it to be. On the other hand, though, ideals and rhetoric do not suffice to give reality to human rights, and it would be misleading to call a human *right* some moral claim that could never be made good in law, for a right is something more and other than a mere aspiration.

This point can be elaborated without recourse to a legal positivist understanding of human rights. The language of human rights, even when applied in a moral rather than a legal context, refers to a distinctive ethical form. The truth which legal positivism highlights, albeit mistaking it for the whole of the truth rather than just a part of it, is that the very concept of a right is of legal origin: as was shown above the rights form has an internal logic and a sociohistorical genesis that cannot simply be disregarded if its deployment in ethical reasoning is to be fully intelligible.

From this perspective, a purely moral argument (as may be devised, 'monologically', whether in the philosopher's study or on the part of campaigners already committed to a particular moral goal) would not suffice to establish such a right as a human right; it would be necessary, though, since there has to be a moral argument that citizens can discuss and as appropriate assent to. Therefore, from this perspective a legal positivist approach is not sufficient. The perspective proposed does not simply rely on empiricist analysis of existing rights; rather, it poses the question whether the new proposed right meets the same standards of normative rationale as those rights which—even from an empiricist perspective—are already recognized as genuine; and perhaps too—or minimally—that it does not conflict in any fundamental way with them.

Hence, a further point to note is that whereas a purely moral case for the genuineness of a particular human right would either succeed or fail (once a moral framework for its evaluation is established), an empirical case admits of qualified and partial answers, since the institutionalization of rights can assume many forms. Thus as is illustrated by Christopher Miller, the question is not a simple and straightforward one: 'when is it meaningful to speak of the existence of an environmental (or, for that matter, any other fundamental) right: when it is first declared by a body like the United Nations; when it is translated into national law; or only when that law has been found to offer an effective remedy after that right has been infringed?' (C. Miller 1998: 4). The answer I am proposing is that it is *meaningful* from the start of the process alluded to—and even, of course, before that, when the right exists as a purely moral idea—but the point is that the meaning changes in the course of the process. Nevertheless, I would add that something that is meaningful about early stages resides in the prospect of later stages being reached. The question might then be thought to be which meaning should matter, but my answer is that they each matter but for different reasons or purposes.[8] Statements about rights can relate to a range of levels of normative ontology. A right can be argued to exist if it exists at any of these levels, among which the following are included: moral argument of philosophers; rhetorical adversions (or 'manifesto appeals') by campaigners, citizens, and politicians; international declarations; international law of 'softer' and of 'harder' forms; regional agreements; provision in states' constitutions;

implemented as statutory (or customary) law; actual enforcement of the laws; real enjoyment by all citizens.

Although some commentators consider it a crucial question which level(s) should be privileged when seeking to determine the existence, and thus genuineness, of a human right, on the view I am advancing each of these levels (as well as others that have not been differentiated among them here) is relevant to (but not on its own sufficient in) determining the genuineness of a human right in the sense of genuineness that I am taking to be the standard of assessment for the environmental right in question. Rather than conceive these levels as ones one must choose between, and rather than privilege any one or other of them, I think it is more appropriate to say that a genuine human right is one that within its own logic, and because of actual pressures, undergoes (or is capable in some sufficiently robust sense of undergoing) the process from ideal to practice, whereby it passes from the status of a well-founded moral aspiration, through exhortatory declarations, into legally binding instruments and effective enforcement—which, in a world of separate states, is most appropriately achieved by being constitutionalized. To take this view of the ontological status of human rights is to acknowledge that human rights have emerged—and continue to emerge—in determinate historical and social contexts, without this negating the admissibility, and indeed the necessity, of moral reasoning, perhaps even in the language of natural law, as part of the self-understanding of that context as a normative one.[9]

In seeing the emergence of human rights as a historical process with a normative logic that can be understood 'from within', a purely moral argument abstracted from any consideration of how it might be implemented is not enough to make a case for human rights, as distinct from a general moral goal, any more than a positivist survey of the rights people happen to enjoy suffices to explain whether those rights are appropriately referred to as *human* rights.

The question regarding the genuineness of a new human right accordingly becomes that of whether this process, as just described, can reasonably be said to be under way, and whether there is any significant obstacle or problem that might cause the process to be truncated or diverted. Some obstacles of brute force can truncate the process, but in this book I am only examining questions of principle, and thus at impediments for which some legitimacy or justification can be claimed.

In what follows I ask first if a right to an adequate environment can be conceived as a universal moral right (which is the starting point of the process), and then survey some of the available evidence relevant to the question of whether it is in the process of firming up as a real norm of positive law.

1.3 A universal moral right to an adequate environment

This section makes and defends the claim that a right to an adequate environment genuinely is, if any rights are, a universal moral right—that is, a moral right that can and should be universally institutionalized. To demonstrate its genuineness in this sense I propose to examine it in the light of the three tests of a genuine human right proposed by Maurice Cranston. Since Cranston's aim was to restrict the range of genuine human rights, essentially, to classical liberal civil and political rights, it is reasonable to consider these tests a suitably stringent set in terms of which to test the case for a human right to an adequate environment. I show that these tests—of moral paramountcy, universality, and practicability—do not pose any problems for this right that they would not also pose for traditional liberal rights. I shall first briefly indicate why the right can pass these tests and then discuss the central line of objection that focuses on the problem of identifying and justifying the duties that correspond to the right.

1.3.1 Why the right to an adequate environment meets the criteria of a genuine human right

If a test for a genuine human right is that it protects human interests of 'paramount moral importance', then, given that environmental harms can threaten vital human interests, this aspect of the case can quite readily be made. Indeed, as James Nickel remarks in affirming this, environmental problems can reach a level of severity, causing such widespread and large scale damage to the health and welfare of a community, that is matched by few human rights violations other than programmes of mass extermination.

> Severe air pollution kills some people, shortens the lives of others, and makes still others recurrently sick. These interests in life, health, and a minimal level of welfare are already protected by a number of human rights, such as rights against murder, torture, or physical injury. Severe pollution is a significant and frequent threat to the fundamental interests that human rights protect; the right to a safe environment aims to protect people against severe pollution and its consequences, and should therefore be accorded a position equal to other human rights that seek to prevent these consequences.   (Nickel 1983: 290)

Although Nickel here refers particularly to *severe* threats, and advocates a right to a 'safe' environment, the same reasoning can support a right to an *adequate* environment (granting that standards of 'adequacy' require negotiation as mentioned earlier), just as classic civil rights protect interests of varying degrees of strength. On the grounds of moral importance, then, there is no good reason to deny the status of a human right to the 'right of each to an environment adequate for health and well-being', since the lack of what this right substantively stands for would be a detriment to humans comparable to that protected against by many established human rights.

Can the right to an adequate environment be conceived as a genuinely universal right? In the sense that the interests it is intended to protect are common to all humans, it clearly can be; so with regard to its universality in this sense it is not vulnerable to any relativist critique that would not also apply to any other universal right. The critical questions about universality apply not to the right, though, but to its corresponding duties. For just as having an interest is not sufficient for having a right, so the universal applicability of an interest is not sufficient for affirming a universal right. Rights imply corresponding duties, and on one account of universal rights these must correspond to universal duties. This is what Cranston, for instance, claims. 'To speak of a universal right', he says, 'is to speak of a universal duty' (Cranston 1967b: 96). On this view, each and everyone only has a right that is genuinely universal if each and everyone is also under the duty that correlates to it. Inasmuch as the right of each to an adequate environment can be understood to imply that each also has the duty to refrain from harming the environment of each other, it qualifies as a universal right in this sense. The right to an adequate environment thus in fact fares better by this standard than human rights such as healthcare, education, and social rights generally, in that the correlative duty, being purely negative (i.e. a duty to refrain from certain actions), can be conceived as unproblematically universalizable.

However, when the test of practicability is also applied, the appeal to that universal duty looks less promising. If each and every individual is supposed to have a duty not to harm any other individual's environment, the critical question is how this duty is to be implemented and enforced; and how, indeed, it is even to be intelligible as an action-guiding principle. Environmental problems are generally the result not directly of individual actions but of complex collective practices; to change those practices may require government action more akin to that necessary for the provision of social rights (for more on which see Chapter 2). This gives rise to serious problems of practicability, especially as the requisite measures are likely to impose actual and opportunity costs. Of course, problems of practicability cannot be held to detract from the moral importance of the right, if this has been independently established, but they do bear on its status as a right, for that entails duties; and since ought implies can, there cannot reasonably be said to be duties to perform actions that are impossible to perform—or even clearly to specify. So when viewed under the aspect of practicability the issue of duties looks potentially to undermine the genuineness of the right.

However, I shall argue that this is not a problem which is peculiar to environmental rights and which does not affect the classical liberal rights. To show this will require looking again, a little more closely, at the understanding of rights.

1.3.2 *Defending the case means critically assessing the relation of rights to duties*

To begin with, the thesis espoused by Cranston about the necessary universality of duties has to be critically examined. For what I wish to explain here is why a universal duty, in his sense, is not always—or even generally—either (*a*) necessary or (*b*) sufficient for the universality of any human right.

(a) From the point of view of the practicability of a right, it is not necessary for its universality that the right correlate to a universal duty in the sense discussed above. In a contemporary response to Cranston, D. D. Raphael distinguished what he called a 'strong' sense, of the expression 'a universal moral right' from a weaker sense: in the weaker sense it means a right of all, but not necessarily against all, and may correspond to a duty of some only. Raphael remarked that economic and social rights, as well as the political right of participation in government, are universal rights in the weaker sense (Raphael 1967: 65). To call these stronger and weaker senses, though, is still to concede too much to Cranston's view. If a duty *applies* so that every right holder is protected by it, then it makes no difference to the right's 'strength' whether the duty is held by all or only by some; as Henry Shue more recently encapsulated the point, universal rights 'entail not universal duties but full coverage' (Shue 1988: 690). If the distribution of the duties is sufficient to fulfil the rights, then the rights are universal in a plain sense which does not admit of a subdivision into strong and weak senses.

It is thus a mistake to suppose that a universal right has to correlate with a universal duty in Cranston's sense. There is nothing in the logic of rights that precludes the possibility of a universal right corresponding to duties held only by some other parties, or even by a single individual. The mistake about universal rights arises, though, from a mistaken presumption about the nature of rights as such. It is a mistake to say, as Cranston does, that to speak of a right is to speak of a duty as if these are simply two sides of the same coin (or a single relationship described from two perspectives). There is, to be sure, a category of rights for which it is the case that the right and its correlative duty constitute a single relation such that the right is nothing other than what the duty demands and vice versa. This is the category of rights analysed by Wesley N. Hohfeld (1918) as 'claim–rights', which arise in bilateral legal relations which are such that, by definition, the meaning of A's right is equivalent to B's duty. This category does not, however, comprise what Hohfeld calls 'privileges' and what others refer to variously as rights of action, liberty rights or liberties, or rights of participation. As Hohfeld explains, when A is at liberty to do X, the only reference to a duty this implies is the absence of a duty on A 'not to do X'. If A does not succeed, or even attempt, to do X, there has been no failure of any duty. If the liberty to do X is sufficiently important to count as a human right, then it needs to be protected by a 'perimeter' of duties on others not to interfere, and perhaps also to enable A to do X. These duties are not correlatives of the right, though, and which particular ones are required to protect it can only be decided by reference to practical necessity, not deduced from the idea of the right itself. Nor does correlativity apply to those other two general categories of rights—that are of particular practical relevance at the constitutional and human rights level—which Hohfeld calls powers and immunities. In all these other cases, then, the relation between a right and the duties necessary to give it effect is not one of straightforward correlativity.

The correlativity thesis (which Cranston's view of universal rights presupposes) does not hold in a straightforward way for *any* rights in a human rights or constitutional context, since these are never simple bilateral relations: they typically involve a 'cluster' of right/duty relations, and can also often include the 'second order' relations of powers and immunities. It is not the case that to every right there corresponds one single duty which is necessary and sufficient to secure the substance of the right: 'Many rights ground duties which fall short of securing their object, and they may ground many duties not one.' (Raz 1986: 170–1). Thus a further point, particularly relevant to the implementation (including constitutional) of rights, is that there need be no closed list of duties which correspond to the right.

The existence of a right often leads to holding another to have a duty because of the existence of certain facts peculiar to the parties or general to the society in which they live. A change of circumstances may lead to the creation of new duties based on the old right.... This dynamic aspect of rights, their ability to create new duties, is fundamental to any understanding of their nature and function in practical thought. (Raz 1986: 171)

Thus one may know of the existence of a right and of the reasons for it without knowing who is bound by duties based on it or what precisely are these duties. For example, one may know that every child has a right to education, and therefore that there are duties to provide children with education, but one may have not formed (in advance) any particular view on who has what duty. Similarly, then, one can claim that there is a right to an adequate environment without necessarily being able to pinpoint (in advance) which duties it entails.[10]

Now it might be thought that a problem with this view is that there could turn out to be intractable difficulties in the way of actually assigning the duties. However, it has to be stressed that this is an issue of practicability rather than an objection of principle, and that as such it applies even to rights which appear—on an abstract view—not to be subject to such difficulties. To show this is to show—which is the second point of this subsection—why universal duties are not sufficient in general to ensure the practical enforcement and enjoyment of human rights.

(b) It has been acknowledged that a universal negative duty would not suffice to make good the environmental right in practice, but what I wish to emphasize now is that this is also the case for other negative rights—even for such an apparent counter-example as the right not to be tortured. For that right, it is certainly true that if every human refrained from torturing, the substance of the right would be universally enjoyed; but it is also true that if every human refrained from harming others' environment, the right would be universally enjoyed. A relevant difference between the two kinds of right may be supposed to arise, however, with the acknowledgement that there is no credible sense, given the socioeconomic organization of the world as it is, in which the abstention from certain actions by individuals can suffice to protect the environment. In fact, though, the contrast with the right not to be tortured is not so stark on this point as might be supposed. Each of us who belong to that fortunate majority of humankind that never come under any instruction to abuse the detainees of a ruling force are fully complying with our negative duty to refrain from torture, but simply in so complying we are doing nothing whatsoever to fulfil the human right of those humans who are subject to its violation.[11] I would go so far as to say that the fact we are under the duty has no practical relevance to the abuse-sufferers—and it is practicability rather than underlying normative principles which is at issue in the alleged contrast. Thus, as with the environmental right, a universal negative duty does not suffice to make good in practice the right not to be tortured. The reasons why it does not are also comparable: the circumstances under which a right not to be tortured is violated are not brought about simply by numbers of individuals failing to recognize their negative duty, but rather are a result of a systematic organization of power within which specific responsibilities are murkily dispersed (Hayward 1995: 158–72). So if the causality of environmental harms is complex and collective, so too is that of human rights abuses which are, by definition, systematic—it is this, after all, which distinguishes human rights violations from crimes. To secure the right not to be tortured, the universal negative duty does not suffice and what is required, in Cranston's words, are processes of socialization and democratization. It is these which institute and give substance to the rule of law that makes universal respect for human rights possible. Cranston himself sees these processes as distinct from genuine human rights, but that is an oddly unrealistic view to take: the rights he recognizes as genuine, such as a right of freedom from slavery, for instance, were only attained through such processes (no doubt in the face of objections from certain quarters regarding their impracticability); moreover, globally, those processes are not yet anywhere near universal completion even for the classical liberal rights.

So I claim that the right to an adequate environment is universal. There are problems of practicability to solve, but my argument is that these are problems that *can* be solved—with requisite political will; and that the moral argument has it that there *ought* to be the attempt to solve them, and thus that there *ought* to be that political will.

This, then, completes the case for the right as a universal *moral* right.

1.4 International recognition of a human right to an adequate environment: the precedents

The general idea that humans have rights in relation to the environment is quite a recent one. It did not figure in the early proclamations of the 'rights of man', and even in the mid-twentieth century, the UN Declaration made no mention of it, and nor did the European Convention on Human Rights. Indeed, traditionally, to the extent that human rights were conceived as having any implicit environmental reference at all, they included rights to acquire property in and dispose freely of the natural world as resources. Environmental rights go against the grain of this tradition by setting limits to human appropriation and use of the natural world. To be sure, the idea of environmental *constraints* on property rights is not entirely new (Brubaker 1995). It is also the case that ever since claims of rights relating to healthy working and living conditions have been recognized, a connection to environmental concerns has been implicit. But the idea of environmental rights as having a moral and legal status equivalent to that of established civil and political rights, or even to that of social and economic rights, has only started to be given any general credence at all over the past thirty years or so.

The first authoritative statement supporting the idea of environmental human rights appeared in the 1972 Stockholm Declaration agreed at the UN Conference on the Human Environment:

Man has the fundamental right to freedom, equality, and adequate conditions of life, in an environment of a quality that permits a life of dignity and well-being, and he bears a solemn responsibility to protect and improve the environment for present and future generations.   (Principle 1)

Although the Stockholm Declaration was legally a non-mandatory document, the thinking it represents has become increasingly diffused. A number of non-binding but widely accepted declarations supporting the individual's right to a clean environment have subsequently been adopted. Environmental rights have figured in regional agreements. The 1981 African Charter of Human and Peoples' Rights has provided 'All peoples shall have the right to a general satisfactory environment favourable to their development' (Article 24). The 1969 American Convention on Human Rights in the Area of Economic, Social and Cultural Rights (Protocol of San Salvador) includes in its 1989 Additional Protocol a similar provision: 'Everyone shall have the right to live in a healthy environment...' (Article 11—in Kiss 1992: 35) The link between human rights and environmental protection was given a further impetus with the Brundtland Report of 1987, which presented the basic goals of environmentalism as an extension of the existing human rights discourse, and proposed the formulation of the right which is taken as canonical here: 'All human beings have the fundamental right to an environment adequate for their health and well-being' (WCED 1987: 348). Additionally, an international treaty particularly worthy of mention is the 1989 UN Convention on the Rights of the Child, which has been almost universally ratified, and which provides, in Article 24, a right of the child 'to the enjoyment of the highest attainable standard of health', to be implemented through, inter alia, 'the provision of adequate nutritious foods and clean drinking water, taking into consideration the dangers and risks of environmental pollution'.

These various developments, combined with the fact that the fundamental significance of environmental protection has come to be reflected in the enacted constitutional law of a large number of countries, encouraged the UN Sub-Commission on the Prevention of Discrimination and Protection of Minorities to undertake a study of human rights and the environment. The Final Report of the Sub-Commission in 1994 (the 'Ksentini Report') offers a conception of human rights and the environment which captures the spirit of Principle 1 of the 1972 Stockholm Declaration. Based on a survey of national and international human rights law and of international law, which found regional and international human rights bodies to be increasingly willing to accept complaints of human rights violations based on ecological considerations, the report's most fundamental conclusion was that there had occurred a shift from environmental law to the right to a healthy and decent environment. This right, the report argues, is part of existing international law and is capable of immediate implementation by existing human rights bodies. The Sub-Commission went on to propose a declaration of 'Principles on Human Rights and the Environment' (see above, pp. 29–31) which 'would give environmental rights an autonomous and explicit character which, by and large, they lack in present international law' (Boyle 1996: 44). These principles proclaim, *inter alia*, that 'All persons have the right to a secure, healthy and ecologically sound environment'. The *Draft Declaration of Principles on Human Rights and the Environment*, suggests Popovic, might serve 'as a vehicle for development of a formal, binding international legal instrument that protects environmental human rights' (Popović 1996a: 497).

However, to date, no such internationally binding instruments have been created. Moreover, the human rights perspective on environmental protection has not been unwaveringly maintained. Twenty years after the Stockholm Declaration, the

1992 Rio Conference on Environment and Development, for instance, which in many senses was the successor to the Stockholm Declaration, avoided the terminology of rights in its declaration that 'Human beings are at the centre of concerns for sustainable development. They are entitled to a healthy and productive life in harmony with nature.' Alan Boyle sees this failure to give greater explicit emphasis to human rights as 'indicative of continuing uncertainty and debate about the proper place of human rights law in the development of international environmental law' (Boyle 1996: 43). Boyle also notes, though, that the Rio Declaration does not entirely abandon the territory of environmental rights, and in one respect it makes a significant contribution to their development: 'Principle 10 does give substantial support in mandatory language for participatory rights of a comprehensive kind':

At the national level, each individual shall have appropriate access to information concerning the environment that is held by public authorities, including information on hazardous materials and activities in their communities, and the opportunity to participate in decision-making processes. States shall facilitate and encourage public awareness and participation by making information widely available. Effective access to judicial and administrative proceedings, including redress and remedy, shall be provided.   (Ref in Boyle 1996: 60, n. 75)

The development of procedural environmental rights was given a highly significant impetus with the Aarhus Convention, which, developed under the auspices of the UN Economic Commission for Europe (ECE), was signed in June 1998 by thirty-five countries from this region, which covers the whole of Europe as well as parts of Central Asia, the United States, Canada, and Israel, although the North American countries opted out of the process. This agreement represents probably the most important step yet taken towards environmental rights protection: it establishes rights—to information, to participation in decision-making, and to access to justice in environmental matters—which it expressly affirms are aimed at securing the right to a healthy environment. Although the Convention is only binding with regard to these procedural rights, it does expressly recognize in its Preamble, as the reason for these rights, 'that every person has a right to live in an environment adequate to his or her health and well-being'.

So, while it would be premature to assert that international law definitely recognizes a human right to an adequate environment, there have been sufficiently significant moves in this direction to support a prima facie case for asserting that an environmental human right is emerging in international law. For effective implementation, though, it is crucial that the right be given the force of a constitutional provision.

1.5 Conclusion

In this chapter I have explained why a right to an adequate environment can and should be considered a genuine human right: as a moral right, it is on a par with established universal human rights in terms of passing the requisite tests; and as a positive right it is in the process of acquiring an equivalent status. While recognizing that it would be premature to reason as if it already had that status in international law, I believe that a strong enough case has been made to motivate the question whether there are good principled reasons to truncate rather than promote its further development through constitutional implementation.

Notes

1. In the Philippines, the *Oposa Minors* case (see Chapter 6) put the right 'to a balanced and healthful ecology' to this end.
2. Because throughout this book the right to an adequate environment will be conceived as a right of individuals, some comments here are in order about the suggestion that, since environmental concerns are generally collective concerns, environmental rights are archetypal examples of collective rights and ought to be considered *group* rights (which are sometimes referred to as a 'third generation' of rights). First, it is important to distinguish between rights relating to collective interests in general and group rights more specifically. The idea of group

rights applies in relation to issues regarding which groups as such are in some sense the irreducible 'agency' or bearer of the interest in question—for example, a language, culture, or 'way of life'—and where it is in some sense the *identity* of the group, and its survival or self-determination as a group, which is at stake. Environmental interests are not generally of this kind. To be sure, there are particular cases where an identifiable group in that sense does have specific environmental interests that are peculiar to it and not shared by others—and these cases are paradigmatically those regarding indigenous peoples. Hence, it is not inappropriate that in this specific context the Ksentini report alludes to group rights. In this respect, though, the 'group rights' asserted of indigenous peoples are more closely akin to the sovereign rights of nation-states over their natural resources than to the human right to an adequate environment.

In other contexts and more generally it would be a mistake to think of environmental rights as group rights in the specialist sense. The temptation to do so arises in cases which share certain features of the indigenous peoples cases in that environmental harms afflict an identifiable social group within a society. But as long as the group is *of* that society, and is not in some politically meaningful sense a distinct 'people', then the environmental harms afflicting it should be regarded as an aggregate of the individual harms of the members comprising it. There is nothing lost or distorted in taking this approach and something gained. Nothing is lost, since class actions are always possible on the basis of individual rights. Nothing is distorted, since there is no burden of having to 'prove' that the persons concerned constitute a group in any sense other than the relevant one of being victims of common harm. Something is gained, for them, since while class actions are possible on the basis of individual rights, the contrary is not possible. Something which is gained or preserved more generally is part of the key rationale for human rights as such: human rights, being rights held by each human in virtue of being human, are necessarily rights of each human; part of the normative force of the human rights discourse is to preclude the merging of any individual human's interests into a larger unit to which any special benefits or burdens might then be applied.

Finally, the focus on individual rights should not be mistaken for a commitment to 'individualism' in any moral sense that might reasonably be characterized pejoratively; the commitment is rather to the universal applicability of certain fundamental values that hold

good for each and every human being in virtue of fundamental characteristics they share and independently of what ends they pursue or
associations they form.

3. See, for example, Dobson (2000: 51–61); the distinction first received
an influential formulation in Norton (1984).

4. Here, the weak/strong distinction could be presented as a distinction
between a more/less *enlightened* conception of human interests—see
Hayward (1998*a*, *b*).

5. I should stress that in criticizing one aspect of Pogge's *conception* of
human rights my aim is a circumscribed one. The broader argument
he develops is an important one deserving of serious attention in its
own terms.

6. For an influential statement of this widely accepted point see Hart
(1984).

7. For an elaboration of the meaning and justification of this principle
see, for example, Habermas (1990: 43–115).

8. This view is not inconsistent with the proposal of Alston (1984) for
procedural criteria for determining the genuineness of a human right
at the level of international law, since this proposal has determinate
purposes in mind. He also recognizes that human rights can be
argued for in other ways and that ultimately their genuineness
beyond the level of philosophy is a political matter.

9. Compare Ernst Bloch (1961) on natural law 'from below' and its relation to human rights.

10. Lest it be thought that there is any tension here with what I said in
the critical discussion of Pogge above, some further clarification may
be in order. I maintain (in contrast to Pogge) that a putative moral
right needs to be understood as supplying a determinate normative
direction to be given effect in law. The truth, which the correlativity
thesis skews, 'is that any genuine right must involve some normative
direction of the behaviour of persons other than the holder' (Martin
1993). Exactly how that direction translates into determinate duties
of determinate parties for any particular right, however, is a subsequent question that cannot be answered simply by analysing an
abstract statement of the right. The normative direction could be
understood as implying whatever duties are necessary to respect, protect, and fulfil the right in question (Viljanen 1994: 61). Shue, too,
says 'there are no one-to-one pairings between kinds of duties and
kinds of rights. The complete fulfilment of each kind of right involves
the performance of multiple kinds of duties.' (Shue 1980: 52). For

Shue, these are duties to *avoid* depriving, to *protect* from deprivation, and to *aid* the deprived.

Sometimes, according to Rex Martin, constitutional rights can be conceived, implemented, and enforced without any reference to duties as such at all. He claims, for instance, that the basic constitutional right of Americans to free speech 'does not create an area of free choice by imposing obligations on others; instead it does so by imposing a normative disability . . . on Congress. The First Amendment "deprives Congress of the authority . . . to enact laws requiring or prohibiting speech of certain kinds."' Thus, although the right to freedom of speech has a conceptual correlative, this is not a duty but a legislative disability; in this case, then, the right itself is what Hohfeld would call an 'immunity'. He continues: 'More generally, the most important means of institutionalizing some rights may be to create second-party disabilities (or, sometimes, to create what Hohfeld called liabilities rather than duties)' (Martin 1993: 31). Legal liabilities, viewed ethically, are equivalent to the idea of responsibilities referred to by Raz (1986; see also Hayward 1995: 168–72).

11. Thus, insofar as a human right is considered a moral right, as it is in the present discussion, I reaffirm my agreement with Pogge that an institutional understanding of it is appropriate. I do also continue to maintain, though, the 'familiar' institutional understanding which requires the right's juridification in a suitable form, and do not accept Pogge's suggestion that all moral human rights can be understood as 'negative rights'.

2

Constitutionalizing the Right to an Adequate Environment: Challenges of Principle

The claim of this chapter is that any state which is constitutionally committed to the implementation and protection of human rights ought to constitutionalize a right to an adequate environment. There are two ways this could be argued.

One would be along the following lines: all human rights ought to be constitutionalized; the right to an adequate environment is a human right; therefore the right to an adequate environment ought to be constitutionalized. As I show in the first section, though, while there is something to be said for this argument, it is nonetheless vulnerable to the objection, directed against its major premise, that there is no reason why all (or even any) human rights ought necessarily to be constitutionalized. I show that this objection can be met, but only by delimiting the category of 'all human rights' so that it includes only those already recognized as such by states in international agreements, which means that the right to an adequate environment no longer falls unequivocally under it. I also emphasize, though, that the argument advanced on this basis is problematized rather than completely defeated, since circumstances can be envisaged under which the right to an adequate environment did receive the requisite recognition.

Nevertheless, to make a case with more immediate applicability, the rest of the chapter relies on a different supporting argument for its central claim, namely, that regardless of what reasons there might be why a state ought to constitutionalize *all* human rights, if a state is committed to the constitutionalization of *any* human rights as fundamental rights, then it ought to be committed to the constitutionalization of the right to an adequate environment. This argument does not proceed from premises about the nature of human rights and the imperative to constitutionalize them, but is rather an argument for an equivalence between a right to an adequate environment and those rights which already have fundamental constitutional status. There is at least a core set of human rights which are included as fundamental rights virtually without fail in any modern constitution.

This core includes: the right to life, freedom from torture, freedom from arbitrary arrest and detention, the right to be presumed innocent, the right to privacy, freedom of movement, the right to property, freedom of thought, conscience and religion, freedom of expression, freedom of assembly and association, and the right to participate in government. (Alston 1999: 2)

Having already made the case for the right to an adequate environment as a similarly fundamental universal human right of paramount moral and social importance, I will argue that there is no compelling reason of a normative kind to withhold that same constitutional status from the right to an adequate environment.

This argument can be challenged by sceptics. In particular, it will be pointed out that there are other human rights, for which powerful normative arguments can be advanced but which are not unambiguously embraced in international law, that are not unfailingly to be found in all constitutions, and when they are may be provided for in the form not of a right but of a general policy statement. Accordingly, Section 2.2 assesses the argument that provisions relating to the right to an adequate environment should be made constitutionally only in the form of a policy statement and not as a fundamental right. I show that the reasons advanced for this conclusion do not succeed in undermining the argument of equivalence.

In Section 2.3, I address a counterargument that would seek to qualify rather than undermine the equivalence. This counterargument starts from the observation that there are other human rights, for which powerful normative arguments can be made and which have wide recognition in international law, that are indeed included in constitutions but are provided with a lower status and less binding force than those of Alston's core set, or may be hedged in with various caveats and qualifications to similar effect. These are constitutionally classed, in contradistinction to *fundamental* rights, as *social* rights. In light of this, the counterargument would claim that the right to an adequate environment is more similar to and so should be placed with those rights of the second order—the 'social rights'—rather than among the fundamental rights. A problem with this particular argument, however, is that it relies on a distinction—between fundamental and social rights—that at the relevant level of conceptual analysis is flawed, since the two categories cannot be so delimited as to be mutually exclusive. This means that even if in some respects the right to an adequate environment resembles some of the rights classed as social rights, this would be an insufficient principled basis for denying it fundamental status. Furthermore, one also has to take into account the ways in which the right to an adequate environment does not resemble a social right. These considerations are brought together with the other conclusions drawn up to this point in the final section to show how it can be affirmed that the right to an adequate environment ought to be constitutionalized as a fundamental right.

2.1 Why the right to an adequate environment ought to be constitutionalized

The general reason why the right to an adequate environment ought to be constitutionalized is that it is a human right; and human rights, as was mentioned in Chapter 1, can be so understood as requiring implementation as fundamental rights, the most stringent form of normative commitment, in a state's constitution, in order that they can be given full effect. Yet, this understanding, as we also saw, is not without its dissenters.

The argument to be examined initially is—expanding a little on the simplified version stated in the introduction—this: all human rights ought to be provided as fundamental rights in the constitution of any modern democratic state; the right to an adequate environment is a human right; therefore the right to an adequate environment ought to be provided as a fundamental right in the constitution of every modern democratic state. The focus of attention will be on its major premise—'all human rights ought to be provided as fundamental rights in the constitution...'—since this can be challenged on the grounds that there is no reason following from the normative logic of human rights that dictates that they ought to be constitutionalized (in any particular canonical formulation, or even at all) as fundamental rights. I shall show that this challenge necessitates a reformulation of the premise, but not its abandonment. However, the problem that then follows is that in picking out reasons *why* the major premise can be held true we are obliged to qualify the characterization of 'human rights' in such a way that the right to an adequate environment can no longer be unequivocally included among their number, and thus the minor premise is called into question. Yet, even if the argument does not directly succeed, it is nonetheless worth rehearsing because, in showing why it does not succeed at the present time, the conditions under which it would are revealed, and these are conditions which, while not currently obtaining, could nevertheless feasibly be envisaged to hold at some point in the future. In the closing part of the section, I briefly set out the reformulated version of the argument that will actually be relied on in the remainder of this chapter.

2.1.1 *Assessing the claim that 'all human rights ought to be constitutionalized'*

A general justification for the premise—'all human rights ought to be provided as fundamental rights in the constitution of any

modern democratic state'—is the normative claim that a commitment to human rights principles entails a commitment to enforce
them and the further claim, which has an empirical dimension,
that the appropriate way to enforce them is to enshrine them
among the highest imperatives of the state as provided in its constitution as fundamental rights, since only these provide sufficiently
stringent guarantees of a commitment to their enforcement.
Against this, it can be argued that whether or not, in any given circumstances, it may be 'appropriate', it is not *necessary*. That is, there
is no necessity following from the general normative logic of
human rights for any of them to be constitutionalized as fundamental rights of the constitution.

   This has been argued by Jeremy Waldron, for instance, who has
pointed out that the desiderata of human rights can be expounded
in more general or more specific ways. On the one hand, they can
be articulated in terms of a few moral fundamentals, such as
autonomy and well-being, which are quite abstract and general
in character;[1] on the other, the implications of those fundamentals
can be spelled out in quite specific rights. As Waldron illustrates:
'A right to the protection of one's home against unreasonable
searches is likely to be based on the importance accorded to a
deeper individual interest such as privacy. A right to privacy may
in turn be based on even deeper premises about the importance of
autonomy and self-governance' (Waldron 1993: 21). The familiar
lists of human rights emerge at an intermediate level between the
more abstract and more concrete: 'As we move from deep abstract
premises to particular concrete recommendations, we may find
ourselves saying things like "People have a right to free speech" or
"Everyone has a right to elementary education"...' (p. 22). If the
normative logic of human rights derives its moral force from the
fundamental premises, then it leaves as an open question how
much specificity constitutional statements of their human rights
commitments should have. Waldron puts the point a bit more
strongly than this, though, saying that it even leaves as an open
question whether they should be included as *rights* in a constitution at all, since 'there is no necessary inference from the premises

of a right-based moral theory to the desirability of constitutional rights as a particular political arrangement' (p. 20), and 'a concern for individual rights may lie in the foundations of a theory, leaving it an open question what those foundations entail at the level of political and constitutional construction' (p. 21).

Before assessing this argument it is worth stressing that to deny that there is a *necessity* for all or any human rights to be constitutionalized is not to show that none ought to be, as Waldron and others (e.g. Bellamy 1995) have further claimed. The reasons in support of this more radical claim will be considered and rebutted in Chapter 4.

The aspect of Waldron's argument which I shall here examine purports to establish that the moral commitments represented by any given human right do not entail that a state should provide for meeting them by means of a constitutional right. What Waldron argues is that the normative claim

(1) P has a (moral) right to X

does not entail

(2) P (morally) ought to have a legal right to X

but only that

(3) The law ought to be such that P gets X. (p. 24)

Waldron is surely correct about this. But the denial of (2) does not require arguing since it would be an irrelevant claim anyway. This is because a constitutional right is a distinct kind of normative entity from a legal right. A legal right is, as Waldron himself notes, 'a highly specific type of institutional arrangement', whereas a constitutional right only implies that some specific institutional arrangement ought to be put in place in order to secure the substance of the right; it does not need to specify the type of arrangement. I thus have no reason to demur when he illustrates his point by saying 'a moral claim that people have the right to shelter is a claim about the importance of their getting shelter. It is not a claim about the importance of their being assigned shelter in accordance with a specific type of legal or bureaucratic procedure' (p. 25).

Constitutional rights do not have to specify any particular type of legal or bureaucratic procedure.

The relevant question therefore is whether (3) entails the further proposition

(4) P (morally) ought to have a constitutional right to X

It is possible to deny that (3) strictly entails (4), since the requirement that 'the law ought to be such that P gets X' can in principle be met by means other than the provision of an express constitutional right to X. Proposition (3) can reasonably be understood as articulating an obligation on the state to ensure that a certain entitlement, benefit, or protection (X) is secured for the individual P, and it is reasonable to say that states' obligations are properly enshrined in their constitution, but it might be argued that this obligation could in principle be provided in the form of a policy statement rather than a right.

However, the question would have to be posed of whether there is some good reason why a policy statement would be required but a right would not: if it has been accepted that the aim or desideratum in question is appropriately expressed in the form a moral right, why should it not retain the form of a right when it comes to receive constitutional recognition? Waldron states that '[t]he fact that there are rights in the foundations does not mean that there need to be rights, so to speak, all the way up' (p. 22). However, I would suggest that there must be at least a presumption that it does mean this when the moral rights in question are human rights. That presumption can be justified by the following thought. In the deepest moral foundations in question there are interests which are deemed so important they ought to have practical recognition in the form of rights, this form being uniquely well-suited to protect and promote those interests because of the duties on others that it implies as an imperative. At this level of ethical thought, one need entertain no specific hypotheses about the form of social organization within which persons are related or therefore about the specific form of the duties concerned. The thought thus envisages no cut-off point for the imperative to retain the form of a right short of finding as good or better a way of protecting the fundamental interests.

Nevertheless, as previously acknowledged, such a thought, as it moves from fundamental interests to specifying increasingly detailed and particular manifestations of them, must at some point find the normative force of the moral human right 'runs out'. What I wish to maintain, though, is that its force does hold good at least up to the point where the fundamental interests find canonical expression in international human rights agreements. To take these formulations as definitive may seem arbitrary from a purely moral point of view, but if we are considering specifically what a state ought to be committed to it is not. If a state's constitution is not seen as a hermetically isolated domestic matter, if the state is seen as also having binding international obligations which it has to incorporate domestically, then for it to take over those obligations in the form in which it has recognized them is not arbitrary. My claim then is that proposition (3) broadly captures what international human rights obligations mean for a state, and what domestic courts understand them to mean. Part of that understanding would be the entailment of (4) since this preserves the necessary congruity between a state's obligations *as framed* internationally and as enforced domestically. Viewed in this light the provision of a policy statement could be seen as a partial, provisional, or imperfect recognition of the obligation. A right is what ought to be provided, and a right in substantially the same formulation.

Taking this line, though, does mean that in order to preserve the major premise of the argument under consideration in this section it has to be reformulated so as to hold that 'all human rights *that a state recognizes in its international treaty obligations* ought to be provided in a similar form in that state's domestic constitution'. On this formulation, the validity of the premise does not depend directly on moral first principles but on the intermediate moral deliverances of the thirty or so human rights—as found in the international and regional charters and conventions—which are already accepted as valid by states.[2]

Of course, this revision of the major premise then necessitates a corresponding amendment to the original formulation of the minor premise—'there is a human right to an adequate environment'—if the argument is to be maintained. Yet, what was shown in Chapter 1 was that even though there is a moral case for seeing the right to an adequate environment as a human right, and some reason to think it is emerging in international law, it is not at present generally recognized as belonging among the obligations that I am now invoking as the basis for constitutionalizing the rights which states do recognize. Therefore it cannot at present truly be asserted as a minor premise that of any state 'a right to an adequate environment is a human right *which that state recognizes in its international treaty obligations*'; therefore the conclusion that this right ought to be recognized in any state's domestic constitution cannot directly be affirmed on the basis of the argument being canvassed. That argument has been worth defending, though, since it need not be entirely moot, given that the right is in the process of emergence, and given that its recognition by at least some states is a factor in its emergence.

The argument reformulated   In the rest of this chapter, I shall put the above argument aside and defend the reformulated claim that *if* a state recognizes that *any* human rights ought to be constitutionalized as fundamental rights, then it should recognize that the right to an adequate environment ought to be constitutionalized as a fundamental right. An argument for this reformulated claim is clearly not moot since the kinds of state to which it applies do actually recognize at least some human rights (i.e. Alston's core set—see Introduction) as fundamental rights of the constitution, and in doing so they make express reference to the normative status of human rights as the reason why they do. My argument for the claim is, briefly stated, that the right to an adequate environment does not differ in any salient respect— other than its not already unequivocally having that status—from those established rights. For the rest, the considerations advanced in Chapter 1 for its status as a human right come into play: the content of the right is stated at the appropriate level of generality— it is not too specific to be applicable in any constitutional context, yet it is clearly distinct from any other human right; and it conforms to the requirements of a generalizable right in being of universal applicability and of considerable moral and social importance. (Furthermore, the fact that it appears to be emerging as a recognized right in international law, while not as yet providing decisive affirmative support, is a relevant consideration.) Given, then, that states also recognize that environmental protection should have some constitutional provision, an objection to my argument would have to show that the right to an adequate environment ought to have a lesser constitutional status than that of a fundamental right. There are, in practice, two main alternatives: to provide for it by means either of general policy statements or of rights that do not have fully fundamental status in the constitution. In the next two sections, I show in turn why arguments for these two alternatives do not succeed.

2.2 Why environmental protection should not be constitutionalized only in the form of a policy statement

Those who resist the constitutionalization of environmental rights do not normally attack the principle that enhancing environmental protection is a desirable social aim; and seldom would it be argued nowadays that no mention at all of this general aim should be included in constitutional documents, perhaps in the form of a general policy statement. The focus of resistance is on proposals to make this into a constitutional *right*. For a choice, which those debating the introduction of environmental protection into a constitution must consider, is 'whether to declare an enforceable, environmental fundamental right or to include a statement of public policy' (Brandl and Bungert 1992: 86). The latter type of constitutional provision contains directives and guidelines for governmental action. Unlike fundamental rights which, at least according to traditional liberal theory, limit governmental intrusions into the private sphere, statements of public policy encourage government action. While a public policy statement may be binding as to the end to be achieved, it normally remains to the state legislature to decide the means of implementation. A statement of public policy and a fundamental right would thus have different effects in constitutional litigation: 'although the existence of a statement of public policy must be given some consideration in a constitutional complaint as well, only a fundamental right grants the individual the legal remedy of a constitutional complaint' (Brandl and Bungert 1992: 32).

In practice, it has to be noted, the distinction between fundamental rights and policy statements is not always clear-cut. Constitutional provisions can be so worded as not to fit clearly into either category, and, as Brandl and Bungert have found, this is often the case with environmental provisions, in that most of these 'are not prototypes of fundamental rights, nor are they prototypes of statements of public policy. Rather, the formulation of each environmental provision falls somewhere along a continuum between the subjective fundamental right at one extreme, and the objective statement of public policy at the other' (Brandl and Bungert 1992: 18). Furthermore, the language used in constitutional articles can sometimes provide a misleading guide to the actual character of the provision. On the one hand, the language of fundamental rights can be used in a constitution for a provision which in practice can only have the effect of a policy principle; and the positioning of the right also affects its practical import, so that an apparent right can be undermined by other provisions of the constitution. On the other hand, policy principles can have the effect of rights if other qualifying or supporting articles of the constitution so affect the reading of the provision. Thus, the real application of a constitutional right is not necessarily evident on the face of its wording, or even in the wording of the document as a whole: 'the efficacy of a particular environmental constitutional provision is directly related to the overall character and conception of the constitution' (Brandl and Bungert 1992: 7). Such ambiguities and uncertainties, it may be argued, arise not merely from contingent features of particular constitutions and their contexts, but from a more general conceptual feature of constitutional provisions, namely, that fundamental rights can be viewed as the 'flipside' of policy principles when these impose obligations on a state. Viewed in this way, the two are not necessarily mutually exclusive alternatives (Popovic 1996b: 361–2).

Nevertheless, a significant conceptual distinction can still be drawn, as Brandl and Bungert observe, between 'a personal right which is enforceable by the individual', or a 'subjective' right, in other terminology, and 'an "objective" provision, proclaiming a state goal which must be respected in every balancing decision made by the government, but which is unenforceable by the individual' (Brandl and Bungert 1992: 7). The former is typically justiciable, whereas the latter has a more 'programmatic' character, reflecting general goals of the legislature rather than determining specific judicial outcomes.

Now some argue that if environmental provisions are to be constitutionalized, then they should have the form only of a policy statement and not of a fundamental right. The reason would be that policy statements, as objective goal-orientated provisions, are inherently better suited to the aims of environmental protection than are individual rights-based instruments. Environmental quality appears on this view to have more the character of a public good than that of the appropriate substance of an individual right, and hence would be more fittingly seen as a general social objective than as a matter of individual rights. The identifying of environmental harms and the appropriate steps to remedy them, it could therefore be argued, would better be addressed by concerted government-directed action than by individual claims in courts. Thus Günther Handl, for instance, believes that a generic environmental right would be an ill-considered proposition in that it would make broad environmental policy decisions a central concern of an individual-right-based process which is unsuited to dealing with them. It could defeat the purpose of a right which was intended to benefit all, he argues, if certain parties could use it to pursue their own special interests: 'the focus of inquiry in a case involving an individual complainant is by definition too limited to ensure consideration of all societal interests at stake', and 'a case-by-case development of general environmental standards in response to individual complaints would be a very inefficient process' (Handl 1992: 135).[3] Moreover, if some individuals can succeed in actions benefiting themselves, this may be detrimental to the environmental interests of others (e.g. by having polluting sources transferred to locations with less litigious populations)—which is a notable problem of environmental justice.

In response to these last specific points, it should be noted that there will always be some environmental harms which as a matter of fact do affect particular individuals or restricted groups rather than the population as a whole, and such parties should be allowed to claim appropriate protection. It would be unwarranted, empirically and normatively, simply to assume that no particular citizen—or group—has an individuated interest which differs from that of any other. Furthermore, the fact that a right is available to individuals does not mean that claims on its basis will necessarily be 'individualistic', and in practice such rights can be and are used as a basis for class actions and actions in the public interest.

With regard to the general objection, I will now argue that it rests on a mistaken contrast between the aims of environmental rights and those of established rights. I do not deny that it would seem odd to think of specific environmental goals purely in terms of individual interests; indeed, the inappropriateness may be compounded by the fact that individual environmental interests can vary in significant ways, reflecting differing vulnerabilities and sensitivities to particular inadequacies of environmental quality. Yet, it does not seem odd to say that the point of environmental protection is to secure an adequate environment for everyone, or, correspondingly, that anyone—whether as an individual or part of a group—whose environment is compromised has a legitimate prima facie claim for some form of remedy. There may be a dichotomy in traditional thinking between 'protecting the environment' and 'respecting individual rights', but in practice it tends to break down. As Advocate General Mischo remarked regarding the implementation of a European directive on air quality, 'there are the individuals, ordinary citizens who are thereby given the right that the air which they breathe should comply with the quality standards which have been laid down' (in Holder 1996: 332). Individuals, he stated, have a right to rely on those standards when they have been infringed. To defend an environmental right of individuals is not to deny a need for implementation of appropriately broader, non-individual oriented, policies; and constitutional provision of such a right would clearly not preclude these policies. Indeed, the right and the appropriate policy statements could be mutually supporting.

The argument I wish to advance here is that the contrast appealed to by the objection, between environmental rights and those 'genuinely individual' rights whose object is not thought of first and foremost as a public good, is overdrawn. The aim of ensuring, for instance, that each individual is not subjected to torture or to arbitrary detention is uncontroversially presented as a matter of individual rights, but it can also be taken to imply and be implied by a general policy objective orientated to the public good of a type of society that lives up to certain general standards of human decency, rather than this being something that each individual has to ensure himself or herself. As Joseph Raz argues, the importance attached to fundamental constitutional rights is not necessarily distinct from that attached to the protection and promotion of a certain public culture. 'That culture is in turn valued for its contribution to the well-being of members of the community generally, and not only of the right-holders' (Raz 1986: 256).

At least some constitutional rights are primarily means of formal or informal institutional protection of collective goods. They protect these collective goods inasmuch as damage to them is caused by harming the interests of identifiable individuals... Where harming an individual seriously jeopardises the maintenance of a public good that harm is also a cause of a harm to the community. (Raz 1986: 258).

Furthermore, some of the most established 'individualistic' rights have an inherent public and systemic dimension: regarding property rights and freedoms, for instance, the point is to maintain a system, not only for protection of individuals whose interests are interrelated, but also, in the final analysis, for their very existence as the rights they are.

I would thus claim that the objection to constitutionalizing the specific right to an adequate environment rests on mistaken assumptions about the 'individualistic' character of human and constitutional rights in general. The institutionalizing of rights serves as an authoritative marker that the interests they represent are deserving of special protection; the rights provide institutional recognition of the normative force of these interests, but should not be supposed to have a normative force which exceeds that of those interests. When a right is constitutionalized this means that decisions about the proper weight of those interests are subject to special constraints; it does not mean that the determination of public policy is suddenly abandoned to the vagaries of litigation on the behalf of individuals.

Having resisted the argument that policy statements should be provided *in place of* a fundamental right to an adequate environment, however, I do not deny that they should be provided as a complement to it. As noted earlier, there is a sense in which a policy statement can be seen as the 'flipside' of rights, inasmuch as it indicates the direction of state obligations corresponding to the right. So it is worth emphasizing that policy statements and rights are not mutually exclusive, and it may well be, as Brandl and Bungert argue, that in the case of constitutional provisions for environmental protection, both are necessary.

Thus we should reject the view that constitutional provision of a right to an adequate environment is less appropriate than provision of policy statements. Constitutional environmental protection may involve more than the protection of an individual right to an adequate environment, but it should not provide less. As a human right, it ought to be given explicit constitutional protection for the same reasons that any other human right ought to, and arguments to the contrary do not succeed in picking out reasons why this right should be considered an exception to that general principle.

2.3 Why a substantive right to an adequate environment should not be provided with lesser constitutional status than a fundamental right

I turn now to consider the argument that if a right to an adequate environment is to be constitutionalized, it ought to be provided with the lesser status sometimes accorded to 'social rights' rather than be included among a constitution's fundamental rights proper. I shall in due course challenge the rationale for placing the environmental right under the category of 'social rights', but the main argument of this section is directed against the very idea that a clear distinction ought to be drawn between fundamental and social rights in a constitution.

Certainly, it has to be acknowledged that in practice a distinction is as a matter of fact drawn between social and fundamental rights. Modern constitutions tend to have a relatively similar format, being divided into separate parts that deal with matters relating to the powers of government, the representation of the people, and rights. Within the part on rights, it is quite typical for a chapter setting out civil and political rights to be separate from a chapter containing provisions for other, generally more substantive, rights, including social, economic, and cultural ones. The chief difference between the two sets of rights is that the former are taken to be directly justiciable individual rights whereas the latter are normally interpreted more as manifestations of political programmes and are not necessarily directly enforceable by courts. This separation of two classes of rights has particular salience to our present concerns because in many constitutions that include environmental rights these are actually placed in the social rights chapter and not accorded fundamental status. Some of the implications of this practice are considered in the next chapter; the question here, though, is whether there is any clear conceptual or normative underpinning for that distinction.

The distinction is invoked to claim that treating social rights as fundamental rights is in some way inherently problematic or

self-contradictory.[4] This claim depends on establishing clear criteria for distinguishing social from fundamental rights. The criteria
appealed to come to rest on a basic distinction between 'positive'
and 'negative' rights. In this section, however, I show that this distinction breaks down and cannot support the social/fundamental
dichotomy. This means that the argument for classifying environmental rights as social and not fundamental rights falls by
default. There is, however, another argument of relevance to the
right to an adequate environment which presupposes (at least
tacitly) the validity of this distinction. This argument, which will
be considered in the latter part of the section, is that, because a
substantive environmental right is vulnerable to the kinds of
difficulties affecting social rights, constitutional environmental
rights should be *procedural* rights only.

2.3.1 Why the distinction between fundamental rights and social rights is conceptually problematic

As others have argued, the traditional objections to according a
fundamental status to social rights do not pick out all and only
social rights as these are classed in contradistinction to civil and
political rights. It is of relevance regarding the right to an adequate
environment to show that the reasons for discriminating between
two classes of constitutional right in fact reflect particular political
priorities rather than anything inherent in the nature of the rights'
substantive aims.

I shall begin by briefly sketching the standard view that maintains the traditional objections. Fundamental rights are typically
taken—at least in liberal democracies—to include classical civil
and political rights and freedoms (most prominently rights of
property, freedom of contract, freedom of speech, and freedom of
religion). Civil and political rights provide guarantees protecting
the individual's sphere of freedom from state interference; they
protect basic freedoms which are to be enjoyed equally by all and
are considered to be neutral with respect to controversial matters
of social policy. Social rights, by contrast, which include rights to

positive state protection of human well-being, such as the right to social security, to decent housing, to leisure, and to food, are not necessarily justiciable rights but may be only a statement of desirable social goals which the state should aim to achieve if—and to the extent that—it can.

Civil rights[5] were developed as a constraint upon the unwarranted interference of governments with the everyday lives of their citizens; social rights, by contrast, place a positive obligation on governments to ensure that their people can live and work in conditions suited to a basic level of human dignity. Thus a key distinction is held to be that between state involvement and state abstention. Social rights are claimed not to be a proper object for legal protection because they require the state to *do things*, that is, they commit the state to a positive course of action. This is supposed to distinguish social from civil and political rights, which would be mere *negative rights*, as they only restrain the action of the state, but do not mandate any specific course of action. Thus, those who seek to explain why social rights ought not to be considered fundamental rights in the constitutional sense invariably do so by invoking a distinction between 'negative' and 'positive' rights.

Before considering how that distinction can support an argument against the constitutionalizing of fundamental social rights, though, we should first note that, as many authors have pointed out, it is misleading to suggest that one category of rights, called 'negative' rights, do not entail a requirement that the state *do* something. Henry Shue, for example, illustrates the point that even 'negative' rights do require the state to do something by reference to the archetypal case of such a right, a right to physical security:

it may be possible *to avoid violating* someone's rights to physical security yourself by merely refraining from acting in any of the ways that would constitute violations. But it is impossible *to protect* anyone's rights to physical security without taking, or making payments towards the taking of, a wide range of positive actions. For example, at the very least the protection of rights to physical security necessitates police forces; criminal courts; penitentiaries; schools for training police, lawyers, and guards; and taxes to support an enormous system for the prevention, detection, and punishment of violations of personal security. (Shue 1980: 37–8)

A demand for physical security is thus not normally a demand simply to be left alone, observes Shue, but a demand to be protected against harm; it is a demand for positive action, and a demand for social guarantees against at least the standard threats. That the need for positive protective measures applies to classic liberties too has been affirmed even in courts: in the influential landmark case of *Airey* v. *Ireland* (2 Eur.CtHR Rep.305(1979)), for instance, the European Court of Human Rights held that 'fulfilment of a duty under the Convention on occasion necessitates some positive action on the part of the State' (para. 25).

So the issue is not simply whether the state must do something, but has rather to do with the nature of what it must do in the two cases. On traditional accounts, all the state must do to protect civil and political rights is pass laws and impose certain restraints on government; to secure social rights, by contrast, it must introduce programmes of provision that entail the allocation of resources. The initial statement of the contrast might therefore be qualified so as to grant to opponents like Shue that the actual provision of a 'negative right' may require the state to perform positive duties and that these carry administrative costs, while nonetheless maintaining that in the case of social rights, over and above those unavoidable costs, there will be the substantial costs which are, at least according to this argument, the very purpose of the rights. In drawing the contrast this way, the positive duties and burdens associated with a 'negative right' can be seen as providing merely 'peripheral' protections; those associated with a 'positive right' can be seen correlating directly and essentially with its 'core'. The claim of a clear and significant distinction between positive and negative rights can thus be preserved in this qualified version by maintaining that the costs incidental to or arising from full protection of civil and political rights differ both in degree and in principle—or quantitatively and qualitatively—from the costs of social rights, since in the latter case, transfers of resources are their very point. Even this qualified version, though, I shall indicate, does not succeed.

On the quantitative side of the question, social rights are taken, by those who resist their constitutionalization, to imply an undefined claim upon economic resources, and thus potentially to represent an unreasonable cost against other social objectives. To this it can be replied, however, along the lines Cecile Fabre (2000) suggests, that social rights do not give their right-holders the right to claim unlimited resources, but only guarantee the set of resources needed to fulfil the basic needs individuals have as humans and as members of a given society.

On the qualitative side, though, a further and distinct objection of principle to constitutionalizing positive social rights is that if courts were to adjudicate on the basis of these rights they would in effect be making budgetary decisions which exceed their constitutional competence,[6] since the requisite balancing and expenditure are not a competent matter for rights-institutions but for the government. This issue will be considered more fully in Chapter 3, but here I will merely raise the question of why it is thought that such decisions *ought* not to be made by the judiciary. For if the point of social rights is to secure citizens in the enjoyment of adequate *basic* living conditions, then this aim is not overambitious for any 'well-ordered' constitutional democracy; and any state which fails to secure it has failed in a basic duty. A court which rules that a social right has been violated does not have to prescribe specific policy measures for rectifying the situation: but if certain social groups have been severely disadvantaged by government policies, then they have been let down by the other branches of government, and it is only right that the judicial branch has the competence to require their plight to be remedied. To deny this, recourse to arguments about constitutional competence can be seen as in fact disguised advocacy of a more libertarian, less welfarist, political philosophy (Viljanen 1994). Indeed, to pursue the line of this denial consistently would mean claiming that social rights are not human rights at all, which is different from claiming they are human rights which only ought to have second class constitutional status, and such a claim falls outside the scope of the present inquiry.

Thus far I have shown that arguments against constitutionalizing social rights which depend on even the qualified version of the positive/negative rights distinction do not clearly succeed. My final observation is the more decisive one that these arguments are mistaken in their most basic assumption. The distinction they invoke depends on a claim that it is the very point of social rights to allocate or transfer resources. However, that is not their point at all. Their point is to secure citizens in the enjoyment of rights associated with adequate living conditions; they only entail a transfer of resources as a *means* to that end where it is not already being achieved. So for social rights, just as for the classic liberal rights, the question of resources can appropriately be conceived as having only an instrumental bearing.

This consideration reinforces the point that the comparative onerousness of negative and positive rights cannot be decided a priori. If practicability is the issue, and if this is mainly a question of costs, then the *whole* of the costs need to be assessed, regardless of whether they are conceived as arising in relation to the 'ends' or the 'means' of the right, its 'core' element or supporting 'peripheral' protections. It then has to be recognized as perfectly possible, for instance, that in a well-ordered state with low unemployment and limited inequalities of wealth and income, the costs of implementing social rights are less than would be the costs of protecting civil rights in a state marked by significant inequalities which generate pervasive threats to persons and property (Shue 1988).

Therefore, arguments which appeal to the positive/negative distinction to explain why civil and political rights ought to be more fundamental in a constitution than social rights are inherently problematic. More than this, though, they are also seriously incomplete. Some of the most important civil and (especially) political rights cannot be classified as either positive or negative. This is true of rights of participation. I shall not explore at length the general point here, but its relevance to environmental rights merits clarification. For there is a widely held view that environmental rights should be rights of participation only, not a substantive right to an environment of a specified adequacy.

2.3.2 *Why environmental rights should be substantive and not merely procedural*

Some legal theorists see the best way forward for environmental rights as lying in the provision of procedural rights rather than of a substantive right to an adequate environment (e.g. Handl 1992; Douglas-Scott 1996; Macrory 1996). Procedural environmental rights are essentially participatory rights in that they formally empower citizens to demand information relating to the environment, to participate in decision-making processes, and to apply for judicial means of redress. Unlike a substantive right to an adequate environment, they do not entail any direct obligations on the state regarding substantive environmental protection measures. The reasons given for favouring procedural rights have chiefly to do with relative practicability and ease of enforcement, which are issues to be discussed in the next chapter. The question here, though, is whether there is any principled normative justification for commending procedural environmental rights as a substitute for, rather than part of the means for fulfilment of, a substantive constitutional right to an adequate environment.

The usual argument in favour of procedural environmental rights is that they are less problematic to justify than a substantive right to an adequate environment because they do not commit governments to the achievement of specific substantive outcomes, but only to allowing the possibility of a hearing to those (whoever they are) who seek to influence outcomes. Yet, it would not be a good argument of principle to advocate procedural rights *simply* because they are less stringent or less demanding than a substantive right. A good argument to that effect would have to claim that the demands of the substantive right are excessively stringent, whereas those of procedural rights are as stringent as reasonably possible. To maintain the first part of this claim would in effect be to give credence to the 'social rights' objection to the substantive right (and thus to assume that my arguments above can be rebutted). What I shall show, however, is that if credence *is* given to that objection, then even procedural environmental rights will not be immune to it if—as required by the second part of the claim—they have any of the stringency of a substantive environmental right at all.

It might be supposed that procedural environmental rights are immune from the social rights objection because that objection targets positive rights, whereas procedural rights resemble negative rights insofar as they do not commit the government to 'do' anything (other than administratively, as, on the qualified version of the positive/negative distinction, negative rights are admitted to do). Yet, although procedural rights are not positive rights, they are not negative rights either. The procedural/substantive distinction does not map onto the negative/positive distinction. Negative rights, no less than positive rights, directly imply substantive ends, and ends that can be specified by reference to important interests of individuals. The end implied by a duty to refrain from an action is as substantive as that implied by a duty to act (the violation of a right not to be tortured, for instance, is not merely the violation of a procedure).[7]

Since procedural rights do not directly entail any substantive duty at all, it might be supposed that this would make procedural rights even less problematic to defend than negative rights. But that is not the case.

The reason why negative rights are immune from the criticisms directed at positive rights is that they do not intrinsically place any demands on the state which go beyond mere constraints on its powers to interfere with citizens' freedoms. These are freedoms of individuals to pursue a personal and private life unimpeded by state interference which are protected by negative rights—rights correlating with negative duties on the state. The use made of these freedoms, when it does not infringe others' freedom or contravene the law, is a matter of indifference from the point of view of the state. We can refer to this indifference as 'neutrality' with regard to the goods persons may happen to pursue. The freedoms which procedural rights serve to support (and indeed allow substance to), and which we may refer to as participatory rights, differ from those personal freedoms in important respects. Participatory rights are freedoms to take part, to *act* in the public realm, within fora and organs of the state itself. These are rights whose 'content' is closely defined by the state in terms of the procedures available for their exercise.

Viewed superficially, rights of participation may seem less demanding on the state than negative rights because they do not directly entail claims on the state, as both negative and positive rights do, either to its forbearance or its action. As 'active' rights, they differ from both positive and negative rights, which can be categorized as 'passive' rights, in that to be enjoyed they have to be exercised by the right-bearer. If the right-bearer happens not to exercise an 'active right' the state cannot be said thereby to have failed in any direct duty. Yet, for active rights to be enjoyed *as* rights, the state must fulfil positive duties to provide enabling conditions as well as negative duties to refrain from impeding their exercise. The duties of the state are thus more determinate and circumscribed than is the case for rights of a merely negative character. The state's procedural duties, moreover, are not neutral in the way that its purely negative duties can be conceived as being. That is to say, the procedures cannot be neutral with respect to the ends of government itself, for those ends define the very purpose of the procedures. These ends can only be conceived in the substantive terms of such practical ideals as democracy, justice, order, stability, economic freedom, and so on. In this respect, the duties on the state are by no means less demanding than for negative rights.

In a deep sense, then, participatory rights, and the procedures through which they are exercised, presuppose determinate substantive commitments on the part of the state. It is only if the ends of government are presumed to be beyond serious contention that participatory rights can reasonably be assimilated to purely negative rights and both held to be immune from contentious 'positive' obligations. For where there is contention, the 'pure procedures' may justifiably be perceived as systematically favouring substantive outcomes of one sort rather than another, as serving to provide substantive benefits to some which to others may in some way be objectionable. This would make 'procedural rights' subject to similar kinds of contestability that are claimed to affect social rights.

What is at issue, therefore, in characterizing certain specific procedural rights as *environmental* procedural rights, if this is anything other than an empty expression, is a question of the very ends of government. It is the question of whether these ends should include giving weight to environmental interests even when these come into conflict with established interests such as economic freedom and private property. Procedural environmental rights either imply a modification of the substantive ends of government or they do not. This forces the issue against those who see these rights as even a partial substitute for a substantive right to an adequate environment, since a 'less stringent' modification would still be a modification. It cannot consistently be maintained both that the procedural rights in question are distinctively environmental and that they are entirely neutral with regard to the potential outcomes of their exercise.[8] If there is any reason at all why *environmental* information, decision-making, and justice should be given any special provision in the constitution over and above that for information, participation, and justice more generally, it can only be the reason, which is actually stated in the preamble to the most important agreement to date on procedural rights, the Aarhus Convention, that 'every person has the right to live in an environment adequate to his or her health and well-being'.

If explicit acknowledgement of this substantive environmental right is accepted as the reason why there should be constitutional provision for procedural environmental rights, then the argument that procedural rights only should be constitutionalized, because the substantive environmental right somehow illicitly skews outcomes, loses not only normative force, but even conceptual coherence. If that reason is not accepted, then there would seem to be no reason of sufficiently compelling normative force requiring environmental procedural rights to be constitutionalized as a matter of course at all. So confronted with the social rights objection, procedural and substantive environmental rights stand or fall together. Having already rebutted that objection in principle, I therefore conclude they stand together.

In short, then, there is no reason why environmentalists or citizens in general—or indeed the state which is charged with representing their interests—ought to rest content with procedural environmental rights only. If procedural environmental rights ought to be treated as fundamental, there is no normative reason why substantive rights ought not to be.

2.4 Conclusion

In this chapter I have sought to show that there is no convincing argument against the case that a human right to an adequate environment ought to be a *fundamental* constitutional right. In addressing the counterarguments, I have not sought to deny that some of the demands of the right to an adequate environment could be constitutionalized in the form of policy statements or procedural rights. Nor have I denied that some of the demands may be akin to those of 'social rights' which some authors deem—albeit mistakenly on my view—to be other than fundamental. What I have sought to deny is that in the full range of its applications as implemented, the fundamental right should be restricted to instruments of those kinds.

In fact, a fundamental right in a constitution normally consists not of a single legal position but of a cluster of legal positions which correspond to different types of right which can be combined in a variety of ways (Viljanen 1994). In the light of the foregoing analyses of the positive/negative and substantive/procedural distinctions, we are brought to recognize three general types of rights: passive rights which are negative; passive rights which are positive; and active rights. The three types of right each correspond to a core modality of imperative: proscription, prescription, and permission. The following classification of constitutional rights from Günther Witzsch corresponds to this threefold typology:

1. As rights of defence (*status negativus*), i.e. the right of a person... against the encroachment by the state on his general individual freedom of conduct, for example the freedom of speech;
2. As rights of performance (*status positivus*), i.e. as rights to demand from the state positive actions or services to preserve or enhance his individual freedom, for example the right to the supply of food or shelter in order to guarantee his right to life or physical well-being;
3. As rights of participation (*status activus*), i.e. rights to have access to the management of the state, to his share in participating in public affairs, for example the right to vote.   (Witzsch 1992: 9)

Something that is important to note about this typology is that the types of rights are differentiated according to the three basic modalities of imperative as distinguished in deontic logic (Scheinen 1994: 76); they are *not* differentiated according to their respective objects (e.g. to life, or to health, or to an adequate environment). Certainly the right to an adequate environment cannot simply be assigned to any of these types, and in fact it implies specific rights of each type.

A generic right to an adequate environment can be understood to entail for its effective constitutional implementation a range of more specific rights of positive, negative, and active types. There is a widely held view that environmental rights are necessarily 'positive' rights, or what Witzsch calls 'rights of performance', and there can indeed be positive obligations on the state to the extent that the state is required to establish regulations, and perhaps to direct resources, for the provision of environmental quality which, without its action, would not be provided. Yet, the right could also be fulfilled as a 'right of defence', implying negative duties. Witzsch suggests, for instance, that a subjective right to a healthy and decent environment may issue in a right of defence 'in a case where the government sets up a coal burning power plant whose fumes infringe the individual's enjoyment of any outdoor activities' (Witzsch 1992: 10). Indeed, a negative characterization of environmental rights would be particularly appropriate whenever what is at issue is a requirement to secure freedom and protection from humanly caused ('anthropogenic') environmental harm: this would imply a negative right in exactly the sense that rights of bodily integrity do. Finally, as we have already noted, a substantive environmental right can be promoted by means of procedural rights, or rights of action. These procedural rights are often discussed as *alternatives* to a substantive right to an adequate environment. But they can, and I have argued should, be seen as part of it, since while they cannot suffice to meet its ends, their normative direction does derive from those ends. If the necessity of procedural rights is *derived* from the ends of a fundamental substantive right, then whether or not the latter is expressly stated in a constitution, it nevertheless does provide normative underpinning. If the generic right can be inferred from procedural rights, then there is no good reason not to state it expressly.

In this chapter, then, I have shown that if a state is committed to the protection of any human rights as fundamental constitutional rights, and to any constitutional provision for environmental protection at all, there is no reason of principle to deny fundamental constitutional status to the right to an adequate environment.[9]

Notes

1. Some see autonomy or freedom as *the* fundamental right (see e.g. Hart 1984); Waldron refers to autonomy and self-governance as two possible candidates; autonomy and well-being are frequently cited (see e.g. Fabre 2000); Shue sees liberty, security, and subsistence as the three basic rights.
2. This is certainly not arbitrary. For the reasons why those and only those rights that have been through a rigorous process of attaining this sort of formal recognition, should be accounted genuine human rights for legal purposes, see Alston (1984).
3. On the specific point about the inefficient process I shall have more to say in Chapter 3.

4. Brandl and Bungert (1992) suggest that the idea of a 'social fundamental right' is misleading, 'because such a right cannot ward off governmental encroachment as can a classical-liberal fundamental right' (p. 13). They note that in a debate in (West) Germany in the 1970s about a proposal for an environmental right it was argued this would have the character of a 'social fundamental right' and it was objected to because 'due to its programmatic character, this right would create more illusions than realities and, therefore, might result in public distrust and a setback in environmental consciousness' (p. 24). As a contrast to this 'received wisdom' it can be noted that even when a right to an adequate environment has a 'non-fundamental' positioning this does not necessarily prevent courts treating it as fundamental, as happened in the Philippines case of *Oposa Minors* (see Chapter 6).

5. On the standard view, it is not only civil rights but 'civil *and political* rights' which are taken to fit this description. I have not reproduced this formulation in the text because it glosses over a distinction which is of manifest significance both historically and conceptually. Historically, at least in the West, where this view has its roots, the achievement of certain liberal civil rights preceded the development of democracy and its associated political rights (Marshall 1950); the latter development was the outcome of a protracted social struggle. Conceptually, the assimilation of civil and political rights glosses over a basic distinction of deontic logic and involves a categorical confusion which will be highlighted in the second part of this section and further explained in the section that follows.

6. Jackman and Porter (1999), however, argue that including social and economic rights in human rights legislation does not give courts and tribunals unrestricted authority to determine social policy. Neither, they say, does it send a message to tribunals and courts that they should abandon their concerns about judicial deference.

> Rather, the inclusion of social and economic rights in human rights legislation will provide much needed guidance to courts and tribunals about when it is appropriate for them to intervene in matters of social and economic policy.... The question is not whether courts and human rights tribunals should have a role in these areas, but rather, in what circumstances should they intervene and to what purpose? (Jackman and Porter 1999: 62)

> They quote John Ely: 'The whole point of the approach is to identify those groups in society to whose needs and wishes elected officials have no apparent interest in attending. If the approach makes sense, it would not make sense to assign its enforcement to anyone but the courts' (Jackman and Porter 1999: 64).

7. This is true even without entering considerations about how the act/ommission distinction itself can be hard to maintain in practice, which would be especially significant in environmental contexts where negative refraining from environmental harms can imply real acts against the pursuit of economic development.

8. Hence I think Douglas-Scott is mistaken when, after highlighting familiar problems with enforcing a substantive right, he writes of procedural rights: 'Even if the introduction of such rights cannot dictate the desired result, it may have other legal effects, such as a liberalization of the standing rules or a shifting of the burden of proof onto those whose action may damage the environment' (Douglas-Scott 1996: 113). As we shall see in Chapter 3, liberalizing standing and shifting the burden of proof do in fact involve substantive issues, and there is no clear reason to think such changes are implied by procedural rights without the support of a substantive right to an adequate environment.

9. On this basis I cannot literally claim to have ruled out the possibility of some further objection being devised, but taking constitutions as they are and can currently be conceived as being, I believe the objections considered and rebutted do exhaust the possibilities. Against any hypothetical suggestion that different alternatives, currently not conceived of, might arise, I would set the more tangible consideration that a right to an adequate environment is in the process of emergence, and that the likelihood of its becoming an acknowledged international obligation of states—and thus of providing a more direct vindication of this chapter's central claim—is far more conceivable. One further source of doubts would be whether the alternatives rejected as such in this chapter might nonetheless suffice to achieve the ends of a fundamental right to an adequate environment, but this issue is addressed in Chapter 5.

3

The Challenge of Effective Implementation

The previous chapter showed that there is no objection of principle to constitutionalizing the human right to an adequate environment, but the critical argument to be addressed in this chapter is that there are in practice such difficulties standing in the way of its being effective and achieving its ends that it would not be prudent to constitutionalize the right. Proponents of this argument make the reasonable point that what really matters is not simply what is written in a constitution but the measures to achieve effective implementation and enforcement. The critical claim they make is that a constitutional right to an adequate environment can generate expectations which are illusory because it cannot in fact be effectively enforced. The reason given is that there are peculiar difficulties in translating the aspiration of the right into effective legal rights that citizens can rely on in courts: there are difficulties of making this right justiciable—that is, of making an admissible case on its basis in the first place; and even where a case can be brought, there are peculiar difficulties in the nature of environmental issues which make success on the merits unlikely.

In the first two sections of this chapter I examine these difficulties, showing that while in many jurisdictions at present they may be real ones, they are not insurmountable and do not arise because of anything inherent in the nature of rights or of environmental problems. What surmounting them does involve, though, is not only improving citizens' access to justice—which critics do not necessarily object to—but also ensuring that courts have the requisite institutional and constitutional competence, which critics consider to be, respectively, unfeasible and undesirable. In Section 3.3, however, I show that there is no serious obstacle to the development of the requisite institutional competence, which, if necessary, can be achieved through the establishment of specialist environmental courts. Where more serious issues arise is in the bearing of the development and exercise of that competence on courts' constitutional competence. What I go on to show in Section 3.4, though, is that the salient issues of courts' constitutional competence arise not only for environmental rights, but also for human rights more generally. I argue that those who object that environmental rights are doomed to be ineffective have not fully appreciated what is involved in the constitutional protection of human rights.

Ultimately, then, the argument of this chapter is that resistance to the constitutionalizing of a right to an adequate environment cannot be justified by any claims that it would be ineffective or exceed courts' competence which would not also apply to other fundamental constitutional rights. I also point out that judicial enforcement of the right is not its only purpose, and may not even be the most significant one; however, since its credibility for other purposes must depend to some extent on its potential effectiveness as a legally enforceable right, it is to this issue that the chapter is for the most part addressed.

3.1 The necessary conditions for judicial enforcement of constitutional rights, and claims that these cannot be fulfilled for the right to an adequate environment

This section examines the difficulties involved in trying to make a right to an adequate environment justiciable. Constitutional entrenchment of a right does not of itself mean that this right can be directly and successfully invoked by a citizen in a court. Whether and how a constitutional right might be relied on by an individual claimant appealing to it as the basis for a decision in their favour depends on a number of factors. Precisely which will vary from jurisdiction to jurisdiction, but some issues of general principle can be identified that lead to the positing of three necessary conditions for the justiciability of a constitutional right: (a) the definition of the standard of protection set has to be unequivocal; (b) the authorization to the courts must be unconditional; (c) the provision must confer a right of action on individuals. The aim of this section, accordingly, is to assess claims that in the case of constitutional environmental rights these conditions can be particularly difficult, or even impossible, to fulfil.

(a) The first potential obstacle to the implementation of an enforceable constitutional right to an adequate environment, then, would be that its general aim is so vague that it cannot be formulated sufficiently clearly and unambiguously to guide the choice of appropriate implementation strategies, let alone dictate a particular result in cases where enforcement is at issue. A constitutional right is directly justiciable when the definitive statement of it has the clarity and imperative force equivalent to statutory or customary law that is capable of conferring actionable rights. Yet, a problem frequently referred to by commentators is that it is notoriously difficult to get clear and unequivocal interpretations of locutions like 'decent' or 'adequate' environment.

It is the *general* nature of typical constitutional formulations that is taken to signify ambiguity or lack of precision, yet this may not be a decisive objection, since it is not an issue peculiar to environmental rights. The general nature of a provision need not necessarily lead to a failure to fulfil the requirement of precision, since a provision can be unambiguous even if expressed in general terms (Holder 1996: 327),[1] and thus sufficiently precise to be relied on by individuals and applied by courts. As Schwartz notes, many of the constitutional provisions on rights that have been developed in the last fifty years could have been—and often were—similarly disparaged for vagueness. The ability of courts to construe a vague term in a constitutional provision is well documented: as José Fernandez notes, 'courts have confidently defined the meaning of such terms as equal protection, due process, and cruel and unusual punishment, terms as vague as those which have prompted courts and others to determine that environmental rights provisions are too ambiguous to be self-executing' (Fernandez 1993: 372, see also 369). The approach to this issue commended by Kiss and Shelton 'is to accept the impossibility of defining an ideal environment in abstract terms, but to let supervisory institutions and courts develop their own interpretations, as they have done for other human rights' (Boyle 1996: 50–1). The proposed standard of '*adequate* for health and well-being', notes James Nickel, 'provides a general, imprecise description of the level of protections against environmental risks that States should guarantee. Risk standards should be specified further at the national level through democratic legislative and regulatory processes, in light of current scientific knowledge and fiscal realities' (Nickel 1983: 285). So the broad aims of environmental rights may require fleshing out in terms of definite environmental standards that are not directly specified at constitutional level, but this particular issue is not an insurmountable obstacle to justiciability (Boyle 1996: 51).

(b) For a constitutional right to be justiciable, however, the authorization to the courts must also be unconditional: it does not suffice that the general aim of the provision be unequivocally clear; the means for the achievement of the aim must also be provided with directly binding force. This may not be the case if enabling legislation is required for the right to take legal effect and the legislature has a margin of discretion to decide if and how to introduce it. In the language of US jurisprudence, this is the question of whether the constitutional provision is 'self-executing': whether, in other words, it supplies 'a sufficient rule by means of which the right which [the provision] grants may be enjoyed and protected... without the aid of a legislative enactment' (Fernandez 1993: 333). In the United States, the doctrine of self-execution is sometimes relied on by judges who appear to prefer to err on the side of judicial restraint in circumstances of potential conflict with other branches of government. As Fernandez has illustrated, this is particularly likely to occur in cases where state constitutions purport to grant a right to a clean environment. Fernandez, and other scholars he cites, suggest that state courts have thereby often thwarted the apparent intent of the state constitution to provide an enforceable right (Fernandez 1993: 334). In such cases, then, the language and general intent may be unequivocal, but the right is not judged by the courts to be unconditional.

The requirement of unconditionality is usefully illuminated by examining the three classes of constitutional provision that can be distinguished according to whether the type of imperative that they transmit to the legislature can be classified as non-mandatory, mandatory, or mandatory–prohibitory (Fernandez 1993: 341–2). Non-mandatory provisions are not self-executing because they do not order a particular result, impose a duty, or create an obligation; they merely state an expression of public sentiment or a public policy for the legislature to effectuate at its discretion. Such provisions are unlikely ever to be justiciable. Mandates which are 'enabling' or have a 'positive tenor' and order a particular result, grant a right, or impose a duty or limitation may or may not be self-executing depending on whether the mandate is expressed in a form susceptible to judicial enforcement. By contrast, negative mandatory provisions, which typically impose limits or prohibitions on legislative authority, are almost always self-executing.[2] In general, then, the requirement of unconditionality is normally quite readily fulfilled by constitutional rights which are conferred by a 'negative mandate'. (Such rights broadly correspond to the type discussed in the previous chapter under the heading of 'defensive' rights.) In an environmental context, such rights would correspond to the disabling of the legislature from passing laws that would have a clear, direct, and foreseeable effect of compromising environmental quality. It would also apply to administrative decisions that had such an effect. Yet, in practice it is unlikely that all environmental rights issues will be considered to be defensive ones. For while at a conceptual level it might be possible to construe all environmental rights as defensive, in practice, as noted in Chapter 2, they will often appear as rights of performance.

However, it is not necessarily the case that the latter cannot be justiciable. Even in the US context, which is not the most favourable to judicial enforcement of rights of performance, Fernandez has noted that 'the need for legislative action to provide an enforcement procedure has not always resulted in a judicial declaration that a provision is not self-executing' (Fernandez 1993: 346). In fact, he records, some courts consider it their obligation to act when the legislature fails to respond to a constitutional call: for example, Chief Justice Hughes of the New Jersey Supreme Court proclaimed that '[j]ust as the Legislature cannot abridge constitutional rights by its enactments, it cannot curtail them through its silence...' (Fernandez 1993: 349).

Evidently, then, how courts decide the question of when a right can be enforced has as much to do with their broader views on political issues regarding the constitution as with legal technicalities. The conditions to which the justiciability of a constitutional right may be subject are contingent on general constitutional principles and the interpretation of them in a determinate context. In any given constitutional context there may be reasons for setting conditions on the justiciability of environmental rights: but such would be reasons to support a claim that environmental rights *should* not be unconditional; they could not tell for a claim that environmental rights *cannot* be unconditional.

(c) Nevertheless, a constitutional mandate can be unequivocal and unconditional but not provide a ground of individual complaint. To be justiciable, the provision must also confer a right of action on individuals. If the provision is framed as a right which is to be enjoyed by all citizens, then one might assume that the condition was thereby automatically met. However, a constitutional right can be intended to confer general protections on the citizen body, and thus on each individual comprising that body, but it might nevertheless be envisaged that this should be achieved by means of general mandates to the government to take appropriate steps to secure the protection, rather than by conferring a direct right of action on each and every individual citizen in the event that those steps are not sufficient. In other words, the aim of the provision could be—or be conceived of as being—protection of the environment in the interests of all rather than as conferring a benefit on individual citizens.

Thus even though it must be supposed, as we had occasion to note in Chapter 2, that a provision intended to benefit everyone cannot be intended to benefit no one, the question is whether there is any peculiar difficulty in allowing a right of action—to any individual or group—relating to the provisions of a constitutional environmental right. In most jurisdictions, in order to bring a civil action or to seek judicial review, the complainant has to have the necessary *locus standi*. This is normally understood to require that he or she has 'sufficient interest' in the matter which the court is being asked to hear. Interpretations of this requirement vary, however, not only between jurisdictions but even within them. Among English judges, for instance, there has not been an entirely uniform view as to where the interest of environmental groups lies. In particular, there is the question whether environmental groups are seen as collectively representing individual interests, or as representing public interests, including the protection of the environment.[3] The issue of standing, nonetheless, is one area where liberalizing moves in favour of environmental rights are generally proceeding well. In England, for instance, Grosz has 'found no reported case in which an applicant with a sound point of law has been denied relief on the ground that he does not have sufficient interest' (Grosz 1995: 195). More generally, and especially in states signatory to the Aarhus Convention, standing rules are not a major obstacle to environmental campaigners. Thus, there would appear to be no objection of inherent impracticability on this score.

There are, however, still those who object to such developments and who argue, with specific reference to proposals to make the proposed constitutional environmental right justiciable, that this would open the 'floodgates of litigation', entailing unrealistic and unworkable demands on the courts (e.g. Ruhl 1997: 48). Yet one thing to note is that this argument, which is presented in the form of a practical problem, is in fact based on a speculative conjecture which, as Andrew Roman notes, 'ignores the reality that litigation is far too expensive, traumatic and inconvenient ever to become a popular pastime' (Roman 1981: 17); indeed, Paul Stein (1995), a founding and long-serving judge of the Land and Environment Court of New South Wales, which has open standing, reports no flood of litigation. To respond to the argument more directly, though, in the event that a multiplicity of actions were to be brought, 'the courts could use procedures such as test cases or class actions to reduce their burden on the court system' (Roman 1981: 18). Certainly, 'it is a poor principle to say that the courts should reject a large number of potentially meritorious cases simply because there is a large number.' (Roman 1981: 18) It has to be said that professed worries about opening the floodgates to litigious busybodies who threaten to undermine the legitimate activities of hard-pressed businesspersons or to overload the courts ring very hollow in view of the prodigious expense involved in engaging in such a pastime.

Indeed, as Grosz observes, the most serious barriers to fair and effective environmental litigation are the cost of litigation and the risk of losing (Grosz 1995: 207). Writing of the situation in England, which is not untypical, Day (1995) notes the problem that if applicants lose a case, they have to pay not only their own costs, but also those of the defendants, who may well have employed a 'Rolls Royce defence'. Moreover, there are financial considerations that can have a bearing on the material outcomes of an action even where it is taken and eventually succeeds. In particular there is the problem which arises from the requirement to make what is known as a 'cross-undertaking in damages'.

In order for the judicial review to be effective, it is often essential that the respondent or a third party be prevented from acting in reliance on the alleged unlawful decision until the case has been resolved ... The major difficulty for the applicant, which arises in seeking an interim injunction or stay in cases where the order would have financial consequences for the respondent or a third party, is a requirement to give a cross-undertaking as to damages. This means that the court requires the applicant to undertake to pay the costs incurred by the respondent or third party as a result of the order, in the event that the case is not upheld at the final hearing. (Day 1998: 207–8)

The significance of this was illustrated in the case of *R. v. Secretary of State for the Environment ex parte RSPB* (1995). The RSPB eventually won its case to preserve Lappel Bank from development, but by that time, because the RSPB had not been able to make the undertaking necessary for an injunction, the developers had turned Lappel Bank into a car park.

In this section, then, I have sought to show that while there are potential difficulties in fulfilling the necessary conditions of justiciability for a constitutional right to an adequate environment, there is no impossibility of their being met. The more concrete obstacles bearing on the potential for effective exercise of the right are not so much the technical requirements for its justiciability as those which arise from the position of disadvantage—in various ways, but not least costs—that environmental citizens occupy in relation to more powerful interest groups whose rights at present are more firmly established.

3.2 The peculiar difficulties of enforcing environmental norms

Nevertheless, even if the right can be made justiciable, so that claims advanced on its basis are admissible in courts, there remains the question of what it may effectively achieve in view of the difficulties in establishing the merits of cases aimed at environmental protection. The difficulties that can arise when environmental cases come to court can be illustrated by reference to private civil actions seeking remedies for environmental harm or public interest suits aimed at environmental protection. These difficulties arise particularly from the need to establish the causation of the environmental harm in question and the legal liability for it. The nature of environmental problems is such that their causes are often difficult to identify with the degree of certainty necessary to determine definite liabilities for them and thus support legal action against specific alleged polluters; it is correspondingly difficult to assign specific duties to individuals or firms which would be correlative to the right to an adequate environment. This clearly presents a serious problem for citizens seeking to hold alleged polluters to account, where what has to be shown is that the owners of a particular source of emissions are responsible for the adverse effect on the health of the specific individuals making the case. The burden of proof on the complainant and the need to establish fault on the part of the defendant constitute real obstacles to successful civil actions. The question for this section is how these obstacles bear on the enforceability of a constitutionally guaranteed human right to an adequate environment. I shall suggest that they show up issues that rather than making the right unworkable are ones that the right could help in surmounting.

The burden of proof A notorious difficulty bearing on the potential effectiveness of environmental rights is that of establishing causation in cases of environmental harms. In civil actions a major issue is the burden of proof that falls in environmental cases on the plaintiff, who must show that but for the action of the defendant the injury and damage would not have been suffered. If there are various possible causes of an injury, and alternative explanations that are as likely (or more so) for the injury, then the test is failed. 'Cases of environmental pollution are notoriously difficult to prove, whether due to chemical poisoning, radiation, electromagnetic fields, or whatever. The primary reason for this is the difficulty in showing that the illness was caused by the particular pollutant' (Day 1998: 298). This is especially so when the effects accrue over a long time period. The lack of success in actions relating to Sellafield in England, for instance, attests to the problem, as Martyn Day describes.

For example, in the early 1980s it was discovered that there was a tenfold excess of childhood leukaemias in the village of Seascale, only two miles from the Sellafield nuclear reprocessing plant. It is generally accepted that radiation is one of the only known causes of leukaemia, and that Sellafield has discharged into the air and sea more radioactive waste than any other nuclear facility in the western world.

Despite it seeming on the face of it that the plant must be to blame, the fact that childhood leukaemia is the most common childhood cancer meant that in the ensuing claims the plaintiffs' lawyers had to try to disentangle the prospect that there might be other competing causes of the cancers. In the end, the judge in the case came to the view that, although radiation was a possible cause, there were other possibilities and that the standard of proof had not been reached.   (Day 1998: 298)

Now the difficulty of proving that a particular environmental threat is being caused by a specific industrial plant, say, could be mitigated by altering the burden and standards of proof required. Day himself—as a practising plaintiffs' lawyer—suggests that a more equitable system 'would be for the plaintiff to have to show that there is a *prima facie* case that the injury has been caused by the defendants, but that thereafter the onus should shift to the defendants to show that they are not responsible, rather than being on the plaintiffs to show the defendants are responsible' (Day 1995: 191). Yet, this suggestion may not appear so equitable from other perspectives. Certainly, a stakeholder from industry, observes Paul Bowden, 'will not be attracted to the idea that because he is supposedly large, rich, a corporate entity and not well-loved, it should be for him to "prove his innocence"' (Bowden 1995: 181). Rather, he will complain that '[w]hat those who propose a reversal of the burden of proof argue is that they would like the courts to take a less rigorous view of evidence; to reach "common sense" conclusions rather than tackling the detail of the basic scientific issues... to take a "quick gut feel" as to causation issues' (181–2). In reply to this point, however, it can be argued that it is in fact not a less rigorous view of scientific evidence which is required, but, rather, a more sophisticated view of the limits of actual and possible scientific knowledge (Wynne 1994),[4] (which might sometimes vindicate commonsense) and an incorporation of this view into the principles of justice as administered.

The problem of proof regarding causation in the light of scientific uncertainties is in fact a much broader and more pervasive issue than shows up in civil actions alone. It is one which is recognized as lying at the very heart of environmental policy-making. The precautionary principle, which has attained the status of a principle of customary international law and has come to play an important role in the environmental law of a growing number of states throughout the world, and is a central policy principle in European Union (EU), addresses this very issue. There is no universally accepted definition of the precautionary principle, but one widely cited characterization of it is the following:

> When an activity raises threats of harm to human health or the environment, precautionary measures should be taken even if some cause and effect relationships are not fully established scientifically. In this context, the proponent of an activity, rather than the public, should bear the burden of proof.   (Jan. 1998 Wingspread statement)[5]

The precautionary principle would not operate at the level of the burden of proof in civil actions, though, as 'it is a principle concerned with ex ante regulatory action rather than ex post private law remedies' (Fisher 2003: 105). It operates outside the sphere of bipolar litigation, as an administrative rather than adjudicative principle, and is taken into account in approving applications for developments which stand to have environmental impacts. But its recognition as a justiciable principle, particularly for the purposes of judicial review, allows the possibility of challenging the legality of the decisions which allowed some of the kinds of problem which become the cause of civil actions to arise in the first place—on the grounds of not having applied the principle—as well as, more importantly, challenging decisions affecting developments that carry a threat of future harms. Application of the principle can thus help head off the problems associated with having to prove causation, without the perceived unfairness or arbitrariness of simply reversing the burden of proof when causes of civil action reach the court.

Yet, the precautionary principle is not automatically treated as justiciable even in jurisdictions which are committed to recognizing it. This may in part be because its precise meaning is the subject of contestation, but for Elizabeth Fisher it is not so much the vagueness of the principle that prevents its being used as a justification for substantive and merits review but perceptions of limits of courts' competence to apply it. She notes that 'courts engaging in merits and judicial review have not used the principle as a justification for intensive and searching review because, as presently argued, it is viewed as beyond judicial competence...due to the fact that the precautionary principle is often characterised as one of substantive impact' (Fisher 2001: 330). If the principle is interpreted as a procedural one, requiring that due consultations and so on be carried out, it is more likely to be taken as justiciable, but it is also unlikely to be effective as a challenge since, as Fisher has found, in most cases where the principle is raised 'the court will conclude it is relevant, and then argue that the decision-maker has already applied it' (Fisher 2001: 325). The actual standards applied by the decision-maker would not have been closely scrutinized. Courts will tend to be deferential since they are hardly competent to strike out too far, 'to go beyond their traditional role of interpreting and enforcing the law and themselves take on the job of giving some substance to the [precautionary principle]' (Marchant 2003: 1802).

It is for want of a principled framework for deciding what is precautionary that reviewing courts tend to be deferential. As Marchant observes, it would be unrealistic to expect a consensus on the meaning of the precautionary principle to arise spontaneously through the experience of applying it. Rather, any progress toward agreement would likely come only through a deliberate and concerted effort to better define it (Marchant 2003: 1802). Courts require guidelines to follow, and these could be developed if there were a constitutional right to an adequate environment. The recognition of this right would shift the presumption in favour of development which has tended to inhibit courts from challenging decision-makers' own—unaccountable—assessment of risks. The real challenge for implementing the precautionary principle, as Fisher says, 'lies with understanding what can and should be the role of the courts'. And this is evidently a challenge with a constitutional dimension. The precautionary principle 'forces a very hard look at the way in which we are governed and the way in which public decision-makers are held to account' (Fisher 2001: 334).

So while the precautionary principle may not literally reverse the burden of proof, it does shift presumptions about who has to prove what when making decisions involving potential environmental impacts. The requirement of recognizing the precautionary principle as a justiciable principle would be strengthened rather than weakened by recognition of a fundamental constitutional right to an adequate environment which, indeed, could be argued to be indispensable for it (Odhiambo 1998). Viewed in this light, therefore, the need to deal with problems of proof can appear as a reason telling in favour of the right rather than against it.

Standards of liability   Another issue bearing on the prospects of success in environmental cases is that of how liability for environmental harms should be apportioned. While in most jurisdictions some industries are subject to statutory regulation which can impose strict liability on polluting firms, there are difficulties in seeking remedies for environmental harms when these fall outside the scope of such regulations. In the United Kingdom, for instance, the legal principles underlying civil liability for environmental damage have developed piecemeal in common law under a range of different torts, but all the torts most used in environmental cases 'are now influenced to a significant degree by fault-based theories of liability' (D. Howarth 2002: 490). Those who are critical of fault-based liability, including those who seek to use law for public interest environmental ends, argue that it is inappropriate because it violates the 'polluter pays' principle, a principle that now ranks alongside the precautionary principle as a cornerstone of environmental policy.

So while some commentators think that tort law can be developed so as to assist in the creation of public interest environmental law (e.g. Harding 1995), others are less sanguine: 'Successful actions in tort in respect of chronic health detriment to third parties from pollutants dispersed into the environment, under conditions which fall short of accidents, remain conspicuous by their paucity' (Miller 1998: 13).[6] The need to prove fault is taken to be a key stumbling block: the plaintiff must prove that the defendant owes the plaintiff a duty of care; that the duty has been breached; and that the breach of that duty has caused the injury and damage for which the plaintiff is claiming. In practice there can be real difficulties for plaintiffs seeking to establish that the three conditions hold. A duty of care, where this is not provided for a specific industry by statutory regulation (which may impose strict liability), is subject to certain restrictions of reasonableness. In English common law, for instance, there is a general duty of care which courts have taken to come into play 'where it can be reasonably foreseen that injury might arise from the person or company's action to people reasonably close to what is happening and where they are directly affected' (Day 1998: 294). The issue of foreseeability has thus become central to this duty. Since it is often difficult to prove that a defendant was aware or indeed should have been aware of the potential of its chemical(s) to cause a specific illness, personal injury claims can be met with the 'state of the art' defence:

A manufacturer or user of chemicals will argue that the medical and scientific evidence was not widely available, that it was found in often obscure medical and scientific journals. The company will ask how could it be expected to have knowledge without considerable research, and without taking advice from experts in subjects relating to rare diseases. (Day 1998: 295)

This defence could in principle be removed, and the hurdle of fault itself simply abolished, by the imposition of strict liability. It would then be the fact of injury or harm, not its foreseeability or any other question of negligence, which made it the polluter's responsibility to pay for the adverse consequences to others, and the environment, of the actions from which they have drawn the benefit.

Nevertheless, general support for the Polluter Pays Principle at the level of policy does not automatically translate into support for the principle of strict liability as a legal principle. Bell and McGillivray write critically of allowing the defence of unforeseeability:

In the interests of doing justice to defendants, the common law does not always seek to redress any damage caused by such accidents. Clearly, this is contrary to the general thrust of the polluter pays principle. (in D. Howarth 2002: 490)

Howarth, however, objects to criticizing environmental tort law on this ground. If 'in the name of justice, tort law allows defendants to win' (D. Howarth 2002: 504), he writes, then the question to ask is what is wrong with that conception of justice. He makes the claim that if, behind a Rawlsian veil of ignorance,[7] 'people should choose the rule they would apply if they did not know which position they were to occupy in society (in this case, plaintiff or defendant in a nuisance case) it seems very unlikely that people would choose Bell and McGillivray's position in preference to the reciprocity rule chosen by the common law' (D. Howarth 2002: 505).

I think this is certainly a good way to pose the question, and clearly places it as one to be addressed at the level of the most basic institutions of society, as set up and maintained by its constitution. It is indeed a question of distributive justice—being concerned with the distribution of benefits and burdens across society. Granting that this is a reasonable question, however, there are two points to make about Howarth's suggested answer to it. First, since the Rawlsian 'original position' is intended precisely to reveal what principles should govern relations between persons on the assumption that they must be reciprocally acceptable, to assert simply that they would choose the reciprocity rule begs a key question. The relations of reciprocity Howarth actually assumes to hold—*in reality, not behind the veil of ignorance*—are between parties who could equally likely be polluters as victims of pollution in the normal course of their activities. This hardly maps the full range of possible scenarios deliberators should reflect upon in the 'original position', and it excludes all those in which there are relatively rich and powerful polluters and relatively poor and powerless victims. The second point, then, concerns the reasons to dispute Howarth's claim that persons would not in fact opt for the principle of strict liability. If we take seriously the suggestion that a Rawlsian procedure be applied, then we should recognize that in deliberations behind 'the veil of ignorance' people would seek to 'maximize' the position of the worst-off representative persons—conceiving the worst off here in terms of most meagre share of social goods or greatest share of social burdens—and that the victims of environmental harms could well be thought worse off than corporate operators who have to meet a burden that has arisen as a result of benefits they themselves have accrued in causing it. Nor would deliberators in a Rawlsian 'original position' necessarily be swayed by utilitarian considerations about the inhibiting effects on industry of its being subject to the principle of strict liability for environmental damage, since the position of the worst off individuals would not necessarily be eased by the putative wider social benefits. In short, the view Howarth thinks it likely deliberators would take is actually the least likely on Rawlsian assumptions.

It would thus appear that if there is a case of justice for the polluter pays principle then there is a case of justice for the principle of strict liability for environmental harms. Certainly, in a world where companies are not under any obligation to distribute unforeseen profits to third parties, it is hard to see why third parties should be obliged to bear the brunt of companies' unforeseen costs.

Proposals for such changes to the allocation of liabilities, though, relating as they do to quite fundamental questions about the basic principles of justice in society, raise, as does the precautionary principle, issues of a constitutional kind. As was articulated in the House of Lords decision in the *Cambridge Water* case, which accepted the polluter's unforeseeability defence, it was for parliament rather than the common law to abandon the foreseeability principle. This is not an unreasonable view to take, but it serves to highlight, as Harding (1995) notes, that the key to overcoming the environmental limitations of tort law is constitutional reform.

A role for a constitutional right to an adequate environment would be to provide precisely the kind of mandate to government to make the sort of change to principles of liability which it is not constitutionally proper for the judiciary to initiate.

The general conclusion of this section is that the obstacles to success in cases aimed at measures for environmental protection or redress are not inherent in the nature of environmental cases, but rather arise from issues of proof and liability that are set at particular standards and levels and could be altered, so as to give more decisive effect to the precautionary and polluter pays principles, if political decisions were taken to that effect. The question then is how such changes could be effected and justified. At this point, therefore, critical attention has to be turned to the competence of courts.

3.3 The institutional and constitutional competence of courts

If rules of standing are liberalized, along with judicial recognition of the precautionary principle and firm guidelines on implications of the polluter pays principle, the prospects for effective judicial enforcement of environmental rights in civil actions and the scope for judicial review of environmental decisions can clearly be expected to be enhanced. However, it can be argued by critics that the proposed solutions to the difficulties of making environmental rights effective are themselves objectionable, in practice and in principle, not simply because of their potential adverse effects on non-environmental interests, but because they would require courts to do things they cannot and should not do—that is to say, they would require courts to exceed both their institutional and their constitutional competence.

In this section I shall consider the two types of competence in turn. Regarding institutional competence, to the extent that courts do lack the necessary expertise to handle complex environmental cases, a solution would be to create, as a number of states already have, a specialist environmental court. Proposals for specialist environmental courts are particularly interesting in that they can provide an especially focused and deliberate means of imple menting environmental rights (even if the one is not strictly entailed by the other), as well as environmental protection more generally, and so they allow the critical issues to show up particularly sharply. Examining arguments for and against this particular proposal brings into relief what it is objected that courts in general, and not only environmental courts, *should* not do. For if a specialist environmental court provides the solution to the problem of technical or institutional competence, this does not itself answer—and in fact serves to highlight—issues of constitutional competence that would arise with regard to any court, specialist or generalist. For as we have noted, the measures that would enhance the effectiveness of a right to an adequate environment are ones that do raise issues about constitutional relationships.

3.3.1 *Specialist environmental courts*

Due to the complexity of environmental problems and the uncertainties concerning their precise causes and effects, courts can face formidable problems of knowledge when dealing with environmental cases. These cases can often turn into a contest between rival scientific experts which 'typically involve evidence given by epidemiologists and physiologists concerning the long-term consequences of the consumption of chemical and biological contaminants' (Miller 1998: 10). With regard to this it is worth observing that courts do routinely—and not only in environmental cases—have to deal with testimony from experts in order to arrive at judgements. However, if one grants that this problem of complexity is particularly acute in environmental cases, then a solution is to establish a specialist environmental court.

Environmental courts have been established in a number of countries, and are proposed for more. The pioneering example has been the New South Wales Land and Environment Court, established in 1980 as the centrepiece of a comprehensive package of legislation for the environment, with a central aim of giving the

general public a right to participate in the process of environmental planning. The court 'was created as an integrated superior court of record of equal status to the State Supreme Court,
with exclusive jurisdiction to determine disputes arising under
more than 20 separate environmental laws' (Stein 1995: 258).
The court was an innovative experiment in dispute resolution
mechanisms, combining judicial and administrative techniques,
with both legal and non-legal environmental experts. 'The mixed
personnel of the court and its specialist nature (and the substantial use of expert witnesses) have been successful in generating
the expertise and precedents required to facilitate better, more
consistent decision-making' (Stein 1995: 263). In the estimate of
Paul Stein, a long-serving judge of the court, it has had notable
advantages in increasing the fairness, efficiency, consistency, and
cost-effectiveness of environmental decision-making. The court
has also developed a policy on costs, so that while these will
normally follow the event of litigation, 'a number of cases have
held that if the unsuccessful party can properly be characterised
as representing the "public" interest, it may be appropriate not to
make an order for costs' (Stein 1995: 261); undertakings as to
damages for interim injunctions to restrain breaches of environmental law are not required as a matter of course; and generally
the task of the court is conceived as administering 'social justice
rather than simply justice between the parties' (Stein 1995: 262).

The rationality of integrating environmental issues in this way,
and the contribution it can make to ensuring environmental justice in environmental decision-making, has found favour more
widely. For instance, Judge Kremlis suggests that, in the evolving
context of the EU's promotion—post-Aarhus—of access to justice
in environmental matters, the creation of environmental courts
in member states would likely represent best practice in this matter; and McAuslan has argued for an Environmental Court in
England 'with a wide-ranging jurisdiction through which it could
develop, via its decisions, an environmental jurisprudence to help
us forward into the new era of a more conscious and deliberate
balancing of development and environmental protection, and

a more knowledgeable weighing of risks, liabilities and rights' (DETR 1.3.4).

One of the virtues of a specialist environmental court, as emphasized also by Lord Woolf (1992), is that it can be inquisitorial rather than adversarial in approach, taking into account the various interests involved and calling on expertise needed to form a reliable view. As Elizabeth Fisher observes,

> solving problems in the public interest is what public decision-makers are concerned with. Such problems are invariably polycentric, value laden and require the balancing of contradictory interests and factors. The 'facts' are only one element of decision-making and an administrative decision-maker takes a far more active role in information collection. The inadequacies of adjudicative procedure to deal with the complexities of this type of decision-making have long been recognized. (Fisher 2001: 331)

This reasoning underpins a reply to one of the objections to which judicial involvement in enforcing environmental rights is vulnerable. This is the 'courts and capture' objection:

> [this] objection notes that courts are quintessentially reactive and that the principles enunciated in their decisions follow the haphazard course set by the decisions of potential litigants, rather than a strategy of judicial intervention carefully planned in the light of social priorities. It therefore charges that courts can be—and have been—captured by interest-group factions, resulting in mis-directed priorities, and a diversion of policy away from 'real' social and environmental concerns. (Du Bois 1996: 169)

Thus Michael Grieve, for instance, has argued that those who see 'environmental interests as higher values that ought to be exempt from the ordinary give and take of politics...want to push [an] agency further than it is willing to go, and they want a piece of the agenda' (in Du Bois 1996: 169). In response to this objection, though, Du Bois points out that these handicaps are shared by other branches of government. Moreover, the accessibility of courts to special-interest groups is not an indication of any inherent institutional flaw in them. 'If there is a capture problem, it results from the nature of the norms a court has to enforce: it is no accident that Grieve's argument is developed through an analysis of American citizen-suit provisions which are drafted in a manner precluding a flexible judicial response to social priorities' (Du Bois 1996: 171). Specialist courts as described above are precisely set up with the appropriate institutional competence to counteract such problems.

Another objection that has been voiced by Tromans, for instance, is that a specialist environmental court may be, or be perceived to be, subject to bias. Whereas a judge in civil proceedings between two private parties 'must obviously be seen to be utterly impartial', the perception will be, he says, that a court composed of 'environmental judges', judges who have in Woolf's words 'general responsibility for overseeing and enforcing the safeguards provided for the protection of the environment which is so important to us all', will be biased in favour of environmentalism. He suggests this is a problem for specialist environmental courts in a way that it is not for other specialist courts such as the Commercial Court, for instance: 'a judge hearing a case between two commercial parties is not perceived to be biased because he has a commercial law background—indeed that is the strength of the Commercial Court which has contributed to its success' (Tromans 2001: 424). In drawing the comparison in this way, Tromans is very clearly portraying environmental protection as a partisan cause, implicitly denying that the general aim of environmental protection—by contrast with the practice of commerce in general—is an unquestioned social value. He is also implicitly assuming that environmental cases involve simple bipolar conflicts of interests, whereas part of the very point of an environmental court is to get detailed and nuanced views of problems and options and not simply adjudicate in favour of one or other interest as antecedently conceived and presented.

Nevertheless, this is not necessarily what courts are thought properly competent to do. It is too much like making policy. This issue brings us to consider objections which bear more nearly on courts' constitutional competence.

3.3.2 *The constitutional competence of courts*

The 'conscious and deliberate balancing of development and environmental protection' and a 'weighing of risks, liabilities and rights'—let alone the 'pursuit of social justice'—are not what critics think the judiciary should be engaged in at all. If the institutional competence necessary to deal with environmental rights cases is achieved by courts becoming more administrative and less adjudicative in nature, this raises questions about the proper scope of their constitutional powers. Specialist environmental courts thus raise issues of more general relevance regarding the legitimacy of courts engaging in the kind of jurisprudence that seems appropriate in reviewing environmental decisions. Indeed, Fisher notes suspicions voiced in some quarters about 'whether the creation of such a court is really just a "stalking horse for the advance of judicial control of administrative action"—that is the creation of such a court will see more intensive review by both specialist and generalist courts' (Fisher 2001: 328).

Before addressing this further, it is worth noting that concerns about constitutional propriety can in practice actually favour the creation of specialist courts. In Europe, for instance, part of the momentum towards the establishment of such courts arose out of constitutional concerns about the separation of powers of government. These were highlighted in the case of *Bryan* v. *United Kingdom* where the European Court of Human Rights held that the system of planning procedures which involved applications being heard by a planning inspector appointed by the Secretary of State did not meet the requirement of their being heard by an 'independent and impartial tribunal established by law', a requirement deriving from Article 6 of the European Convention on Human Rights. The issues raised by that case are complex and not fully resolved, but the general implication appears to have been thought sufficient in Sweden—where previously the government had also been the last instance in applications cases concerning big environmentally hazardous activities—to warrant creating an environmental court in 1999.

Nevertheless, Stephen Tromans takes issue with this rationale for an environmental court. The question put in *Alconbury*, against the background of the *Bryan* judgement, was whether the Secretary of State could be said to be an independent and impartial tribunal, given that he is a government minister applying government policy and his own political judgement to cases appealed to him. The House of Lords found that in fact there was adequate judicial control exercisable over the decision-making processes, and that 'the European jurisprudence did not require the court to be able to substitute its own decision for that of the administrative authority' (Tromans 2001: 423). In welcoming that 'ringing affirmation of the administrative tradition of this country', which includes a staunch resistance to any form of substantive judicial review, Tromans takes the view that

So long as political systems are broadly perceived as trustworthy, most people (as opposed to specialist lawyers or pressure groups) would probably prefer decisions on matters such as whether and where a regional incinerator is to be built to be taken by politicians rather than by judges. (Tromans 2001: 424)

This speculation is certainly open to question, particularly when in current day Britain 'it is still more difficult to suborn or lobby a judge than a politician or a bureaucrat' (Howarth 2002: 471). The point, though, is that the appropriate nature and scope of judicial powers in a constitutional democracy is a serious matter that cannot be settled by suppositions about 'what most people probably prefer' but requires discussion in terms of principle about who is entitled to decide what—and when, why, and how (see Chapter 4). The basic question it highlights for attention is whether administrative authority should be under the rule of law or not.

On a traditional understanding of this question, a distinction is drawn between 'what gets done' and 'how it gets done': decisions as to the substance of policy are for the government and legislature to take while only issues regarding their equitable implementation are appropriate for judicial consideration or intervention (Barry 1996: 98). Whether this distinction is somewhat arbitrary in general, as Du Bois (1996) suggests, it is certainly hard to maintain once courts are required to rule on human rights claims. These can directly call into question settled constitutional relationships.

The issue can be illustrated by reference to a civil environmental case in England where the plaintiff won by using a human rights claim, in a decision which commentators understandably see as a regrettable one. The case of *Peter Marcic* v. *Thames Water Utilities Ltd* concerned the damage caused to Marcic's property by an overflowing sewer. The water company had not taken steps sufficient to alleviate the problem. Alongside a claim in common law, a human rights claim was advanced on the basis of Article 8 of the European Convention, the right to respect for private and family life and a person's home (for more on the use of this article in environmental cases see Chapter 5). Both the High Court and the Court of Appeal accepted that Marcic had such a claim, and found that while Convention rights were subject to a margin of discretion to strike a proportional balance between the interests of the community as a whole and the protection of individual rights, the statutory scheme for safeguards did not provide a satisfactory means of striking a fair balance. William Howarth criticizes this decision because it

effectively overturns the statutory mechanisms for determining expenditure on sewerage improvement. The resolution of an intricate problem of public service provision and funding, reached by an elected Government, bound to respect the needs of all parties and the broader general public interest, has been reversed by a non-elected court which has determined that the matters at issue fall outside the margin of appreciation which should be allowed to a government.   (W. Howarth 2002: 388)

Construing the *Marcic* decision broadly, he observes, 'the possible environmental liability implications seem impossible to contain' (W. Howarth 2002: 389). Such a potentially massive inroad into liability ought to be

the outcome of a purposeful exercise of making clear and explicit provision for environmental rights, and as a result of an open and comprehensive

debate about their positive and negative implications. What is objectionable is that environmental rights have apparently been introduced by
subterfuge, as derivative forms of traditional civil and political rights and
liberties, and without their cost to parliamentary democracy being
openly and fully assessed beforehand.   (W. Howarth 2002: 389)

Howarth sees this case as having profound constitutional implications concerning the respective roles of Parliament and the courts
in determining the environmental rights of individuals.

Marcic certainly highlights a problem that involves conflict
between Parliament and courts; but what is the solution? For the
time being, Howarth suggests, it is judicial deference to the government's 'margin of appreciation'; longer term, it is a proper
working out of the scope and extent of environmental rights.
There need be no quarrel over the latter point, but it could be
argued that part of that working out is finding the scope and limits of the existing legal situation, which is what could be said was
going on in *Marcic*: here the court actually defined the *limit* of the
government's margin of discretion, and if Howarth's view is that
the balance was struck at the wrong point, that is a matter of
judgement, not of constitutionality. The courts do have a part to
play in this process. There can be no justification for deference to
Parliament if this is at the price of disregarding legitimate rights
from other sources. As Du Bois notes, courts can make 'a vital contribution to the pursuit of justice by exposing the failures of government before the political community' (Du Bois 1996: 172). In
bringing out the significance of budgetary judgements in a public
forum, the courts can be argued to have performed a service for
the transparency of democracy. As longs as courts remain as deferential as Howarth would apparently have them be, environmental
justice and rights in general will hardly be served and nor will the
public be aware of specific instances when they are not.

So the problem illustrated in the case was not want of judicial
deference. The House of Lords, which is hardly an activist body,
was simply trying to accommodate human rights principles into
its reasoning. The problem is that human rights jurisprudence as
such sits uneasily with the doctrine that procedural matters of

'how it gets done' can be clearly insulated from substantive matters of 'what gets done'. The issue here is thus a broader one about the kind of jurisprudential assumptions required for taking human rights seriously. Indeed, what I shall argue is that the issues that arise for courts enforcing environmental rights arise more generally for attempts to take any human rights seriously.

3.4 The jurisprudence of human rights

The issues regarding the constitutional competence of courts do not only apply to environmental rights specifically, but to the more general incorporation of human rights principles into judicial reasoning. Human rights are substantive norms. The significance of this point for the constitutional competence of courts is that whenever such norms have to be taken into consideration in the judicial review of government or administrative decisions (or in interpretation of statutory laws when these bear on civil suits with a human rights dimension), the consideration of those decisions has a substantive dimension. It is this which critics of environmental rights particularly, but also of human rights jurisprudence generally, believe involves courts overstepping the constitutional limits to their competence, exceeding which would be unacceptable activism contravening the principle of the separation of powers.

In this section I seek to show why the jurisprudence of human rights can support substantive review of government decisions without involving unconstitutional activism. This does, though, mean reflecting to a degree on the underlying nature of constitutional relationships in the context of a modern democratic state that takes human rights seriously.

On the restrictive view traditionally exemplified in England, courts have the competence to review whether a decision is one that the administration was entitled to make. But that is construed as meaning they are charged with checking the legality of the decision in terms of the decision-making body's authority to make it and the procedural propriety of the method of arriving at it. The closest courts could come to reviewing the substantive basis of the decision—so it was understood—was on the grounds of 'manifest irrationality' or the test known as '*Wednesbury* unreasonableness' where the court is satisfied that the decision is unreasonable in the sense that it is beyond the range of responses open to a reasonable decision-maker. On this criterion, the actual reasons of the decision-maker do not require substantive examination because the unreasonableness of the decision will be manifest *on its face*, so there is no conflict with the doctrine that such an examination is disallowed (Hunt 1998: 217).

There are legal scholars, as well as eminent English judges, who have long contended that this ground for review is not adequate for dealing with cases involving human rights precisely because the reasonableness or otherwise of a decision will often not be so starkly obvious, but rather will require the careful balancing of a number of considerations. For this reason, courts which have to deal with human rights considerations are ineluctably brought to deploy the concept of proportionality. Proportionality, in public law, has to be understood as the balance between an individual's liberties, rights, and interests on the one hand, and the purpose of the public measure on the other.[8] The reviewing court cannot but take a view of the relative importance of a range of public interests and of the right interfered with. The intensity of scrutiny must also vary according to the importance of the right (Hunt 1998: 217–8). 'The more substantial the interference with human rights, the more the court will require by way of justification before it is satisfied that the decision is reasonable in the sense outline above' (Pannick in Singh 1997: 11).

If courts are obliged to deal with human rights, and they are, then they cannot consistently avoid using the principle of proportionality—whether or not recognized by name—in their reasoning, and as a legitimate ground for review of government decisions. This means the relation between courts and government *cannot* be quite as it is described as being when the description is taken as a benchmark for asserting the unconstitutionality of the kind of jurisprudence involved in adjudicating environmental rights cases. If that cannot in fact *be* the relation between courts and government wherever human rights are taken seriously, then normative arguments about competence which depend on assuming it is cannot be sound.

So the constitutional position needs to be viewed somewhat differently. The restrictive doctrine of the limits to the scope and intensity of judicial review is warranted by the assumption that what the judiciary is essentially doing is correcting legal mistakes in (or dealing with unforeseen consequences of) the way government has gone about formulating, implementing, or executing the acts it decides on. This assumption rests on the deeper assumption that the government, as one body, and as authorized by one people, does not intentionally will contradictory objectives, and so the closest the judiciary can or should come to reviewing its reasons for a decision is to check what was its actual intent when this has become clouded by infelicitous administrative acts or events. The underlying assumption, then, is of the applicability of the image of a single body politic: this is a single sovereign body in which the people, through elections, mandate a legislature to pass laws which the government will execute. Sovereignty is thus assumed to be simple and indivisible, whether reference is to the will of the people as made manifest in the government, or by the customary shorthand of 'parliamentary sovereignty'.

The extent to which, historically, that assumption ever held good is a matter on which I shall not seek to comment, since the point is that today it certainly does not hold absolutely in any constitutional democracy. States sign international treaties, and they incorporate (by various means) international law and conventions, etc.—in particular in the field of human rights. Once a state has ratified any such agreement it has thereby introduced a source of authority into its domestic affairs, which is not the same as its domestic sovereignty. Indeed, in practice, even without such formal state recognition, the authority of international law and of international conventions of human rights are frequently recognized by courts. So in any state that recognizes the authority of international or regional human rights norms—and there is no 'well-ordered' state that does not—the idea that courts can coherently refrain from a degree of substantive engagement with governmental and administrative decisions as is required by deployment of the principle of proportionality is mistaken; and the idea that they should seek to do so rests on an anachronistically monistic conception of sovereign authority.

It is precisely the unwarranted restrictions of that outmoded jurisprudence that constitute the major obstacles to success in cases involving environmental rights. The restrictions affect both environmental and human rights dimensions, and in cases involving either dimension the idea that they can be decided on the narrowest legal basis possible can be inimical to the coherence of legal reasoning. Leonor Moral Soriano takes this to be illustrated in the case of *Duddridge*, a test case for the precautionary principle in England. Here, the legal point at issue was whether European Community law obliged the Secretary of State to apply the precautionary principle. Mrs Justice Smith reasoned that since the requirement of applying the precautionary principle stemmed from a statement of EC policy (Article 130r), not from any binding obligation of Community law, this meant that the Secretary of State had discretion as to whether to apply the principle. Therefore, his failure to do so in this particular instance could not be successfully challenged. It was not that the judge saw insurmountable problems in interpreting the precautionary principle, or even in finding that the 'possibility of harm' was sufficient to justify its substantive application to the case. Her judgement was constrained by the jurisprudence that holds policy to be a matter outside or beyond the law. The applicants' failure in the case was due to constraints taken by the judge to prevent her from engaging in what Soriano refers to as the 'jurisprudence of rights' as distinct from the jurisprudence of 'wrongs': the Secretary of State had not acted illegally, because he had committed no legally identifiable wrong (since he had the discretion according to the law to issue the decision he did); the question of rights, 'the question is the infringement of an individual's right sufficiently justified?'—being an intrinsically substantive matter—is not held to arise. Yet, Soriano criticizes the judge's jurisprudence for its failure to take appropriate account of how principles and rules should not be treated as identical *types* of statement.

This explains why Smith LJ referred to the precautionary principle as if it were a statutory norm... [She] disregarded the different role of rules and principles in legal reasoning: *rules* apply in an either/or fashion and according to deontic logic, whereas *principles* apply in a "more or less" fashion and according to the logic of optimising. This means that principles, such as those requiring precaution in environmental matters, can be more or less relevant to decide an environmental case, but they have to be taken into account since it is one of the elements which makes environmental law coherent. In addition, principles cannot be blindly followed: they have to be weighed. This is only understandable if principles are conceived as requirements to optimise. This means that they are commands which require the highest degree of realisation, and that a more intensive implementation of one principle may reduce the degree of realisation of another, competing, principle, but certainly does not necessarily lead to its wholesale exclusion.   (Soriano 2001: 304–5)

Soriano writes:

substantive considerations, including policy factors and consequences, far from labelling judicial activity as judicial activism contribute to the coherence of legal reasoning and the system as a whole. Indeed, legal reasoning should be understood as an exercise to find coherence, that is, to accommodate all legal (and non-legal) issues that determine the justice of the decision.   (Soriano 2001: 311)

The kind of jurisprudence required for the effective enforcement of environmental rights, then, differs then from the restrictively proceduralist kind that is characteristically favoured on a liberal view of the courts with its distinctive take on their 'neutrality'. To engage in a wholesale critique of that view is beyond the scope of this book, but it is worth observing that the traditional view, according to which the courts should seek to determine intent on the narrowest, most literal, grounds possible, is not neutral in its effects. Resistance to the introduction of fully consistent human rights jurisprudence brings with it the risk of a very selective recognition of which rights are to be regarded as 'fundamental'. In particular, as Hunt remarks regarding the situation in England,

> there is a danger that reliance on judicial development of the indigenous common law may be inherently backward looking. In other words, the rights which the common law is prepared to regard as fundamental are those classical liberal rights, such as the right to property and associated freedom interests, which the common law has traditionally prioritised and against which so much regulatory legislation has been deliberately directed by the administrative state.   (Hunt 1998: 307)

Moreover, at a very practical level, as we have seen, the adversarial system favoured by traditionalists, which views cases as a narrow conflict of bipolar interests, has an inherent tendency to favour those with the resources to mount or defend an action more effectively.

Resistance to taking constitutional environmental rights seriously relies on objections that this involves, in effect, too swingeing a challenge to competing interests and too searching a review of government and administrative decisions. Each line of objection, then, rests on a value judgement—about what is 'too' swingeing or 'too' searching. In the one case it is clearly a substantive value judgement: the rights which environmental rights can compete with—paradigmatically those associated with property and economic development—are taken to have a certain substantive weight that environmental values do not match, let alone exceed. In the second case, however, the substantive value is not so immediately evident, but I have sought to indicate how traditional jurisprudence does in fact tend to promote it.

3.5 The effectiveness of a constitutional right to an adequate environment

This chapter has sought to show that what obstacles there may be to the potential effectiveness of a constitutional right to an adequate environment are at root of a political, not a technical, kind. That is to say, there are technical means of surmounting them which can be deployed where there is the political will to do so. Since this chapter has mainly looked at issues bearing on the justiciability of the right it remains to be emphasized that justiciability is not the only criterion of effectiveness.

A number of purposes can be attributed to constitutions, and the provision of rights that are directly justiciable for individuals is just one of them. Commentators like Cass Sunstein (1993), for instance, who seek to caution against extending constitutional provision beyond the classic liberal rights to include such rights as the right to an adequate environment, tend to stress that a constitution is essentially a legal document, and that the basic point of constitutional rights is to provide campaigners and ordinary citizens with the judicial means to rectify wrongs: either before the event, through injunctive relief; or afterwards, through compensation. Yet, this is not the only purpose of constitutional rights, and if we are to understand how the general aims of constitutional environmental rights are to be achieved, it is not enough to focus solely on the role of courts. For it is not in fact the main purpose of environmental rights, or of human rights generally, to bring about a proliferation of legal suits, much less a generally litigious culture; rather, the aim is to secure individuals in the protection and enjoyment of the substance of the right. The effectiveness of constitutional environmental rights has to be assessed against their general aim, which is to ensure that everyone is more secure in the enjoyment of environmental protections than they would be in the absence of those rights. This can be achieved by individual rights of litigation, by appropriate legislative measures, by properly supported citizen action, and by combinations of these.

It is therefore appropriate and important to note other functions—legal and extralegal—of a constitutional right to an adequate environment. Even within the realm of legal enforcement, some of the functions of a constitutional right are not directly related to individual justiciability. One legal consequence of such a right would be the enactment of further environmental protection legislation: for, while legislation can be inspired by provisions other than rights, being based in rights provides a stronger stimulus than mere policy statements. Even Sunstein grants the possibility that the existence of such a right would prompt legislatures to attend to environmental issues when they otherwise might not. It could also affect judicial interpretation of existing statutory provisions and generally serve to stimulate a more environmentally appreciative application and evolution of legal concepts by the judiciary. This tendency would likely be enhanced by extralegal effects such as positive feedback, 'in that the value which society places on the particular right is substantially increased' (Stevenson 1983: 397), and what Robyn Eckersley refers to as an upward ratcheting effect on political expectations (Eckersley 1996: 220). Stevenson also emphasizes the broader educational role of the right, particularly in fostering a publicly recognized environmental ethic: 'if a constitutional right to a clean environment existed, it would serve to foster a greater public appreciation of the ... potential threats to the environment and, ultimately, to society itself' (Stevenson 1983: 397). Such effects would serve to consolidate the essential aims of environmental protection as being a matter of public interest rather than a partisan cause.

Certainly, the foregoing line of argument tends to presuppose that it would generally be the case that environmental rights are, in Schwartz's words, 'provisions the nation believes to be indispensable to its general welfare'. A necessary condition for the effectiveness of constitutional environmental rights is the existence of the requisite political will as embodied both in the institutions of the state and in the political culture of its citizens. The question of whether this condition is fulfilled is not one that can be addressed in the abstract, since the 'requisite political will' pertains to a specific actual polity.

So my final comment is to caution against supposing that the issue of the effectiveness of a constitutional environmental right can be settled one way or the other by means of purely theoretical argument. For there is a risk of circular reasoning on both sides: just as it would be a mistake to assume that a strong normative case for constitutional environmental rights would necessarily be embraced as the political will of any particular state and its citizens, it would likewise be a mistake to take any current lack of an unequivocal will in their favour as a reason to believe that such a will would never develop. Indeed—and here is a further reason to resist a precipitate conclusion—the existence or otherwise of the requisite political will could in fact be influenced by the outcome of the debates about exactly the matters which have been the topic of inquiry in this chapter.

Yet, there is also a tension—and further practical reflexivity—here. For another part of the point of constitutionalizing a right is to give it some immunity from normal political decision-making processes. I have argued that the kind of jurisprudence required to make constitutional environmental rights in particular effective is also required for constitutionally recognized human rights more generally; but given, as we have seen, that this entails some renegotiation of constitutional relationships, it remains to ask whether what it entails is actually a greater immunity from political governance than should be allowed or welcomed in a democracy.

Notes

1. Fernandez (1993) has critically discussed the timidity on this score of Virginia and Pennsylvanian courts in pointing to the ambiguity of the environmental rights provisions in their state constitutions as an obstacle to judicial enforcement. However the problem with those cases, according to Bruch, Coker, and VanArsdale et al. (2000), is that the aesthetic and cultural dimension of the environmental rights was emphasized, and until the human health dimension is properly established it is over-ambitious and even counterproductive to press for rights relating to less fundamental aspects of human well-being. Once the right to an environment adequate for health is established, they note, courts do appear more willing to protect the environment without requiring an explicit link to human life or health.

2. See Chapter 5 below on similar issues regarding EU directives and direct effect.

3. Contrasting signals emerged from two Greenpeace cases, for instance: in the *THORP* case, Otton J. referred to the large number of Greenpeace supporters in Cumbria as a relevant feature given the geographical

location of the plant in question, and thus considered Greenpeace to have standing because it represented *individual interests* (Soriano 2001: 309); in *R* v. *Secretary of State for Trade and Industry ex parte Greenpeace Ltd*, though, Greenpeace was thought of as representing the *public interest*, and its standing was recognized on this basis.

4. The long-running investigations relating to the Sellafield cases may be instructive of this. The UK Committee on the Medical Aspects of Radiation in the Environment (COMARE) has repeatedly published reports stating that no linkage has been proven between the nuclear reprocessing plant and childhood cancers such as leukaemia in its vicinity. But the report of Schneider et al. (2001: 13) puts the findings another way:

> More than fifteen years of research has established that the excess inci-dence of childhood leukaemia around Sellafield is statistically significant and is continuing. The cause or combination of causes of the observed leukaemia increases are not known. Many uncertainties remain. Radiation exposure due to radionuclide releases from Sellafield cannot be excluded as a cause for the observed health effects.

5. Another widely cited definition is from UNCED's Rio Declaration (1992), principle 15: 'Where there are threats of serious or irreversible environmental damage, lack of full scientific certainty shall not be used as a reason for postponing cost effective measures to prevent environ-mental degradation.' The reference to threats being 'serious or irre-versible' and to precautionary measures being 'cost effective' represent significant qualifications with respect to the definition given in the text. Needless to say, when the principle is invoked in courts it is liable to considerable interpretative contestation.

6. Miller acknowledges that this negative impression may to some extent be offset by cases which have been settled out of court, but the fact of settling itself vitiates the establishment of legal precedents and hence the emergence of legal rights.

7. The reference is to the contractarian theory of justice of John Rawls (1972): see, for example, §§ 3, 20, and 24 on how the 'veil of ignorance' operates in that theory.

8. Formally speaking, this concept was alien to the United Kingdom, although it is a fundamental concept in the European Convention, but Murray Hunt provides detailed analysis to show that developments of English common law since *Wednesbury* brought courts to recognize the principle of proportionality in all but name even before the 1998 Human Rights Act.

Environmental Rights as Democratic Rights

Having examined questions about how effectively constitutional environmental rights *could* be enforced, I turn now to the question of the legitimacy of trying to enforce them at all. This is a significant question because the point of constitutionalizing rights is to set them above the vicissitudes of everyday politics, and this is also effectively to raise them above the possibility of (routine) democratic revision. Because of this, political theorists have adduced various reasons to be cautious about, or even opposed to, the constitutionalizing of rights in general; and these reasons might be thought to apply particularly decisively to the newer rights proposals, such as those including environmental rights, which have not historically been linked with the conditions of legitimate government. The focus of this chapter is on one issue of principle that has been appealed to, both by politicians and by theorists, as a reason for not constitutionalizing environmental rights, namely, that to do so would be undemocratic.

This issue concerns both the environmental content of these rights and their constitutional form *as* rights. While virtually no constitution in the world that has been drafted or amended in the past ten years omits reference to principles of environmental protection, even if not in the form of a rights provision, such principles, it seems, cannot be directly justified by reference to principles of democracy. As Robert Goodin observes: '[t]o advocate democracy is to advocate procedures, to advocate environmentalism is to advocate substantive outcomes' (Goodin 1992: 168);

there is no necessary connection between them such as to guarantee that the former procedures will yield the latter sorts of outcome. Of course, it also does not follow that there is any necessary conflict between environmental and democratic principles, at least if a state's constitutional commitments to environmental protection are presented in terms of general policy statements allowing latitude of interpretation and political negotiation of their practical implications. However, when a constitutional provision is entrenched in the form of a right, this can mean that it is presumed to have a 'trumping' force with respect to other social values and policies if these conflict with it. Thus, the question arises as to the democratic legitimacy of constitutional rights which set certain substantive values beyond the reach of routine political revision and have the effect of pre-empting decisions that might otherwise be arrived at through democratic procedures. To the extent that environmental rights can be taken to embody substantive value commitments, therefore, they would appear to be vulnerable to the criticism that the constitutional entrenchment of them is undemocratic. It is to this criticism that the present chapter seeks to develop an answer.

In the first section I address arguments for the view that the constitutionalizing of any right at all is undemocratic; I show why these arguments are hyperbolic in that they cannot apply with the requisite force to *all* rights, and that they ultimately depend on assumptions about the meaning of democracy that are so problematic that it remains an open question whether they would necessarily apply to *any* rights. The critical arguments certainly seem unsustainable in relation to those procedural rights that are necessary for the very functioning of democracy as such. In the second section the scope of these 'democratic rights' is considered, and it is shown how procedural environmental rights can be counted among them. The question then is whether and how substantive constitutional environmental rights might be defended. In Section 4.3 I investigate whether arguments for the democratic legitimacy of social rights can be applied to environmental rights. However, I suggest, because such arguments are somewhat problematic in their own terms, and because there are also important differences between environmental and social rights, a separate line of defence could be more appropriate. What I argue in Sections 4.4 and 4.5 is that a distinct defence, which is actually more robust than that available for social rights, can be developed on the basis of considering environmental rights as 'negative' rights more similar to established protective rights than to 'positive' social rights.[1] I suggest that substantive environmental rights, in common with some existing and far less controversial rights, can in fact be justified not indirectly, by reference to the material preconditions of democracy, but on the very grounds that democracy itself is justified. Such rights would have a very strong democratic legitimation which could undercut the main criticism altogether.

4.1 Are constitutional rights inherently undemocratic?

If an aim of constitutionalizing rights, in general, is to set them beyond the scope of ordinary political revision, this may be claimed to be fundamentally undemocratic. A number of reasons for such a claim have been set out with particular clarity by Jeremy Waldron in his 1993 article 'A Rights-Based Critique of Constitutional Rights', and this will be the focus for the discussion which follows.[2]

4.1.1 Undemocratic transfer of powers from legislature to judiciary

A major concern of Waldron's is that any proposal for entrenching a constitutional right is in effect a proposal to transfer power from an elected legislature to an unelected judiciary. Since courts do not simply enforce rights, but unavoidably also have to interpret them, 'the courts will inevitably become the main forum for the revision and adaptation of basic rights in the case of changing circumstances and social controversies' (p. 20). We should have

grave misgivings about this prospect: 'our respect for... democratic rights is called seriously into question when proposals
are made to shift decisions about the conception and revision
of basic rights from the legislature to the courtroom' (p. 20).
Waldron's view is that courts should not have powers to make
decisions about the scope and applications of constitutional rights
because such decisions can have politically controversial content,
and political controversies should be settled in political fora.
A democratically illegitimate erosion of legislative power can
follow from the entrenchment of constitutional rights. 'When a
principle is entrenched in a constitutional document', he writes,
this is, in effect, 'a disabling of the legislature from its normal
functions of revision, reform and innovation in the law. To think
that a constitutional immunity is called for is to think oneself
justified in disabling legislators in this respect (and thus, indirectly, in disabling the citizens whom they represent)' (p. 27).
However, while a degree of caution is certainly appropriate, it
seems that the genuine worry here can be overstated. A justified
concern about *too much* power being transferred to the judiciary—
or even being arrogated to themselves by activist judges—should
not lead to a disregard of the democratic importance of the judiciary's *legitimate* powers. Nor should the legitimacy of constraints
on legislators' powers be disregarded. Constitutional rights have
the effect of placing certain constraints on the exercise of law-
making powers, which are also conferred by the constitution, of
the legislature. To be *constrained* in the exercise of a power with
regard to certain specific matters, however, is not the same as
being *disabled* from using a general power; and so Waldron's
claim, as stated, appears somewhat hyperbolic.

It also has to be recognized that the legislature's supposed
monopoly of legitimate law-making is not qualified only by constitutional law. A good deal of law may be made, altered, and interpreted at 'lower' levels too—for example, secondary legislation,
regulation, etc., as well as in institutions of subnational governance.
The legislature is thus also not the only branch of government
to be constrained by constitutional principles and rights. With

regard to environmental decisions, specifically, it has to be noted that many of these are taken not by the legislature but by the executive, and so, as Robyn Eckersley points out,

> in so far as trade-offs must be made, it is better that they be made solemnly, reluctantly, as a matter of 'high principle' and last resort, and under the full glare of the press gallery and law reporters rather than earlier in the public decision-making process via the exercise of bureaucratic and/or ministerial discretion that is presently extremely difficult for members of the public to challenge.   (Eckersley 1996: 229)

Furthermore, Waldron's suggestion that constitutionalizing a right is undemocratic because this indirectly disables citizens from debating or influencing its meaning or status requires some qualification. To be sure, Waldron's claim does not have to be seen as depending on any assumption, which in most contexts would likely be contentious, about the genuine representativeness of politicians; rather, his view takes as the standard of legitimacy the procedural principle of majoritarian rule. Because, in most jurisdictions, to effect a constitutional amendment generally requires more than a simple majority approval, the requirement contravenes that principle. However, this particular objection, that it is difficult to effect constitutional changes, cannot straightforwardly be applied to the initial constitutionalization of a right: precisely because a supermajority will be required to approve it, at the time of approval it would be 'super legitimate' by majoritarian standards. Where his objection applies, though, is to the subsequent immutability of the provision. Circumstances change, as does the content of political will, and the problem lies in disabling future citizens from amending the provision by democratic, that is, simple majoritarian, means.

4.1.2 Undemocratically binding the future?

The focus of Waldron's concern here is the placing of binding constraints on future citizens, limiting their autonomy in policy-making through principles developed on the basis of historically superseded exigencies. While constitutions can of course be amended, this cannot normally be achieved by routine democratic means, and so does not meet the point of principle Waldron wishes to insist on.

Again, though, the objection appears to require some qualification. Although Waldron's argument purports to be directed against *any* canonical list of rights, it does not seem to apply, at least with the same force, to *all* kinds of entrenched rights. As was noted in relation to an earlier criticism, he appears to refer approvingly to 'democratic rights'; and it is hard to conceive of what it could mean for these to be effectively respected without a fairly complete catalogue of at least the standard liberal civil and political rights. The extension of such protections into the future can hardly be seen as an unwelcome binding constraint on future individuals, or as undemocratic, if they constitute 'self-binding' commitments of democracy itself.

However, as we shall see in the next section, Waldron does not accept any rights at all should be entrenched, if the aim is to preserve democracy. He does concede, though, that 'if the people want a regime of constitutional rights, then that is what they should have: democracy requires *that*' (p. 46). So he does not challenge the democratic legitimacy of a contemporary majority constraining future majorities, even if this amounts to 'voting democracy out of existence, at least so far as a wide range of issues of political principle is concerned' (p. 46). He does, however, seek to *dissuade* from such a course.

What Waldron's argument seems to come down to, then, is not that a decision to entrench rights is itself democratically illegitimate; nor does it (because it could not) seek to prove that entrenching rights necessarily harms democracy into the future; rather, the argument essentially amounts to a claim that constitutional rights proponents are imprudent and irresponsible in advocating the removal of protections for democratic decision-making.

4.1.3 Rights proposals have an undemocratic motivational structure?

Waldron seeks to challenge the credibility of his opponents' case by suggesting that there is something fundamentally undemocratic, and perhaps even self-contradictory, in its motivational structure. He thinks that citizens might be dissuaded from following constitutional rights proponents if they consider what attitudes are exemplified by the latter.

> To embody a right in an entrenched constitutional document is to adopt a certain attitude towards one's fellow citizens. That attitude is best summed up as a combination of self-assurance and mistrust: self-assurance in the proponent's conviction that what she is putting forward really *is* a matter of fundamental right and that she has captured it adequately in the particular formulation she is propounding; and mistrust, implicit in her view that any alternative conception that might be concocted by elected legislators next year or the year after is so likely to be wrong-headed or ill-motivated that *her own* formulation is to be elevated immediately beyond the reach of ordinary legislative revision.   (Waldron 1993: 27)

However, this depiction is vulnerable to criticism on a number of grounds. In taking as its target the attitude of a *campaigner* for rights, the quoted claim about unwarranted assurance misses the mark it would need to hit in order to dissuade citizens from agreeing with 'her'. For in the event that citizens consider her arguments, and a majority agree that what she proposes is a matter of fundamental right, then her self-assurance would not be unwarranted in Waldron's terms. Waldron's remarks about 'mistrust' similarly miss their target. It is certainly true that an element of mistrust can be assumed to animate proposals for constitutional rights: those in favour of constitutionalizing certain fundamental rights believe that this protects the interests the rights represent against the trade-offs they might otherwise be subject to under the pressures of expediency that affect ordinary politics. There is a mistrust in the inherent inequities that majoritarian decision-making can generate and tolerate; and a mistrust of any assumption that a majority will always be sufficiently motivated to protect the interests of minorities. Such mistrust is not, in the rights proponent's view, unwarranted (and, indeed, she need not be taken to imply that she exempts herself from it either). Nor are its implications necessarily undemocratic, since majoritarianism has to be justified by democratic criteria, not vice versa. The majoritarian decision-making procedure may be defended as the least worst decision-making procedure under circumstances of disagreement, but this defence would not suffice to establish that a majoritarianism qualified by the constraints of providing certain fundamental rights for everyone was, all things considered, less democratic. To establish this would require an account of the rationale and criteria of democracy that did not reduce, with circularity, to the majoritarian principle.

Here is not the place to offer even a sketch of a theory of democracy, especially since that could immediately arouse the suspicion that it was tailored so that my preferred view of environmental rights would fit into it. Nevertheless, I do think it is appropriate to indicate why the assumptions underlying the view of democracy informing Waldron's swingeing critique of constitutional rights are uncompelling.

4.1.4 *Internal tensions in the majoritarian critique of constitutional rights*

Waldron objects to the presumption of proponents of constitutional rights in appearing to lay claim to a rationality superior to that which animates ordinary politics. His view is that there is no Archimedean point, no privileged vantage point, from which to affirm that superior rationality; and this is sufficient reason to leave matters open to ongoing democratic debate. Yet, he is also ready to lament the unwisdom of a majority, or even of a supermajority, decision arising precisely out of ordinary democratic processes to entrench rights on the grounds that while these people currently have a view of certain fundamental values, and this may appear to them to get at the truth, it is really just one attachment in a likely series; any decision they take can in principle be viewed from the vantage point of a hindsight available to the theoretical commentator but not to them, and viewed, moreover, *as* but one of a likely series of temporary convictions. His own view therefore rests on a mere assumption of the radical mutability of social values that has no firmer ground than the view he opposes.

Indeed, his own view might be thought to be less firmly grounded when we consider the inconsistency manifest in the way he views disagreements among the citizen body. He claims that 'if people disagree about basic rights (and they do), an adequate theory of authority can neither include nor be qualified by a conception of rights as "trumps" over majoritarian forms of decision-making' (p. 20). Yet in circumstances of disagreement, it is far from obvious why he thinks it more appropriate to 'rely on a general spirit of watchfulness in the community, attempting to raise what Mill called "a strong barrier of moral conviction" to protect our liberty' (p. 18). The assumption of radical pluralism extending over time seems to be inconsistent with any appeal to a 'general spirit' of a 'community' or to a liberty that 'we' unproblematically share. Such an appeal seems moreover to disregard basic sociological considerations about why people may not be able to realize their full potential as 'moral agents endowed with dignity and autonomy' or to exercise political influence in the 'processes by which decisions are taken in a community under circumstances of disagreement'. It is precisely a concern that this potential may in many cases be held in check or suppressed by inauspicious socioeconomic or cultural circumstances which underpins the view of those who believe that aspects of social disadvantage are appropriately the substance of rights for the disadvantaged. Furthermore, in advocating reliance on ordinary rights generated by statutory or common law rather than constitutional rights, Waldron also requires us to share his assumption that the existing balance of ordinary rights is a result of, and reflects, majoritarian political will. We are expected to rule out a priori any suspicion—any *mistrust*—that the ordinary legal rights found in any liberal democracy might systematically favour the interests of any particular minority group of society, such as property owners, for instance.

Finally, against the various speculative objections Waldron raises we have to set the empirical historical evidence that tends to suggest that constitutional rights, wherever they have been effective, have served to enhance citizens' access to justice, both procedural and substantive (Epp 1998). This could only be considered a diminution rather than an increase in democracy on a view of democracy that was too impoverished to merit being taken as a benchmark of normative criticism.

4.1.5 Section conclusion

In this section I have defended the general principle of constitutionalizing rights against charges that it necessarily runs counter to democratic principles. I have suggested that such charges can ultimately only be sustained on the basis of implausible assumptions at the level of political sociology and unwarranted assumptions at the level of normative theory. On the basis of more realistic and reasonable assumptions, by contrast, we are able to appreciate why existing democratic regimes, and their citizens, do as a matter of fact accord importance to constitutional rights, even taking these to be in important ways *constitutive* of democracy itself. Certainly, citizens' access to the institutions of justice is an important feature of any constitutional democracy, especially given that their effective ability to influence the legislature may be rather less than Waldron's position implies. Moreover, in order to sustain the claim that democracy is undermined by the attempt to constitutionalize rights, 'democracy' itself has to be defined in terms such that effectively forfeit any claim for it to be a pre-emptive value.

So far, however, I have sought to show only that there is nothing inherently undemocratic about the constitutionalizing of rights in general; this does not imply that there could be nothing undemocratic about constitutionalizing any specific right; it also does not mean that any right could necessarily be considered a 'democratic right' as opposed to being neutral with regard to principles of democracy. In the next section we consider why certain rights may be necessary for democracy, and ask whether these might include environmental rights.

4.2 Democratic rights

It may be persuasively argued that a certain set of rights is necessary in principle for the functioning of democracy. As already noted, even Waldron refers approvingly to generic 'democratic rights', and whatever force his objections may have against other constitutional rights, these, at least, might be thought to be immune. Yet, that is not in fact his view. In order to get clear about the issues here it may be helpful, though, first to clarify what the expression 'democratic rights' is itself to be taken to mean for the purposes of this inquiry.

The expression 'democratic rights' is not to be taken to refer to rights that have been decided on or constitutionalized by democratic means. On the understanding informing this chapter, it is accepted with Waldron that the fact that a right may have a democratic genesis is neither a necessary nor sufficient condition for its being called a democratic right: it is not sufficient, since democratic decisions can have undemocratic outcomes, and one possible sort of outcome is the entrenchment of an undemocratic right; it is not necessary since democratic outcomes, and thus democratic rights, might be secured by undemocratic means.

A contrast between democratic and undemocratic rights, therefore, can be drawn on the basis of a consideration of the effects or function of the rights: democratic rights are necessary to the functioning of a democracy whereas undemocratic rights would undermine its functioning. Rights may be said to be undemocratic, that is, not necessarily in virtue of their object (e.g. social security may not be necessary for democracy yet also not necessarily undermine it, so that a right to it in this respect is only 'non-democratic'), but in virtue of being constitutionalized when it is their constitutionalization itself which undermines democracy.[3] Of course, an indefinitely large variety of definitions of democracy are possible, but for present purposes it suffices to draw attention to a narrower and a broader sort of definition. On a narrow definition, democracy consists in a set of procedures for arriving at decisions; on a broader definition, democracy would be seen not simply as a set of procedures or mechanisms but as a type of society, complete with certain value commitments regarding not only the procedures for reaching decisions but also regarding desirable outcomes.

I propose to consider rights that are democratic according to the former conception of democracy as democratic rights in a strong sense: these are rights that are necessary to the very functioning of a democracy—of any democratic regime at all—and thus can be considered constitutive for democracy. Democratic rights in a weaker sense would be rights that happen to be necessary for (or even simply conducive to) the realization of the substantive principled goals of a given democratic regime, but which are not necessary for every conceivable regime that has a well-founded claim to be considered democratic in the stricter sense. For the moment, I shall be concerned only with the question of whether and how any constitutional rights can be considered democratic rights in the stronger sense.

4.2.1 Democracy's 'self-binding' rights: procedural rights

It can fairly readily and, I think, persuasively be shown that certain rights are a part of what Michael Saward calls democracy's 'self-binding commitments' (Saward 1998: esp. ch. 5). Such rights do not have a merely contingent relation to democracy, but are a necessary and constitutive part of it. Thus certain political rights, for quite evident reasons, would appear to be necessary for any democracy worthy of the name: if there were not a constitutionally assured and equal right of citizens to vote, the political system could hardly be considered democratic; nor could it be if there were not a right to stand for political office, or to associate and communicate with regard to elections, and so on. In general, then, certain rights of political participation can be conceived of quite readily as democratic rights.

These participatory rights can be distinguished in important respects from other types of constitutional rights. The rights which can be claimed to be strictly constitutive for democracy are essentially, or at their core, 'rights of participation', or 'rights of action'. What is conceptually distinctive about this type of right is that it is fulfilled if and when its holder performs the action which they have a right to perform; no action of any other party is directly at issue in the basic specification of the right; if the right-bearer fails to perform the action, no duty has been violated. Its fulfilment does not immediately or directly depend on the fulfilment by any other of a duty to act or forbear. Yet while the actual exercise of participatory rights may depend entirely on the will or ability of the bearer, however, the possibility of exercising them—and indeed the very existence of them as rights—depends on the existence of the requisite institutions and procedures. If these institutions and procedures are ones that are required for democracy to function, then the rights exist for the same reason that the democracy does. Rights of participation can thus be argued to have the same justification as the corresponding democratic procedures within which they are exercised. They can be conceived of as *procedural* rights as distinct from *substantive* rights, as rights relating to procedural requirements for the functioning of democracy in general rather than substantive requirements that a particular democratic regime might seek to meet. It may therefore be thought that even if substantive rights might be vulnerable to criticism as undemocratic, procedural, participatory rights are not.

However, this argument has been resisted by Waldron. His root objection to what he dubs the 'proceduralist gambit' is that the distinction between substance and democratic procedure is not a clear-cut one: 'People disagree about how participatory rights should be understood and about how they should be balanced against other values.' (p. 39). 'Many of the values we affirm in our opinions about democratic procedures are also values which inform our views about substantial outcomes' (p. 40). To be sure, at the most fundamental level, the commendation of any procedure has to do with its fittingness as a means for achieving a certain sort of substantive outcome, otherwise it would have no point; it is also likely that the more detailed a specified procedure is, the more it may be taken to steer towards one particular sort of outcome rather than another. Nevertheless, the most basic procedural rights set out in quite general language at the constitutional level are likely to be indeterminate with regard to any controversial outcome involving a conception of justice or the good more particular than the maintenance of a democratic system of government. Furthermore, even if no procedure could be completely indeterminate with regard to outcomes, it is not clear why Waldron thinks there may be any more democratic alternative to entrenching certain procedures, for, as Fabre points out, '[i]f constitutionally entrenching *any* procedure is undemocratic and therefore unacceptable, it logically follows that there should be no constitution at all' (Fabre 2000: 144). Waldron simply does not address this implication.

It therefore seems to me that we can accept with Waldron that there can be no procedures that do not relate to a substantive purpose, and nevertheless argue that the substantive purpose of certain procedures can be to enhance democracy. While there may be disagreement about how well—or even whether—they achieve this, the disagreement does not have to be seen as one between defenders of democracy and their opponents, but as one between competing views of what democracy entails. Certainly, if we consider the actual purposes of certain procedural rights— which might include promoting public debate, extending the range of issues of which citizens have knowledge, and expanding the possibility of their exercising influence over those issues, for instance—there seems no overwhelming reason why they should be objected to in the name of democracy rather than supported by it.

If we are therefore entitled to assume that some procedural rights may be defended as functionally necessary for democracy, the question to consider now is whether that defence would extend to *environmental* procedural rights.

4.2.2 *Environmental procedural rights*

The most significant developments in actual environmental rights provision to date have centred on procedural rights with respect to matters of specifically environmental substance. These rights—of access to environmental information, participation in environmental decision-making, and access to justice in environmental matters—have received widespread support from environmental campaigners, have been recognized as workable rights by legal commentators, and have been increasingly endorsed by governments. They have received a considerable impetus from what is probably the most significant agreement to date in the field of environmental rights protection, the Convention on Access to Information, Public Participation in Decision-Making and Access to Justice in Environmental Matters, generally known as the Aarhus Convention.

The Aarhus Convention was conceived with the express aim of promoting democracy as well as protecting the right of everyone to live in a healthy environment. Rights of information are clearly a prerequisite of effective democratic citizenship; and democracy is enhanced by increasing government and industry transparency and accountability on environmental issues. Opening up access to justice in the environmental field to members of the public is a democratic necessity given that the implementation and enforcement of environmental protection laws is a task which governments alone cannot fully accomplish: in a democratic society based on the rule of law, individual citizens and their various associations have a role to play in this field too, and it is one that governments should recognize and support. If the aim of these rights is to improve citizens' effective access to justice as well as to democratic decision-making mechanisms, they would hardly fall foul of Waldron's concerns about rights that 'disable citizens'.

It is worth noting that the agenda of Aarhus was in significant part determined by a concern to get newly independent states of Central and Eastern Europe closer to EU standards of environmental protection, and the democratic component was considered crucial to this end. Drafters and commentators alike claimed that the experience of the former communist bloc testified to a direct correlation between deficits in democracy and environmental quality. Access to reliable information on the environment and recognition of the role of NGOs in raising the level of public awareness of environmental issues were seen as prerequisites to developing a 'civil society' of democratic citizenry.

It is also worth noting that the small number of governments that were obstructive in negotiations for the Aarhus Convention did not seek to justify their resistance with Waldron-style arguments about democracy; their concerns were rather substantive economic ones about how the proposed rights could be used to block development decisions and counter rights of economic freedom more generally. In thus seeking to reserve those substantive decision-making areas from the influence of citizens, their aim could be seen as one of seeking in effect to *dilute* the Convention's democratic content.

If the aim of such rights is to open up new areas of public debate, to bring an increased range of decisions into the sphere of influence of citizens, and to provide a counterbalance to the substantive values promoted by existing rights, then they have a prima facie claim, certainly not automatically invalidated by Waldron's general objections, to be considered democratic rights. It is therefore hard to deny the democratic legitimacy of procedural environmental rights.

However, it may be argued that they have this legitimacy only insofar as they are seen simply as a logical extension of existing democratic rights: hence the opening up of information and justice with regard to environmental decisions could be nothing other than a specific application of more general democratic principles.

On this view, environmental rights would have no legitimacy other than that shared with other procedural rights. Yet it can be argued, and in the Aarhus Convention it is explicitly stated, that those procedural rights are underpinned by a fundamental substantive right to live in an environment adequate for health and well-being. How democratic are that fundamental right and other substantive rights it might generate?

4.3 Substantive environmental rights as democratic rights

Substantive environmental rights—a fundamental 'right to an adequate environment', and rights derivable from this—do not appear to be democratic rights in the sense that procedural rights can be claimed to be. It is in principle possible to offer a complete description of a democratic regime without necessarily making any reference to the quality of its physical environment. Many constitutions of the past omitted any such reference, without this being considered a source of democratic deficit; and even if no recently promulgated constitution omits reference to the importance of environmental quality, whether as a public policy objective or even as a right, this might still be distinguished from democratic objectives more strictly construed. Nevertheless, certain objectives of social policy are entrenched as constitutional rights, and, according to some theorists, this entrenchment can be defended by reference to the requirements of democracy. Their argument is not that such rights are necessary to democracy in the strict sense of being constitutive for democratic decision-making processes, but that they represent necessary preconditions for the effective functioning of a democratic regime. After briefly examining this argument we will consider whether it points to a democratic justification for environmental rights.

The preconditions argument seeks to establish democratic legitimacy for rights that are conceived as means to the ends of securing effective democratic rights rather than as rights that could be described as representing democratic ends in themselves. Such rights are not directly democratic rights in such a strict sense that a description of democracy which omitted reference to them would necessarily be an incomplete description. Nevertheless, they are rights which appear to be material requirements for the effective functioning of a fully developed democratic regime. For instance, it is widely accepted that a right to education, while not strictly necessary for the existence of democratic decision-making processes, is nevertheless a necessary condition for effective political participation: any conception of democracy that required or allowed the citizenry to be ill-informed and uneducated would not be a conception worthy of deployment as a benchmark of legitimacy. Some theorists extend this reasoning to argue that further substantive rights are necessary for the effective functioning of rights pertaining to democratic procedures. Thus rights to health, housing, and welfare (even including basic income) have been defended as necessary preconditions of democracy. Michael Saward, for instance, writes that

a citizen may...be so lacking in basic human needs—food, shelter, clothing—that her or his possession of the right to basic liberties is so hollow as to be wholly symbolic. For this reason, I have included in the list of unambiguously democratic rights one to a basic income, sometimes referred to as a guaranteed minimum income...The basic income is an essential condition for the effective exercise of other basic rights and freedoms of democracy.   (Saward 1998: 99)

Saward's claim, then, is that the capacity to make effective use of democratic rights is undermined where certain basic social and economic rights are not met.

However, this line of argument has been considered problematic even by supporters of constitutional social rights. Cecile Fabre, for instance, has raised two doubts about it (Fabre 2000: 122–5). First, insofar as it rests on the suggestion that people have a right to food, housing, and so on in order that they can participate politically, it seems to miss the real point of such rights: rights to health and welfare are important for reasons that have nothing to do with political participation. Second, the connection between meeting people's needs and their capacity to participate in public fora is too tenuous: rights to relief from extreme need might be justified on the grounds that they are necessary for political participation, but fully adequate welfare rights mean more than what is required simply to enable a person to haul himself or herself to a voting booth, and she doubts that these could be justified in terms of what is needed to enable people to participate politically.

So how do matters stand with regard to environmental rights? Robyn Eckersley has suggested that the preconditions argument can be used to support environmental rights:

there are certain basic ecological conditions essential to human survival that should not be bargained away by political majorities because such conditions provide the very preconditions (in the form of life support) for present and future generations of humans to practice democracy. In one sense, they might be seen as even more fundamental than the human political rights that form the ground rules of democracy.   (Eckersley 1996: 224)

However, as others (e.g. Dobson 1996) have pointed out, if certain ecological preconditions have to be met, there is no necessary reason why they have to be met by democratic means. Thus rights that flow from the ecological preconditions argument are not necessarily democratic ones. Ecological preconditions may be important (as a number of values other than democracy may be), and sensible people in a democracy may in fact agree that decisions to protect them need to be taken; but if they do not happen to agree to this, then it would be *un*democratic to have a right going against their expressed will and preferences. It would not be an adequate response to this objection to insist that ecological preconditions are so important—with human lives, and hence their democratic society, depending on them—that they simply must be protected by rights, since this would be to beg precisely the question that the democratic critic believes requires a democratic answer: for whether it is in fact so important is for the democratic participants to decide, and if they choose some other value, such as free choice, over survival, *that* is their democratic right.

It therefore appears that the preconditions argument is as problematic regarding the democratic legitimacy of environmental rights as it is for social rights.

However, a slightly different line of argument could be developed, adapting what Norman Daniels has put forward in the name of 'relative rationality' (Daniels 1975: 276). The basic argument would be that if it is rational for a democrat to affirm equal civil and political rights, then it is also rational for a democrat to affirm the equal worth of those rights. This argument can be invoked in support of social rights on the grounds that the actual worth of civil and political rights is seriously compromised for the socially and economically disadvantaged sectors of society. So if democracy is recognized to imply certain self-binding rights, then these rights themselves imply further, substantive, rights.

Nevertheless, while the 'relative rationality' principle itself may be persuasive, its deployment in the argument for social rights is problematic in that it depends on additional assumptions that are challengeable, namely, that assuring the equal worth of political rights depends on a redistribution of income and wealth such as is brought about by guaranteeing certain social rights. Against this, it could be argued that relative rationality could be respected by means of more rigorous procedures protecting political rights from external socioeconomic influences,[4] for instance, rather than by supplementing them with social rights. Thus, whatever its merits as an argument for social justice, this argument is not necessarily stronger than the preconditions argument as a specifically democratic justification for social rights. The argument also shares with the absolute preconditions argument the problem of potentially yielding a conclusion about substantive outcomes that in practice might be democratically opposed.

Nevertheless, when we consider how the relative rationality argument might work in relation to environmental rights, matters may look a little different. It could be argued that if it is rational to affirm procedural environmental rights, then it is rational to affirm all the necessary conditions for achieving the ends for which they were introduced. Such ends would not be specific substantive environmental conditions, but an equal right of all to participate in establishing what those conditions should be. This seems an impeccably democratic principle. However, before seeing how this argument could be developed in favour of substantive environmental rights, it is necessary to indicate how these can be so conceived that they are not vulnerable to the kind of criticisms that have been seen to apply to social rights.

4.4 Environmental rights as negative rights

Thus far have I have examined the case for substantive environmental rights on the assumption that they should be treated as a subspecies of social—or 'positive'—rights. I now address the question whether they might not also, or even instead, be assimilated to negative rights. If they can, this is potentially significant given that negative rights are generally considered to be more readily justifiable on democratic grounds than positive rights; the question of the democratic legitimacy of negative environmental rights will be examined more carefully, though, once the basic case for them has been set out and defended against foreseeable objections.

The basic reason for seeing a right to be free from humanly generated environmental harm as a negative right is that, like negative rights generally, it would entail the proscription of certain activities which others might otherwise engage in. Saward (1998) suggests that a green democratic right could be expressed as a negative right thus: 'The state must not deprive citizens, or allow them to be deprived, of an undegraded environment'. Thus, just as individuals have a right not to be subject to the kinds of harm wrought by practices of torture, unlawful detention, and so on, they may equally be thought to have a right not to be subject to comparable sorts of harm which might be wrought through practices which assail them, for instance, with toxic pollutants.

It therefore seems appropriate to view a right to an adequate environment as a negative right to the extent that the demand it implies is not that the government has to 'provide' a clean environment, but that it prevent private parties—and its own agencies—from polluting or despoiling what would otherwise have been, without the need for any positive action, an adequate environment.

Nevertheless, a number of objections to this view have to be considered. An initial objection of a relatively minor sort is that, in practice, such a right might be advanced in circumstances where the environment has *already* been compromised, and so the demand based on it would not literally be preventative: the demand might be for rectification of or compensation for harm that has already been done rather than for prevention of some impending harm. Yet even in these circumstances it is possible to maintain, in point of normative principle, that the right should be classified as a negative one: compare, for instance, the case of a regime engaged in systematic torture or murder of its citizens; here the fact that the harm is already being done, and thus requires remedial rather than preventative action, does not in any way diminish the normative case for the citizens' right to be free from the harm.

It may be further objected, though, that the normative principle is an abstract one which simply does not carry through with regard to the implementation of the right by means of determinate duties. Thus whereas in the case of a regime engaged in rights abuses such as torture the demand is for restraints on actions occurring under the auspices of the state, in the case of protection from environmental harms, by contrast, the demand is for positive programmes of action by the state. The thought is that in the former case the state needs only to cease what it is doing for the right to be fulfilled, whereas in the latter case the state has to undertake positive activities to fulfil the right, which can be more problematic in various ways. In particular, the environmental protection programme may require the diversion of resources to its accomplishment. Yet, while this may (sometimes) be the case, this in itself does not mark off environmental from more established negative rights, since any institutional protections are going to

require resourcing. If there is a relevant difference between negative and positive rights on the question of resources, it lies in the
fact that for negative rights an allocation of resources is necessary
only as a means to the end represented by the right, whereas for
positive rights the redistributive allocation is itself inherent in the
aim of the right.[5] Thus typical positive rights such as welfare rights
directly entail a redistribution of economic resources. The right to
an adequate environment, however, is not a right to a particular
share of economic resources, and so does not need to be seen as a
positive right on this ground. While social rights necessarily presuppose the existence of a welfare state and developed economy,
all that environmental rights necessarily presuppose are the existence of the natural world and a normative order which recognizes rights. It therefore seems appropriate to speak of a negative
right to be free from interference effected in the medium of the
environment.

It is difficult to envisage, though, that a negative environmental
right could be an *absolute* right in the sense of requiring a complete absence of interference, where 'interference' is measured as
'degradation' of the environment. For one thing, a completely
undegraded environment cannot be exactly what is at issue, since
an environment may be degraded to some degree and yet still be
adequate for everyone's health and well-being. In fact, it can be
argued that a degree of environmental degradation is unobjection-
able if it occurs through developments which are aimed at the *promotion* of people's health and well-being. As Joseph Sax argues, for
instance, 'leaving free from pollution' could entail unrealistic—
and largely undesired—diminution or elimination of economic
activity; and he thinks it implausible to suggest that unless a society hardly transforms its environment at all it should be branded
transgressive of fundamental human rights (Sax 1990: 95).

What about freedom from degradation of the environment to
the point that it actually does cause *harm* to individuals, though?
Should this, at least, not be considered an absolute normative
imperative? The problem here, too, as Mark Sagoff has indicated, is
that protection from environmental harms cannot be formulated

as an absolute imperative in the way that protections of more
established negative rights can. He notes that although laws
aimed at protecting citizens from environmental threats do
resemble, for instance, child labour, civil rights, and anti-
discrimination statutes 'insofar as they identify moral evils and
seek to minimize or eliminate them' (Sagoff 1988: 197), they nevertheless also differ in important respects.

Pollutants and the risks they cause are evils, but unlike child labour and
racial discrimination, they are to some extent necessary evils, because
they inevitably accompany beneficial activities we are unwilling to do
without. What is more, even a single instance of discrimination, voting
fraud, or sexual harassment is a crime to which Americans are opposed as
a society... In controlling pollution and other risks, however, a conception of diminishing returns applies: As pollution levels approach zero,
further reductions, as a rule, cost more to make but may be less important
from a moral point of view.   (Sagoff 1988: 197–8)

Environmental protection, then, is not an all-or-nothing matter.
'We cannot entirely eliminate hazards created by people': writes
Sagoff, 'rather, we must accept some risks that are insignificant,
uncertain, or impossible to control; we must accept others
because the costs of controlling them still further, *even from an
ethical point of view*, are grossly disproportionate to the additional
safety we gain' (Sagoff 1988: 198, emphasis in the original). Hence
Sagoff argues that 'No one has a right to a completely risk-free
environment or to be protected from *de minimis* hazards even
when they are caused by man' (Sagoff 1988: 219).

However, while I substantially accept this assessment of the less
than absolute character of environmental rights, I would dispute
that this is a peculiar feature of environmental rights which is not
shared by the other rights mentioned. For instance, the unequivocal crimes that may be associated with discrimination, sexual
harassment, and so on, have always to be distinguished from more
minor sorts of offence that society requires individuals simply to
live with; and the general point here is simply that in its actual
implementation the 'harm principle' always has to be set against a
principle of *proportionality*. So if the negative environmental right

neither could nor would need to be a right to be free from absolutely any harm or risk thereof, it could nevertheless be understood as a right to be free from *'unacceptable'* harm. This, after all, is the essence of established negative rights: even such a right as that to be free from torture conforms to this principle rather than to a principle of freedom from any harm whatever. Therefore the negative status of environmental rights cannot be denied on this ground either.

There are, of course, peculiar difficulties in arriving at serviceable definitions of 'unacceptable harm' in the environmental field. There are certainly immense technical difficulties in trying to quantify harms and risks in a field which is so thoroughly permeated with uncertainties. However, the point about the criterion of 'acceptability' is that, whatever the current state of scientific knowledge, certain risks, as currently perceived, either are or are not deemed to be acceptable on the basis of *political* decisions. The question that has to be asked in the present context is whether democratically legitimate decisions about the acceptability of risk would be enhanced or compromised by constitutionalizing negative environmental rights.

4.5 The democratic legitimacy of negative environmental rights

In a self-governing society a risk may be an acceptable one if it is knowingly and willingly assumed by those affected by it. As Sax observes, since 'self-government is at the core of democratic government, and genuine choice is a key to self-government, assur-ing that risks taken are the product of such genuine choice is fundamental to the legitimacy of environmental decisions' (Sax 1990: 97). So what does it take to make a choice legitimate? 'It is not necessary that each individual personally consent to every risk, nor that risks taken be equally imposed on every individual. No society could undertake any sort of activity if it awaited unanimity, or if it had to promise that the benefits and detriments of every program would be entirely equal across the population' (Sax 1990: 97).

But if we cannot demand unanimity and complete equality, there nonetheless is a democratic case for insisting 'that decisions be made under conditions of sufficient knowledge and consideration so as to reflect a true choice fully appreciative of the consequences' (Sax 1990: 97). And if benefits and detriments flowing from decisions cannot be shared entirely equally, the parameters of acceptable inequalities at least must be democratically legitimated.

In ensuring that everyone has a say in the specification of acceptable environmental risks, the procedural environmental rights discussed previously clearly have an important role to play. However, procedural rights alone are not sufficient to this end. There are a number of reasons, in any complex and stratified society, why it would not in practice be possible for everyone to participate in the determination of acceptable risk. If it is not practically possible for all to exercise participatory rights with equal effectiveness, then decision-making processes should be so organized that some of the foreseeable consequences of the impossibility of genuinely universal participation are accounted for. That is to say, if some people, especially those from certain disadvantaged sectors of society, lack the knowledge, education, capacity, confidence, time, and so on, to participate effectively in pursuit of their own environmental interests, then, independently of considerations about the need to rectify socioeconomic disadvantages at source, there is a case for saying that their basic interests should in some way be represented in the deliberations of those who do participate.

At the least, as Sax suggests, the majority can be said to owe to each individual a basic right not to be left to fall below some minimal level of substantive protection against hazard. For it can and does happen that risks which are chosen by majoritarian democratic processes fall particularly heavily on certain groups or individuals. 'The most tragic images of environmental harm are those involving hapless victims, those who without sufficient knowledge or involvement and without choice have had risk and damage imposed upon them' (Sax 1990: 97). It is also worth noting that sometimes people, particularly the poor, 'assent' to a heightened risk of environmental harm, if this is the only way they can retain their livelihood; yet such a situation is not only unjust, but also undemocratic, since such people are under an effective material compulsion to accept, and bear the brunt of, decisions in a way that others are not. The basic democratic principle of equal autonomy would thus appear to be violated.

So I believe there is a case not only of justice, but also of democratic principle, that can be made for a basic norm, as suggested by Sax, that 'the least advantaged individual is insulated against imposition of risk below some minimal threshold within his or her own society' (Sax 1990: 101). This norm is most appropriately conceived as a fundamental substantive environmental right. In formulating the relevant norm, one can imagine, for instance, a Rawlsian procedure whereby from behind a 'veil of ignorance' rational agents would determine which risks they would wish to be protected against under any circumstances, and which risks they would be willing to run as a trade-off against certain attendant benefits. This procedure would in effect make it possible to distinguish protective rights, which are on a par with those protecting liberties, from provisions which may be subject to the trade-offs allowed by the difference principle. Rights relating to a minimum environmental standard would come under the same protection as basic liberties, and in this respect they would be akin to existing negative rights in not being liable to any trade-off. For having granted that some trade-offs of environmental quality against socioeconomic advantage might be considered permissible in a democracy, it is nevertheless arguable that certain basic limits to trade-offs are warranted, particularly in circumstances of environmental injustice whereby the economic benefits of some are traded against the environmental detriments of others.

Such a right is not vulnerable to the problem we noted earlier regarding attempts to argue for social rights as democratic rights, whereby opponents can claim that it is not irrational to assent to political rights (i.e. democratic rights in a strict sense) and yet to dissent from social rights, if one can conceive of how procedures in the former sphere can be insulated against substantive disruptions in the latter. For, by contrast, it would be irrational to assent to procedural environmental rights and yet dissent from substantive environmental rights since the former do not pertain to a separate sphere from the latter. In the very specification of *acceptable* environmental risks, procedural and substantive dimensions intermesh.

At this point, however, it is open to a sceptic to respond, echoing Waldron, that if a commitment to procedural environmental rights does entail substantive rights then this is a reason for a democrat to resist entrenching that commitment in a constitution. Should democratic participants not retain a right to dissent from a commitment to such substantive outcomes? In reply to this critical question, the implications of conceiving the right as a negative one must be brought to the fore.

Negative rights are generally considered to be more readily justifiable on democratic grounds than positive ones are. Certain negative rights can reasonably be claimed to be implied by the core demands of democracy: thus civil rights, aimed for instance at protecting citizens' freedom of expression and association, follow with a clear substantive logic from the requirements of a properly functioning democracy. However, this direct connection does not seem to hold for negative environmental rights (for reasons already discussed). Interestingly, though, the connection by no means holds for a number of other negative rights, including some of those which have proven to be the least controversial in democracies. It would be implausible to suppose that rights not to be tortured or arbitrarily imprisoned, for instance, are only respected by democracies because of the practical difficulties of registering a vote under such proscribed circumstances. Indeed, if that were so, then arrangements could be made—such as temporary release on polling day—that would render torture and arbitrary imprisonment consistent with democratic imperatives. Rather than subscribe to this bizarre and abhorrent view, I think, most democratic theorists would accept that there is some stronger normative connection between a range of rights to be left alone and those rights which are more strictly associated with democratic procedures.

In other words, democratic rights in what I earlier referred to as the weak sense of the term, are in practice as vital to a fully fledged democratic polity as rights pertaining to its formal constitution. Certainly, the counterintuitive results of following strict proceduralism to the extreme consequences noted in the preceding paragraph force on our attention the issue of the extent to which procedural democracy has certain substantive normative presuppositions. If such wrongs as torture, servitude, slavery, and so on cannot be ruled out on any grounds other than that they impede political participation, then there can be no more democratic warrant for rights to protection against them than there is for rights to environmental protection. However, I think the appropriate view to take is that these rights can be justified not on the grounds that they are necessary for the effective functioning of democracy, but rather on the *same* grounds that democracy itself is justified.

Finally, then, I wish to argue that a fundamental constitutional right to environmental protection can be supported on the very grounds that Waldron appeals to in defending the claims of democracy against constitutional constraints on it. A central presupposition of that defence is, to put it perhaps somewhat crudely, that individuals have a presumptive right to do whatever they choose to do just as long as what they choose is not proscribed by legislation. In the absence of a proscription, they do not need to produce a justification for what they choose to do, and the onus is on those who would proscribe the action to produce a justification. If we then consider how the presumption itself is warranted, it suffices, I think, without going into the various justificatory explanations that may be given for democracy, to note that a common feature of them would be to deem that individuals have basic rights of autonomy or self-governance (which I take it Waldron has in mind when speaking of the 'democratic rights' that require defending against constitutionalist constraints). Without some such presupposition, even a descriptive account of democracy would be incomplete, and a normative one would be all but impossible. If democracy requires individuals to be considered to have a basic right of self-governance, this implies a presumptive right of individuals to be free of any interference that is not justified on the grounds of being necessary for the functioning of democracy. Unless some substantive reason to the contrary is provided, the presumptive right of non-interference can be deemed to hold with respect to interferences which occur in the medium of the environment as much as in any other medium where individuals' personal or bodily integrity is threatened.

4.6 Conclusion

Environmental rights can assume a variety of forms within a constitution, including the three broad types discussed in this chapter: procedural rights, positive rights, and negative rights; each type, I have suggested, can in principle be claimed to have democratic legitimacy comparable to that of more established rights of these types. Therefore if any constitutional rights at all can be considered to have democratic legitimacy, then a wide range of constitutional environmental rights can. Reasons have also be given for thinking that any normatively elaborated conception of constitutional democracy actually requires full recognition of these rights.

Notes

1. This is an argument at the level of the basic legitimating rationale of a right to an adequate environment, and is distinct from the issue of how rights might be classified for the purposes of constitutional implementation, which was discussed in Chapter 2.
2. Waldron's specific concern in this article is to counter arguments in a British context for a Bill of Rights, particularly if this should be accompanied by US-style provisions for judicial review. However, his arguments for the most part are couched in terms sufficiently general to be of applicability in other contexts too.
3. Here, I am seeking to capture the essence of Waldron's argument, and not necessarily endorsing the distinction so drawn. For a discussion of these issues see also Fabre (2000: chapter 4).
4. For an argument along these lines see, for example, Michael Walzer (1985).
5. I do say 'if' there is a relevant difference: see Chapter 2 for a critical discussion of this question.

5

Is a Constitutional Environmental Right Necessary? A European Perspective

So far this book has addressed doubts about whether there is a normative justification for constitutionalizing a fundamental right to an adequate environment, about whether that right would be effective, and about whether it would be democratically desirable. The challenge for this chapter is to address the doubt about whether, after all, such a right is necessary. The arguments of preceding chapters have depended at crucial points on the assumption that the constitutional context in question is that of a modern democratic state that takes seriously a commitment both to human rights and to high levels of environmental protection; for without such commitments, the potential effectiveness of the right would be undermined. This leaves the question, though, of whether with such commitments there is really any *need* for the right. That is to say, if a state lives up to its human rights and environmental commitments, would it not, in doing so, meet the demands implied by the fundamental right to an adequate environment? For it is possible under certain circumstances for constitutional or legal environmental provisions to have rights-like effects without the need for an express constitutional right to underpin them; and it is also possible for non-environmental rights to have environmental applications.

In seeking to address the question of whether these possibilities hold, and in such a way as to render an express constitutional environmental right redundant, however, there are certain methodological issues that need to be considered. In particular, as will be explained in the first section, the question can be approached neither as a purely theoretical one, nor as a purely empirical one. The discussion of these issues leads on to an explanation of why I have chosen to address the question in the context of states which are subject to European Community law and the European human rights regime. In that section I will also explain how the question is to be approached in the rest of the chapter so as to provide a relevant basis for comparison with other constitutional democracies that take human rights and environmental protection seriously.

5.1 Contextualizing the question

The question for this chapter is a critical one inasmuch as it implies that for any given state its principles of environmental law and existing human rights may between them provide for all the aims of a constitutional right to an adequate environment. It is a question of practical importance for states and citizens seeking to understand whether, in pursuit of those aims, it would be a better strategy to develop existing instruments or to create a new constitutional right. For if the new right were to prove redundant, then constitutionalizing it would do little good and could possibly do harm, since, other things being equal, surplus in a constitution can generally be considered a bad thing in that it may introduce overlapping but potentially conflicting authoritative principles. Yet, it could be equally problematic to try to adapt to environmental rights ends measures which were designed for other purposes, since this can introduce various normative strains which may undermine the force and credibility of the measures in their own proper domain. In both cases, the constitutional position with regard to substantive questions would be less coherent than it ought to be.

Now the question cannot adequately be addressed in the abstract, as a purely theoretical question, since with enough ingenuity one could derive any of the effects of a right to an adequate environment as theoretical implications of a range of

environmental or human rights principles; or, with similar ingenuity, one might find reasons for resisting those implications. The
question really only has purchase in a context where those principles have actual normative force and where such interpretations
have real authority. As meaningfully posed, then, the question is
about how states actually implement and enforce their constitutional commitments in practice. Since no two states do so in an
identical manner, this presents a problem for any attempt to
attain an answer to the question which would have any significant degree of generalizability.

Should we even strive, then, for a generalizable answer? I think
it is worthwhile making the attempt, if only to clarify some of
the requirements a good answer would have to meet. Certainly,
there is a need to have some way of testing and evaluating a
claim, in whatever context it is advanced, that a constitutional
right to an adequate environment would be nugatory. For there
is a good pragmatic reason to be cautious in the face of such a
claim, namely, that states as a matter of fact do not normally fail
to declare rights whose requirements they do actually fulfil in
practice; on the contrary, because by doing so they have nothing
to lose, and something to gain in terms of domestic legitimacy
and international prestige, they are all the more likely to do so in
practice. Therefore, it is not unreasonable to assume that if a state
is resistant to constitutionalizing the right to an adequate environment then this is more likely to be due to concerns that the
right would imply more onerous demands on the state than it
would otherwise be under—concerns that would belie the claim
under consideration. However, this mere assumption does not
suffice to head off an argument, which might also be advanced in
good faith, that for a particular state the right would be nugatory
and that, because surplusage in a constitution is undesirable, it is
therefore a mistake to constitutionalize the right. In this chapter,
accordingly, the focus is on how one might respond to such an
argument.

Clearly the question of whether a constitutional right to an
adequate environment would make an appreciable difference—if

this is taken to refer to the effective enjoyment of the substance of the right—can only meaningfully be asked in specific contexts about actual states, not of states in general or in the abstract, for it requires an investigation of the specific provisions that might in principle serve the same ends. Furthermore, it also requires an investigation of how those provisions are operationalized. For states do not in practice always give full effect to their principled constitutional commitments, and just because an environmental right is formally declared in a constitution this does not necessarily mean the right will be implemented or enforced in a manner adequate to fulfil the aims apparent in its wording. In some states, constitutional provisions in general, and rights in particular, are treated as expressions of aspiration as much as or more than legally binding commitments; and even in states which do generally treat constitutional rights as binding commitments, the rights provided, or some of them, can be hedged in with various qualifications so that their actual implementation does not match the normative intention apparent on the face of the constitutional statement. There is an evident need, therefore, for the inquiry to have an empirical element. But what sort of evidence would provide a definite answer to the question, and how would it be attained?[1]

A problem for assessing the truth of the argument, advanced as an empirical claim in any particular context, is that it involves elements of counterfactual comparison—comparison of what *would* be achieved with a state's express constitutional commitment to a right to an adequate environment with what is, or is not, achieved without one. To be sure, an approach that could be adopted for a state that has already constitutionalized a right to an adequate environment would be to undertake longitudinal studies covering periods before and after constitutionalization of the right to seek evidence of its effects. If such studies can control reliably so as to ascertain that the pressures (whatever they are) that led to the constitutionalizing of environmental rights would not have led to similar effects (if any) even without that formal commitment, they could provide an answer for that state. It has to be said, though, that there is still relatively little experience to go on for such states, and the evidence may therefore not be clear and conclusive even for their own case. Furthermore, this approach cannot be used directly to study states that have not already constitutionalized the right to an adequate environment, and results obtained using it may be of restricted generalizability.

A further limiting factor on a purely empirical approach to the question is that the ways in which constitutional imperatives are interpreted and operationalized in practice depends in part on broader characteristics of the political culture and material constitution of the state in question. An implication of this is that political will itself can be a significant factor in determining whether a right is declared, how it is implemented, and with what assiduousness it is enforced. Political will can have a bearing, in particular, on how seriously a state takes its formal constitutional commitments, and so, since political will can always be in the process of formation, this matter cannot be adjudged purely on the basis of the state's historical track record.

A purely empirical approach therefore would hardly be more adequate than a purely theoretical one to dealing with the question of this chapter. If a purely theoretical approach places no determinable limits on the scope of interpretation of norms, a purely empirical approach is limited to historically contingent interpretations.

The question needs to be treated in a determinate context, but without supposing that the context fully determines the answer to it if contingencies of political will are considered as part of the context. Treating the question as one to which decision-makers or citizens have an interest in finding an answer means recognizing they will be participants in a determinate political context; but *as* participants in the processes of political will formation, there is reason for them to bracket out from their deliberations those variables which may be influenced by the outcomes of those deliberations. But how can these be bracketed out without reverting to the overly abstract theoretical approach? What is required is an empirical anchorage in authoritative norms and interpretations, but without that anchor being sloughed in the contingent vagaries of a given state's material constitution and political culture. In asking whether a right to an adequate environment would be nugatory in a state that provides high standards of environmental and human rights protection, then, we want to be able to make the assumption that the state takes its constitutional commitments reasonably literally. But how could that assumption in practice be warranted? One sort of circumstance where the assumption might be warranted is one in which the state 'has to' live up to its principled commitments, even in the face of countervailing practical pressures. The position of states within the European Union (EU), I suggest, provides a closer approximation to this circumstance than would usually be the case in a more fully sovereign state.

The EU context provides a case of how transnationally recognized norms—including especially those relating to the environment and human rights—can acquire the equivalent of constitutional force in states, even in the face of countervailing political traditions, and with relatively little regard for specific sociocultural–political contexts that could affect the manner of their implementation. The specificities of different states' constitutional cultures play a less decisive role in determining how fundamental norms are implemented than would be the case if the states remained more fully sovereign. This allows issues of implementation to be considered from the point of view of principled imperatives and conflicts rather than relatively contingent technical obstacles arising out of particular national circumstances.[2] As states which are bound by law to fundamental norms which are not necessarily of their own making, the specificities of the individual state's constitutional culture, environmental policies, rights enforcement mechanisms, and so on, can to a certain degree be bracketed out in order to focus on the question whether provision of a substantive environmental right with constitutional force has the potential to add anything to the environmental and human rights provisions that already bind them.

The focus for this chapter, therefore, is on the question whether the existing environmental and human rights provisions which are binding on member states of the EU already provide the protections that a formally declared right to an adequate environment would aim for. In the next two sections, accordingly, I seek to identify the main environmental rights currently enjoyed by citizens of states within the EU, and to assess whether these are such as to render unnecessary the provision of a fundamental substantive right to an adequate environment, entrenched or binding at the 'constitutional' level of the EU. Section 5.2 considers the environmental provisions of foundational treaties and European Community law relating to the environment and shows that the protections they offer, while significant, fall short of what might be expected of a substantive environmental right with constitutional force. The environmental protections afforded by human rights law are then considered in Section 5.3. This examines the scope of substantive and of procedural environmental rights as currently available in Europe. Again though, while some scope for invoking non-environmental human rights for environmental ends is noted, and the potential for citizens to exercise procedural rights to these ends is acknowledged, it is nevertheless shown that a substantive environmental right with constitutional force would not be nugatory.

5.2 Environmental rights in European Community law

European Community law has not expressly endorsed a declared human right to an adequate environment. Nevertheless, the EU is committed both to fundamental rights and to a high level of environmental protection. At the 'constitutional' level of the Union itself, environmental protection has been accorded the unique status of being a required component of the Community's other policies. EC law comprises a considerable amount of legislation that may serve some of the ends which an environmental right would be intended to achieve. It is also worth noting that the European Court of Justice (ECJ) has affirmed the importance of environmental protection in relation to the principles of free trade, which, while declared to be a fundamental right, is not

absolute, and can legitimately be subject to certain limits necessary from the perspective of environmental protection (Shelton
1993: 564). So even if EC law does not expressly provide a right to
an adequate environment, its policy principles and directives
have underpinned developments in case law that suggests that
environmental deterioration can lead to violations of rights.

5.2.1 EC policy principles

The Treaty on European Union, signed at Maastricht, provides that
Community policy 'shall be based on the precautionary principle
and on the principles that preventive action should be taken, that
environmental damage should as a priority be rectified at source
and that the polluter should pay' (Art. 130r2 of EC Treaty as
amended by Treaty of Union 1993). This is an unequivocal statement, with constitutional force, of principles of environmental
protection; and no other program or policy is given this importance in the Treaty. To be sure, the relevant legal provision, Article
130r, only lays down principles upon which Community policy on
the environment must be based; it does not impose any obligation
to act in a particular way by member states, and in the absence of
determinate obligations there is a corresponding absence of rights.
Yet, if policy principles do not directly confer environmental
rights on individuals, their implementation may nevertheless
have rights implications. In particular, the potential of the Polluter
Pays Principle and the Precautionary Principle merit consideration
since, as was discussed in Chapter 3, these principles can contribute
to the effectiveness of environmental rights.

Polluter pays principle

The basic idea of the Polluter Pays Principle is that the polluter
should bear the expenses of preventing and controlling pollution
to ensure that the environment is in an acceptable state. As usually
interpreted, the principle applies so as to attach liability for clean
up to the original agent who contaminates or pollutes. It thus
aims to internalize external costs of pollution by requiring the

polluter to pay in some manner for the costs of the pollution, whether these costs are incurred through a charge on emissions or are in response to some direct regulation leading to an enforced reduction in pollution. In providing an allocative mechanism to internalize negative externalities, it does not require the polluter to pay to an individual right bearer. Certainly, it is in theory possible to invoke the principle in claims for compensation, and there are precedents in other jurisdictions of courts finding that the polluter is liable to pay the cost to the individual sufferers as well as the cost of reversing the damaged ecology. However, it is not obvious that the principle substantially alters the existing basis of civil compensation claims, or, in particular, that it generates rights.

Nevertheless, in order to enforce the principle, a legal regime of environmental liability has to be in place; and rights might at least indirectly be enhanced by tightening the liability regime. This suggestion is of particular relevance in a European context given that at the time of writing the EU has drafted a new directive on Environmental Liability, whose text lays out the main features of a liability regime for damages to the environment. The proposed environmental liability regime could help enhance citizens' environmental rights in a number of ways, in particular by applying the principle of strict liability with respect to activities regulated by EU legislation and by alleviating the burden of proof in cases of environmental damage.

The principle of strict liability is of indirect benefit for citizens' environmental rights in that it undercuts a significant obstacle to success in civil suits: namely, the burden of proving fault or negligence on the part of the polluter. However, the principle does not of itself give rise to rights, and is likely in practice—as envisaged in the proposed directive—to be restricted in application to activities classed as 'dangerous' rather than to any activity at all. This restriction flows from a concern to balance interests in environmental protection against the interests of industry in not stifling innovation.

Regarding the burden of proof, legal actions against alleged polluters often fail because of the difficulties in establishing causal links with regard to environmental harms. Environmental groups have long argued that the burden of proof should be on the defendant, so that after an initial evidentiary hurdle has been surmounted by the plaintiff, there would be a presumption that the defendant's activity caused the damage in cases where the substances or activities undertaken by the defendant are in principle capable of resulting in the type of damage which has occurred. Such a reversal would significantly enhance the effectiveness of citizens' and campaigners' procedural rights. However, due to pressure from industry, and with some justification, as noted in Chapter 3, the environmental liability proposals stop short of reversing the burden of proof, providing only an 'alleviation' of the burden of proof for the plaintiff.

So while the measures necessary for successful implementation of the polluter pays principle would be measures that also enhance (procedural) rights of concerned citizens and campaigners to hold polluters to account, the principle itself does not directly generate environmental rights.

Precautionary principle

The Precautionary Principle may look to be a more promising basis for generating rights. Christopher Miller writes that this a 'powerful and comprehensive principle which, in conjunction with the right to information on discharges and rights conferred by other directives, would appear to endow citizens of the European Union with something akin to the United Nations' "fundamental right to an environment adequate for [human] health and well-being"' (Miller 1995: 389). According to the principle, when an activity raises threats of harm to human health or the environment, precautionary measures should be taken even if cause and effect relationships are not fully established scientifically. The principle thus brings about a significant reversal of presumptions that would otherwise apply: it embodies a presumption in favour of ordinary citizens' right to protection from environmentally hazardous activities, and places the burden of proof on proponents of a new technology, activity, process, or chemical to show that it does not pose a serious threat.

However, does or could the principle provide a basis for rights citizens can actually rely on? One thing to say is that interpretation of the principle is subject to considerable contestation; and issues of interpretation arise at each stage of the specification and operationalization of the principle. To begin with, the prima facie case for precaution—the existence of threats of serious or irreversible environmental damage—has to be established, but the principle itself does not supply clear guidance as to the degree of proof required before the principle becomes operational.[3] Even when the genuine possibility of the threat is established, this does not mean that the proposed activity is necessarily prohibited. Rather, it is treated as a factor to be taken into account in a cost–benefit analysis. A problem in trying to identify cost effective measures in environmental cases is that the effects are non-established. Hence, there are scientific uncertainties; but the uncertainties also have a political dimension, since any comparison of costs and benefits involves contestable assumptions about where, when, how, and on whom each should fall. Thus even with regard to a threat of serious or irreversible environmental harm, there is no guidance inherent in the principle as to the weight to be given to such a factor in reaching a final decision in conflicts between environmental and economic values.

So although the status of the precautionary principle, within the EU and more generally, seems well established, and despite its undeniable importance in imparting substantive meaning to environmental rights, the inherent uncertainties involved in interpreting and applying it mean the principle cannot in itself be considered a source of rights or to make a fundamental environmental right redundant; on the contrary, those uncertainties rather suggest the need for an independent standard to appeal to, regarding socially acceptable risks, which arguably a constitutional environmental right is most suited to supply.

I would therefore conclude by reaffirming what was discussed in previous chapters, that there is a significant difference between policy principles and rights, and that provisions for the former in general do not suffice to meet the more stringent demands of the latter.

5.2.2 Directives

Most EU environmental laws are directives, a form of law which is designed to impose obligations on member states while being flexible enough to take into account differing legal and administrative traditions. Directives are binding on all member states, but the choice and method of aligning each national legal and administrative system is left to the discretion of the member state. Because directives specify general goals, they are not necessarily or primarily intended to confer rights on individuals. Nevertheless, legal scholars have adduced reasons to think that some directives are capable of generating rights. Some argue this on the grounds that directives are capable of direct effect, and that a necessary condition for the direct effect of a directive is that it does bestow rights on individuals. Alternatively, where direct effect is not possible, rights may be generated from directives via the principle of state liability as established in cases such as *Francovich* v. *Italian Republic* [1992] ECR I-5357. I shall consider these two lines of argument in turn.

Direct effect

The doctrine of direct effect was developed by the Court of Justice of the European Community (ECJ) as a response to the question of whether directives have effect in member states without the latter introducing implementing legislation. The doctrine has been formulated, in a case where an environmental directive was at issue, in the following way:

> wherever the provisions of a directive appear, as far as their subject matter is concerned, to be unconditional and sufficiently precise, those provisions may be relied upon by an individual against the State where the State fails to implement the directive in national law by the period prescribed or where it fails to implement the directive correctly. (Case 8/81 *Becker* v. *Finanzamt Muenster-Innenstadt* [1982] ECR 53)

There are parallels between this doctrine and that of the 'self-execution' of constitutional or treaty provisions, with the requirements of unconditionality and precision applying to each. In practice, as was noted in Chapter 3, the requisite conditions for self-execution are more likely to be found to obtain for 'negative mandates' than for 'positive' ones—that is, for mandates that put some constraint on the state as opposed to those which yield a positive obligation on it—and this informal requirement seems to be broadly borne out for directives of EC law too. Ludwig Krämer (1996) identifies three main groups of environmental directive with direct effect that generate rights. One consists of provisions containing clear-cut negative mandates, namely prohibitions, such as can apply to discharges of certain dangerous chemicals into the groundwater for instance. A second group of environmental provisions in EC law, which fix numeric maximum values, maximum concentrations, limit values, and so on, have the tenor—if not the form—of negative mandates in that their imperative is 'do not exceed'. A third category consists of obligations for the administration to act, but these examples of 'positive mandates' are fewer. The most significant point to note in the present context, though, is that not all, or even the majority, of environmental directives have direct effect. Thus, as Somsen observes,

the programmatic nature of much of EC environmental law will still often prove an insurmountable obstacle for individuals seeking to rely on those provisions before their national courts. Even where environmental directives are directly effective, there remain doubts about the extent to which community law prescribes the national procedures and remedies for the enforcement of those rights. An 'enforcement gap' can therefore be said to exist in the sphere of EC environmental law, which could seriously undermine its effectiveness.   (Somsen 1996: 138)

We turn then to consider the suggestion of Somsen and others that the principle of state liability might serve to narrow this enforcement gap.

State liability and environmental rights: the significance of *Francovich*

Commentators who argue that environmental rights can and do flow from directives which are not directly effective do so by reference to the principle of state liability, as developed by the ECJ in *Francovich* and subsequent landmark cases. In *Francovich*, the Court of Justice listed three necessary and jointly sufficient conditions of state liability for not correctly implementing a directive: first, the rule infringed must be one established for the protection of individual rights; second, the scope of such rights must be ascertainable in the light of the directive in question; third, there must be a causal link between the damage suffered by the plaintiff and the violation imputed to the member state (Caranta 1993).[4]

The significance of *Francovich* with regard to environmental rights is however a matter of some debate. There are differences of opinion, particularly, on the question of when an environmental directive entails the granting of rights to individuals. In Christopher Miller's view, and especially because of the essentially programmatic nature of directives, the 'rights' they give rise to are in effect a legitimate expectation that state obligations be honoured; but a legitimate expectation is not a right. Somsen, though, maintains that even on a restrictive interpretation of a 'right', there are a number of environmental rights which flow from directives primarily concerned with the protection of human health against the adverse effects of certain types of pollution that could be protected by the *Francovich* remedy.

Nevertheless, environmental cases, as Miller has observed, are not typically the sort to which *Francovich* rulings might be applied. Because many environmental directives, if not directly effective, allow states a margin of appreciation, they do not fit the *Francovich* criteria for state liability. Rather, they would be judged in accordance with the Court's doctrine on state liability for breaches of Community law as further elaborated in subsequent judgements, most notably in *Brasserie* and *Factortame*, which cover cases where, unlike *Francovich*, a directive leaves a wide margin of discretion in taking legislative decisions. In such cases, the conditions for *Francovich* liability are modified so that instead of the requirement that the contents of the individual's right be established on the basis of the directive, it is required that the breach must be 'sufficiently serious, a manifest and grave disregard of the limits on the exercise of power.' To establish a sufficiently serious misuse of power is an onerous undertaking, particularly in relation to attempts to vindicate environmental rights, since in assessing the proper margin of a state's discretion rights of economic freedom have a more certain status. Moreover, neither *Francovich* nor *Factortame* rulings can be applied if the directive relevant to the case was not intended to confer a right in the first place: to succeed in holding a state liable for a breach of rights requires a prior authoritative statement of those rights.

The main conclusion I draw from this brief consideration of European Community law is that whatever rights may be inferred from directives and even policy statements, it makes a significant difference, particularly in view of how much debate turns on the clarity of statements of the rights to be protected, if the rights are themselves clearly stated with the equivalent of constitutional authority. A genuine commitment to the principles underpinning the policies and directives does, I suggest, imply a commitment to the principle of a constitutional environmental right; the limits on the application of them suggests the need for implementation of such a right.

5.3 Using human rights for environmental protection

It remains to ask, however, whether the commitments of an environmental right can be fulfilled by existing human rights that are recognized within the EU.[5] The EU is bound by its treaty declarations to respect universal human rights principles and, in particular, the fundamental rights 'as guaranteed by the European Convention on Human Rights'—to which all member states, although not the EU itself, are signatories—and 'as they result from the constitutional traditions common to the Member States, as general principles of Community law' (Art 6 Treaty on European Union). Also the European Social Charter, while being a 'soft law' document, provides rights which may have some relevance to our discussion. None of these instruments, however, provides an express right to an adequate environment. More recently, along the way to preparing its own constitution, the EU has produced its Charter of Fundamental Rights, but consistent with its declared aim of consolidating existing commitments rather than adding to their scope or force, the article it includes relating to the environment is not presented as a fundamental right.[6]

Nevertheless, the European Court of Human Rights has shown a growing willingness to recognize the nexus between environmental protection and human rights, and has even implied that a right a to live in an adequate environment may be derived from basic civil and political rights. Existing human rights instruments can be interpreted to address environmental issues not anticipated when those instruments were formulated because of the evolutive and teleological interpretations thought appropriate to apply to the Convention. Among the reasons to think this process may be sustained is that some member states' constitutions do provide environmental rights, and the European Court of Human Rights 'may note the existence of human rights-enhancing practices and policies taken by Contracting States and raise the standard of rights-protection to which all states must adhere' (Acevedo 2000: 446).

In the brief survey that follows, I shall consider the extent to which existing human rights have been so interpreted as to serve environmental protection, looking first at the use of substantive human rights in environmental cases; I shall then consider the implications of the procedural environmental rights provided by the Aarhus Convention, to which all member states and the EU itself are signatories.

5.3.1 The environmental potential of existing substantive rights in Europe

Article 2 of the European Convention provides a Right to Life. While traditionally understood as a protection against (arbitrary) deprivation of life by the state, some commentators believe this right might be invoked by individuals to obtain compensation in the event of death from environmental disaster, in so far as the state is responsible. Thornton and Tromans note that the Article refers to intentional deprivation of life, and since most environmental risks will not be intentionally directed at people, this may well limit the Article's usefulness. Nevertheless, they suggest, 'if the definition of intention is expanded to include the "shutting of eyes to obvious risks", the potential for protection is greatly increased' (Thornton and Tromans 1999: 54). Stefan Weber (1991) even argues that this right is the European legal provision most appropriate to protect the environment, invoking the suggestion that its rationale is the protection of life from all possible threats, including those presented by environmental deterioration. Nevertheless, this is probably a minority view, and it is debatable whether the right also involves positive obligations on the state to preserve or promote life expectancy, for instance, via less polluted water or air. Moreover, while the right to life may have some potential application in the environmental field, it has not yet been successfully invoked (Churchill 1996: 90).[7] It would in any event only seem to apply in relation to drastic and present harms, or at least to direct threats to life, and thus not cover other serious environmental concerns.

Some of the concerns not covered by the right to life might appear to be covered, though, by the right to health, provided in Article 11 of the European Social Charter Part I, which is a right of everyone to benefit from any measures enabling them to enjoy the highest possible standard of health attainable. The Social Charter does not provide for an individual complaint procedure, however, its application being supervised through the submission by states of reports which are examined by the Committee of Experts. The Committee has taken the view that Article 11 requires states to take measures to prevent certain forms of environmental pollution, but this requirement is very general, with an undefined threshold of protection, and so states are generally found to be in compliance with it. Moreover, even if the Committee were to be more critical, its opinions would not be binding. Hence, this right is not a very promising candidate for fulfilling the aims of a fundamental right to an adequate environment (Desgagné 1995: 271; Churchill 1996: 103). Similar points apply to

Article 3 of the Social Charter which provides a right to safe and healthy working conditions (Churchill 1996: 102).

Interestingly, a right that has been used to set potentially important precedents for environmental protection is provided by Article 8 of the European Convention, a right to respect for one's private and family life and one's home. A particularly significant precedent was the 1994 case of *Lopez-Ostra* v. *Spain*.[8] The applicant had suffered serious health problems from fumes from a tannery waste treatment plant, and her attempt to obtain compensation from the Spanish courts had been completely unsuccessful. The European Court of Human Rights held that there had been a breach of Article 8, and this was the first time the organs of the European Convention found a breach of the Convention as a consequence of environmental harm. This judgement may be claimed to have enhanced the legal protection of the environmental victim by opening the door to applying Article 8 to nearly all sources of pollution, and not only to noise emissions as in previous cases. Nevertheless, this right is still ultimately tied to the concerns its words state—that is, private and family life—rather than the environmental well-being of individuals, whoever and wherever they are, in public or private spaces.[9] So while the expansive interpretations of this right illustrate the possibilities for stronger environmental rights—and these have been further illustrated in the subsequent landmark case of *Guerra and Others* v. *Italy* (Miller 1999; Acevedo 2000)—it remains likely that such possibilities can only be fully realized through the instantiation of more specifically environmental rights.

There are thus good reasons to be sceptical of any suggestion that existing human rights instruments applied in Europe provide such coverage as to make an express right to an adequate environment redundant. I would therefore dissent from the claim made by Margaret DeMerieux 'that it is unnecessary to "add" specific environmental human rights to the Convention' (DeMerieux 2001: 521). Her grounds for this claim are 'that there can be derived from a Convention that contemplated neither protection of the environment nor of the individual against harm to the environment, substantial legal protection under the Convention

against environmental harms' (DeMerieux 2001: 521) Yet, showing that sometimes in specific instances existing rights can be
and have been successfully used to environmental ends is not
the same as there actually being a right that can generally and
robustly be relied on. Most environmental related complaints
brought under Article 8, the main focus of attention, have not in
fact been successful (Miller 2003: 113), and even when they have
been it is debatable whether the precedents set really have much
application for environmental issues as such, since the latter are
tangential to the rationale of the right. Miller writes,

> I have no wish to understate the plight of Ms Guerra (or Ms Lopez
> Ostra)...But I believe we should hesitate before further eroding the dis-
> tinction between maladministration and the deliberate and systematic
> invasion of privacy by the state to suppress political opposition (which
> Article 8 was originally conceived to combat). Given the importance of
> the wider struggle for human rights, it is surely unwise to blunt our most
> respected weapons on the less deserving targets. (Miller 1999: 176)

Leaving aside the assessment of particular cases and their deserts, I
would take from this observation the point that if existing rights
cannot reliably find the environmental target then there is in fact
a need for a right with the proper dedicated aim.[10] Indeed, another
source of concern about deriving environmental rights from rights
instituted for quite other purposes is that, in DeMerieux's own
words, it 'depends on the initiative of the adjudicating body'
(DeMerieux 2001: 559) and requires 'a willingness in the adjudicating body to be assertive and perhaps adventurous' (p. 558). This
does not seem a strong or legitimate basis on which to depend in
any context where the creativity of the judiciary is as a matter of
constitutional principle kept within reasonably clear bounds.

5.3.2 *Procedural environmental rights and the Aarhus Convention*

Perhaps the most significant area of development of environmental
rights—in Europe as elsewhere—is that of procedural rights relating to the civil, political, and legal possibilities for environmental

protection. The potential of these rights has long been recognized, and their development was given a further impetus by 'The Convention on Access to Information, Public Participation in Decision-Making and Access to Justice in Environmental Matters,' generally known as the Aarhus Convention (1998). This agreement, to which both the EU and its member states are signatories, represents probably the most important step yet taken towards environmental rights protection: it establishes rights—to information, to participation in decision-making, and to access to justice in environmental matters—which it expressly affirms are aimed at securing the right to a healthy environment.

It is beyond doubt that these procedural rights have a necessary and important role to play; a question, though, is whether they will also, as some commentators believe, be sufficient to that end. In Chapter 2 it was explained why one should not expect them to be, and this I shall now show does seem to be borne out.

Access to adequate information in the environmental field is a *sine qua non* for the successful exercise and enforcement of environmental rights. It expands possibilities for citizen involvement and gives individuals and communities the tools for better environmental protection actions at a local level. An informed public can contribute meaningfully to decision-making on environmental issues and act as a watchdog supplementing governmental environmental management and supervision efforts. Even prior to Aarhus, some significant elements of such a right were already in place; and to pave the way for ratification of the Convention, with its more stringent requirements, the EU has had to prepare a new directive on access to environmental information. Yet, while an adequately enforced right of access to environmental information is an indispensable prerequisite for effective and democratic measures to protect the environment, it is equally clearly not sufficient on its own, since there has also to be scope for putting the information to effective use. This, though, is what the other two procedural rights are intended to enhance.

The practical significance of rights of participation in environmental policy-making, in decision-making processes regarding environmental developments, and in the determination of environmental standards has also long been recognized. The Aarhus Convention acknowledged that greater clarification is needed in defining which environmental issues must include public participation, and that the concept of the interested or affected party should include NGOs as representatives of legitimate collective interests. The Aarhus Convention defines 'public concerned' as 'the public affected or likely to be affected by, or having an interest in, the environmental decision-making; non-governmental organizations promoting environmental protection shall be deemed to have an interest' (Article 2.5). Two positive aspects of this definition are the inclusion of public (persons or groups) with a mere interest in the decision-making process, and the explicit inclusion of environmental NGOs. Nevertheless, the public participation provisions relating to decision-making on policies, plans, programmes, and legislation have been criticized for being so weak as to be more like recommendations—even though these are some of the most important forms of environmental decision-making. Provision of a substantive environmental right, by contrast, could be expected to carry some weight in deliberations at the higher levels of decision-making, as well as to enhance prospects of securing environmental outcomes against competing interests through public influence at other levels.

Another necessary but insufficient condition for effective realization of substantive environmental rights are procedural rights to seek legal redress in the environmental arena. Access to justice includes, quite generally, 'rights to object to ministerial and agency environmental decisions; and rights to bring action against departments, agencies, firms, and individuals that fail to carry out their duties according to law' (Eckersley 1996: 230). With regard to the availability and effectiveness of these rights prior to the Aarhus Convention, three particular problem areas were identified. One was the general slowness of many administrative and judicial appeal procedures. In principle, the demands embodied in the Aarhus Convention would do something to ameliorate this problem. Another, though, is the high fees and costs: the prohibitive expenses include bonds that often are set too high for parties with limited means who are acting to protect the environment. The Aarhus Convention does not appear to offer much to overcome this obstacle which is left to individual states to deal with. A third obstacle concerns restrictions on legal standing to take action. The provisions of the Aarhus Convention have gone some way to ease these restrictions, reflecting the growing consensus that public interest groups whose activities show that they have a genuine interest in protecting the environment should have standing without having to wait for the relevant public authority to take action. Ultimately, though, whether actions admitted actually succeed on their merits depends on the basic principles courts are to apply, and a substantive environmental right could give a steer that may otherwise be lacking.

In all, the Aarhus Convention has certainly set in train real advances for environmental rights, but environmental citizens' organizations have been critical of extensive weaknesses, loopholes, and ambiguities in the text, and have described the compliance mechanism for the Convention as the weakest of any in international environmental law. The Aarhus Convention can thus be immanently criticized for not going far enough to meet its own ends. Its preamble states that 'adequate protection of the environment is essential to human well-being and the enjoyment of basic human rights, including the right to life itself', and it includes express recognition 'that every person has the right to live in an environment adequate to his or her health and well-being'. It stops short, however, of providing means for citizens directly to invoke this right.

It is this last point, rather than specific weaknesses of the Aarhus Convention itself, which I think most significant. It remains the case for the moment, as when Dinah Shelton wrote in 1993, that 'there is no right to a clean environment to be balanced with other rights or with Community policies' (Shelton 1993: 582). Procedural rights alone do too little to counterbalance the prevailing presumptions in favour of development and economic interests. Indeed, procedural rights can cut both ways: they enable parties to both challenge proposed action by the state as well as resist such challenges. Such considerations can reasonably be argued to point to the need for a substantive environmental right that stands above political contestation.

It seems then, on the basis of the considerations advanced here, that a substantive environmental right in Europe would not be nugatory.

5.4 Conclusion

It has been seen in this chapter that environmental rights, of sorts, can under certain circumstances be derived from existing environmental law and human rights law in Europe. Regarding EC environmental law, though, we were obliged to recognize that its provisions, as promulgated through directives addressed to member states, can only generate rights if these are explicitly included in the framing of the directive. Moreover, because there is no fundamental right to an adequate environment explicitly recognized in EC law, whatever particular rights in relation to the environment may be derived from it are not only restricted in their scope to the purposes of the particular directive, but also remain in a weaker position than rights of economic freedom which do have fundamental status. Regarding suggestions that existing human rights can be pressed into the service of environmental ends, we have noted that there is some scope for this, but that it is relatively circumscribed. Furthermore, to expand the scope beyond the current limits would, in the absence of an explicitly recognized fundamental right to an adequate environment, require a degree of judicial creativity that is inherently problematic in the kind of democratic state that is assumed as the normative context of the present discussion.

I therefore conclude that if rights of environmental protection are to have a determinate status in relation to other social goals that are already protected as rights, instead of being seen, as at present they sometimes are, as the values of a partisan cause, they have to be supported by a fundamental right to an adequate environment. A fundamental right would also have a role in firming up the protections that could be achieved through the exercise of procedural environmental rights.

I would also suggest that the arguments presented here have some applicability to states beyond Europe. Among developed states with constitutional democratic governments, at least, formal disparities are not great: EU directives stand in a relation to state laws which is comparable to constitutional mandates within states; its human rights jurisprudence corresponds to international norms. So the issues of justifying and applying the relevant legal principles are likely to be generalizable enough to admit of useful comparisons. Where the arguments may have less purchase, however, is in poorer states which have more serious problems in living up to their formal commitments. There are clearly limits to the usefulness of seeking to hold states to obligations which it is materially beyond their capacity to fulfil. The source of a potentially damaging criticism of the argument of this chapter is that it has focused on affluent states and disregarded their relations to poorer states. This is the issue to be addressed in the final chapter.

Notes

1. I discount the possibility of an approach which would draw empirical comparisons between states that have constitutional environmental rights and states that do not in order to determine which are 'greener'. Empirical evidence can be adduced to suggest that there is not necessarily any positive correlation between the constitutional provision of environmental rights by a state and its actual protection of the environment or associated rights: some of the states with the most impressive environmental rights on constitutional paper compare unfavourably with other states with regard to their actual record in enforcing those, and other, rights. However, such comparisons in themselves tell us nothing about whether any given state would or would not be 'greener' with a constitutional right to an adequate environment.
2. While member states retain a margin of discretion to determine the manner of the implementation of policy principles and directives, for

instance, they do nevertheless have to implement them; and there are also various tendencies at work which push, longer term, in the direction of harmonization of states' domestic laws (Börzel 2002; Olsen 2002).

3. In the *Duddridge* case, which was something of a landmark regarding the status of the precautionary principle in England, the applicants contended that the principle requires precautionary action to be taken where the mere *possibility* exists of *an increased risk* of serious harm to the environment or human health. Against this, though, the court pitted the government's view, and a view more consonant with that of industry, that it could be triggered only by 'risks that are so high and whose costs of correction are so great that prevention is better and cheaper than cure'. (See the competing interpretations of the principle referred to in Chapter 3.)

4. The *Francovich* ruling established the principle that individuals have a right to compensation for loss and damage caused in the case of a breach of Community law for which a member state can be held responsible, separate from the existing doctrines of direct and indirect effect. The case itself was not an environmental one. Francovich and the other plaintiffs were employees of firms in Italy which had become insolvent leaving past salaries and other benefits unpaid. Italy had not complied with a 1980 Directive which aimed at protecting employees in case of insolvency by requiring the setting up of guarantee funds. The Court of Justice ruled that although the Council directive (80/987/CEE) was devoid of direct effects, the Italian state should nevertheless be held liable for the damage suffered.

5. On the status of ECHR rights in the EU, and the question of deriving environmental rights from them, see, for example, Shelton (1993), Desgagné (1995), Acevedo (2000), DeMerieux (2001).

6. The wording and placement of the article about environmental protection make it considerably weaker than a substantive right to an adequate environment. As drafted, proposed Article 44 provides that 'Union policies shall ensure environmental protection, which involves preserving, protecting and improving the quality of the environment, protecting human health and prudent and rational utilisation of natural resources'.

7. For precedents outside Europe, though, see for example Anderson (1996b) and Desgagné (1995); also Chapter 6 below on precedents from Latin America and South Asia.

8. For background to the case see for example Alfred Rest (1997).

9. Thornton and Tromans (1999: 41) summarize the limits to the extent
   to which Article 8 can protect the environment; see also Desgagné
   (1995: 273, 283).
10. This contrasts with the point taken by Miller and others (e.g.
    Thornton and Tromans 1999) which would appear to be that the
    human rights approach as such is not best suited for adaptation to
    environmental ends, which should rather be treated as matters of
    duties.

6

Environmental Rights and Environmental Justice: A Global Perspective

The argument of this book has been that any modern democratic state ought to constitutionalize a right to an adequate environment. The normative drive of this argument has been the affirmation of a right, in the words of the Brundtland Report, of *all human beings* to an environment adequate for their health and well-being. Yet by no means all human beings enjoy the rights protected by modern democratic states. This prompts the question whether the argument serves to promote measures which might improve the environmental protections provided in the 'well-ordered societies' while leaving untouched, or possibly even worsened, the position of the rest of the planet's population. The focus of this final chapter is accordingly on questions about the role that can be played by constitutional environmental rights in the pursuit of environmental justice more generally.

One central argument will be that even if the provision of constitutional environmental rights in any given affluent democratic state cannot be expected in and of itself directly to promote the protection of environmental human rights beyond that state, it can be expected to have indirect effects that are conducive to that end. In order to unfold that argument, though, it is necessary first to say something about why the focus on rights provisions within states is appropriate. For in view of the fact that many of the most serious environmental threats transcend the territorial boundaries of nation-states, and some are literally global, it might be thought that the focus on states' constitutions as the locus for securing environmental rights is inappropriately parochial and possibly even counterproductive in so far as a state may pursue a national environmental interest at the expense of environmental interests of others. The first section accordingly shows how the focus on environmental rights at the level of states is justified on both practical and principled grounds. Practically, and despite any relative diminution of their monopoly of claims to sovereignty, states remain the key sites of legitimate political power, and have the main responsibility for administration of policy and protection of rights. As a matter of normative principle, and notwithstanding tensions between principles of human rights and state sovereignty, some aspects of global justice, including environmental justice, depend on reaffirming sovereign rights, particularly of poorer states, to protect their peoples' interests against forces of economic globalization. A further crucial consideration is that states fulfil an important role in developing international law relating to human rights in general and environmental rights in particular: this means that the recognition of environmental rights even in richer states can contribute to the development of international norms that would require respect for the environmental rights of people globally. Viewed in this way, the provision of constitutional environmental rights by states can be regarded as a necessary condition for the development of global environmental justice.

Nevertheless, it is clearly not sufficient, and meanwhile there remains the question of whether in practice, given the dramatic inequalities of power and wealth between states, the constitutional enhancement of citizens' environmental rights in richer and more powerful states may not in fact be achieved at the expense of those of poorer nations. For while a disadvantaged state may have relatively little capacity to protect its citizens' rights against environmental threats even when these are domestically generated, more powerful states, on the other hand, might be able to enhance their citizens' environmental rights by effectively exporting environmental problems to the poorer countries. In response to this critical question, the second section explains why the interests of poorer countries should not be assumed to oppose the development of constitutional environmental rights in richer countries. It begins by pointing out that there is already a massive 'exportation' of environmental problems from richer to poorer countries, and that if the environmental interests of the rich are better protected than those of the poor this is because the economically disadvantaged have less power to resist the imposition of threats to them. The existing global distribution of environmental harms, and indeed also of benefits derived from environmental services and natural resources generally, is largely a result of market forces operating under a regime of rights that is in principle contested by the right to an adequate environment. In view of the maldistribution of the benefits of development under this regime, moreover, I also argue that it is a mistake to suppose that for countries struggling to achieve the benefits of development environmental protection is a luxury they cannot afford. Much injustice is made manifest in the 'ecological distribution conflicts' (Martinez-Alier 2002) which compromise prospects of development as well as environmental quality; in such conflicts, environmental rights can and must be linked to issues of access to resources more generally. Thus rather than constructing the interests of the worse off as lying in a denial of environmental rights to citizens in better off countries, they should be seen as aiming to secure those same rights for themselves.

That this is in fact how they perceive matters is seen in Section 6.3 which indicates how constitutional environmental rights also have a constructive role to play in less advantaged countries. This section brings forward evidence showing that in poorer states there is a recognition of the importance of constitutional environmental rights, and that some of the most important precedents in this field originate in such states.

The overall aim of this chapter, then, is to indicate why the constitutionalizing of environmental rights can be expected to contribute to the process of building environmental justice rather than detract from it.

6.1 State constitutions and the permeability of normative orders

The purpose of this section is to show how the acknowledgement of the fact that the sovereignty of nation-states is less than absolute does not mean that states no longer have a vital role in promoting the kinds of norm represented by environmental rights. For states remain the key sites of legitimate political power, and have the main responsibility for implementing those norms. States also have the potential to play a vital role in protecting their citizens' interests in the face of the forces of economic globalization that can pose threats to them. Furthermore, as I indicate in the second part of this section, while any given state may not be the originating authoritative source of all the international norms it is called upon to administer, states are nevertheless key agents in the development of international law which is a necessary condition of global justice.

6.1.1 The continuing importance of the nation-state

It is well understood that nation-states today do not dispose of the absolute sovereignty that it was once supposed they did.

Today, it is a commonplace that political developments within and beyond the state have rendered the idea of sovereignty less and less illuminating in characterizing the state's relations with its own people and with other states. Just as the spread of constitutionalism and federalism has compromised the idea that there must be one institutional location at which ultimate legal authority is exercised, so the development of international law has limited and qualified the notion of exclusive domestic jurisdiction. As Stanley Hoffmann wrote many years ago, 'Sovereignty, rather than being a reservoir that is either full or empty, is a divisible nexus of power of which some may be kept, some limited, some lost.' The traditional theory of sovereignty needs to be recognized for what it is (or was): an effort to represent as a timeless truth an important but historically specific feature of the development of the Western nation-state.   (Beitz 1994: 128)

Nevertheless, for all that their sovereignty may not be absolute, states remain the critical sites of political power in the modern world, and for the foreseeable future they will continue to play a pivotal role in the implementation of rights, justice, and protection of the environment. That is true not only domestically, but also with regard to any transnational redistributive measures that might be adopted in the name of global justice. Indeed, the principles, rights, and obligations proposed by the Brundtland Report (WCED 1987: 348–51) that follow on from the fundamental right to an adequate environment are all addressed to states.

It is not just that states matter for practical reasons, though. There is also the point, bearing on the normative justification of states' sovereignty even in relation to transnational norms, that many environmental problems (and all the more so in relation to natural resource issues) are such that poorer states in particular need to be able to defend their sovereign rights against depredations of transnational companies. With regard to this point, it is worth stressing that 'the inalienable right of all States freely to dispose of their natural wealth and resources in accordance with their national interests' is, as declared by the UN General Assembly (1962), a 'right *of peoples and nations* to . . . be exercised in the interest of their national development and of the *well-being of the people* of the State concerned' (UN General Assembly 1962, my emphases). Some proponents of global distributive justice have argued that this right is morally questionable on the grounds that the territorial distribution of natural resources is arbitrary from a moral point of view (e.g. Beitz 1979). But an arguably more significant arbitrariness—to be discussed further in Section 6.2—is how the extent of a state's *command* of natural resources depends less on its territorial endowment than on its stage of economic and technological development: advanced industrial countries are able in all sorts of ways to extract natural resources from poor countries at a minimal cost.

The sovereign right of states has also been subject to another moral challenge, though, on the grounds that natural resources are humankind's common heritage and ought to be preserved into the future, and not simply used up in whatever ways or at whatever rate their current custodians happen to choose; further-more, some natural resources located within political territories have functions within the global ecosystem and thus should not be seen as national property to be disposed of at will. Such consid-erations, however, while certainly implying requirements of restrictions on the scope of states' freedom to dispose of the resources on their territory, do not of themselves undermine a right of sovereignty as suitably qualified by the various declara-tions and agreements that have addressed such issues.[1] Certainly, unless the entirety of the world's bounty were to become as a matter of legal fact the common property of all humankind, it is morally indefensible for the rich industrialized nations in effect to say to nations located in territories endowed with globally sig-nificant ecological resources that 'what is mine is mine and what is yours is ours'.[2]

I should perhaps stress that none of the preceding remarks are intended to suggest that reality necessarily lives up to the normative principle: some of the poorest states do not have the capacity to exercise sovereign rights over their resources in the face of powerful transnational corporations seeking to exploit them; some states do not even attempt to promote the well-being of their people, as opposed to lining the pockets of corrupt leaders, and such states are nevertheless accorded the recognition of the 'resource privil-ege' and 'borrowing privilege', as explained by Thomas Pogge (2002), to sell natural resources and to borrow money in the name of—but to the detriment of—their country and its people. To jus-tify such recognition on the grounds of the principle of sover-eignty is arguably to use that principle in bad faith: for while it may be the case, as Michael Walzer for instance argues, that 'states can be presumptively legitimate in international society and actu-ally illegitimate at home' (Walzer 1980: 222), this means only that there is an absence of justification for invading them in the name of human rights, not that there is the presence of a justification for engaging in lucrative trading relations with them such as can even exacerbate their domestic abuse of human rights.

The point is that sovereignty is not a monolithic *normative* principle any more than it is de facto, in the words cited above, 'a reservoir that is either full or empty'. The appropriate view to take is that the state is—both practically and normatively—an important locus of sovereignty; not the only one, but nevertheless a key one. It is not a case either of defending a view of its absolute sovereignty that has become untenable, or of claiming that the state has been radically undermined either in practice or morally. More constructive and appropriate is to understand its role in relation to other sources of authority.

6.1.2 The permeability of domestic and international normative orders

As has been noted in earlier chapters, it is appropriate under contemporary conditions to take a pluralist rather than monist view of sovereignty and to recognize, in particular, that international norms carry authority within domestic jurisdictions and also that domestic norms, including environmental rights, influence the development of international norms.

This permeability of legal orders is a significant and positive factor for the development of environmental rights.

In the increasingly interdependent world of international agreements regulating how states behave towards their own citizens, states 'internalize' international norms in sophisticated ways, which some refer to as 'indirect incorporation'. International human rights law, as Murray Hunt explains, 'has attained a domestic status which is greater than that of other international treaties but still short of full incorporation, a status that cannot be explained in terms of the traditional premises of sovereignty and dualism' (Hunt 1998: 301). Popović takes the 'indirect incorporation' of international human rights law into legal reasoning of state courts in the United States to 'demonstrate that, binding or not, international human rights principles provide a strong set of norms to inform the content of state law, especially where the state law expresses the same or similar concerns as those expressed by international human rights principles' (Popović 1996b: 372). 'Indirect incorporation is an established and appropriate means of guiding, interpreting and applying domestic law, and it should be no less viable in the specific context of environmental justice claims' (Popović 1996b: 373). Indeed, this is particularly relevant regarding environmental rights given that there are few precedents to go on in any single domestic context.

Developments in domestic law, for their part, contribute to a bottom-up development of international law: 'As more and more municipal legal systems recognize the legal right to a satisfactory environment, that recognition supports the establishment of a general principle of international law and contributes to the emergence of a norm of customary international law that binds all nations regardless of their domestic law' (Popović 1996a: 603).

So the more states that recognize a right to an adequate environment, the more precedents there are to inform the development of international law; this in turn generates normative principles for indirect incorporation into other domestic jurisdictions; and so on, in an ongoing process. Thus part of the answer to the question whether consolidating environmental rights in the constitutions of affluent states would be to the disbenefit of less advantaged states is to point out that the provision of these rights in any constitution enhances rather than diminishes the prospect of their being taken as authoritative for, and perhaps also being provided in the constitution of, other states.

Nevertheless, this is not a complete answer.

6.2 Constitutional environmental rights viewed from the normative perspective of global justice

The question of whether enhancing environmental rights in affluent developed countries would exacerbate existing environmental injustices globally cannot be settled a priori, since it would involve empirical assessment. However, I shall suggest (first) there is little reason to think any adverse impact would be great, and (second) there are significant reasons to think that—especially in the longer term, but not only—the impact of domestic constitutional environmental rights will be beneficial also globally.

One reason for thinking that the impact of enhancing environmental rights in rich countries would not be to significantly worsen existing global environmental injustices is that these are already so bad. The ecological burdens that the rich are able to impose on the poor in virtue of their positions of relative economic advantage and disadvantage are considerable. Joan Martinez-Alier has highlighted four areas in particular where the rich can be said to have an 'ecological debt' towards the poor. One of these is the dumping of hazardous wastes and siting of hazardous plants. Although the injustice of dumping has been recognized by the Basel Convention which restricted the export of wastes from Organisation for Economic Cooperation and Development (OECD) countries to non-OECD countries,[3] the pressure for the export of toxic waste still increases. Meanwhile hazardous industries continue to be relocated from richer to poorer countries thereby obviating any need to export waste (Martinez-Alier 2002: 185). Another major factor of ecological debt is the 'carbon debt', which is arising from the massive and disproportionate emissions into the atmosphere by the industrialized countries. As campaigner Andrew Simms states:

A typical US citizen, for example, uses fossil fuels at a rate 20 times higher than the average Indian citizen, 300 times that of someone from Mozambique, and many times the threshold for sustainable consumption per person. Though less extreme than the US, similar disparities exist for all EU and industrialised countries. As every day passes without a radical shift in consumption, the rich country carbon debt to the global community grows larger. (Simms 2001)

The other two kinds of ecological debt are 'biopiracy' (the use of intellectual property laws to gain monopoly control over genetic resources based on the knowledge and innovation of farmers and indigenous peoples) and 'environmental liabilities' (i.e. the debt acquired through the extraction of natural resources from impoverished countries at a low price and compromising domestic development potential). One could multiply examples of specific environmental injustices in the world today, but a view of them in the aggregate can serve as a perspective from which to appreciate that the injustices referred to under the general heading of 'ecological debt' arise as a result not primarily of citizens in affluent countries enjoying environmental rights, but from processes which on principle the right to an adequate environment opposes. This is not to deny that domestic environmental protection regulations are a factor in decisions to export 'negative environmental externalities', but to suggest that enhancing affluent citizens' environmental rights would have at most only a marginal tendency to augment the weight of that factor. More importantly, though, against this has to be set the weight of the other driving factors. With regard to these, there are four points I wish to highlight.

The first is that the negative environmental impacts of the practices of rich industrialized countries on poorer countries cannot meaningfully be considered in isolation from broader issues concerning the effective command of natural resources. It is true that the factors of ecological debt arise from two distinct sorts of problems: first, the export of raw materials and other products from relatively poor countries sold at prices that do not include compensation for local or global externalities; second, the disproportionate use by rich countries of environmental space and services (for instance, the free use of carbon dioxide absorption capacities). Yet, conceptually it would be artificial, and practically it would be inappropriate, to consider 'environmental bads' and 'environmental goods' as entirely separate sets of phenomena. Freedom from the former and enjoyment of the latter are often 'two sides of the same coin' (since environmental services can themselves be regarded as resources) and may be two ways of describing a single set of circumstances. There is just one biophysical reality to which the various categorizations of environmental goods and bads relate. A unified description of them is therefore appropriate.

In recent years, systematic attempts to account for the biophysical basis and impacts of human economic activity have developed converging methodologies to determine the total amount of biologically productive land and water area required to produce the resources consumed and to assimilate the wastes generated using prevailing technology. This aggregated amount is referred to as 'ecological space'; and the use or 'occupation' of an amount of it is referred to as an 'ecological footprint'. Ecological Footprint accounts express in 'global hectares' the amount of 'biologically productive space with world average productivity' which is 'necessary to maintain the current material throughput of the human economy under current management and production practices'. The Ecological Footprint measures a nation's resource consumption by adding imports to, and subtracting exports from, domestic production. 'Since people use resources from all over the world, and affect faraway places with their pollution, the footprint is the sum of these areas wherever they are on the planet.' With the world's current human population, the available space per person worldwide is calculated to be in the region of 1.7 global hectares. When considering the distribution of actual per capita use of ecological space as calculated with this method, there are several things to note. One is that nearly all nations exceed the 1.7 hectares per capita in their utilization of ecological space (the exceptions being sub-Saharan Africa, India, Pakistan, and Bangladesh, with China on 1999 figures just under that limit). This in itself is an alarming observation which relates to the claim of Wackernagel and Rees (1996) that if all countries achieved 'development' to the level of the richest, four planet earths would be required to provide the necessary ecological space, and further serves to underline the point that an adequate environment for anyone cannot be assured unless all natural resource impacts are considered in their totality. Another thing to note is that, as one would therefore expect, the footprints of most countries also exceed the available ecological space attributed to their own territory (the exceptions being those countries like Australia or Canada which are relatively well-endowed with natural resources in proportion to their populations). So even if one assumes that rights of sovereignty over territorial resources ought to be absolute, then on this basis most of the best-off countries are running an ecological deficit. For Japan the deficit is of the order of 4 hectares per capita; for the United States it is almost the same; in Western Europe it varies between around 2 (Austria) and 3.8 (UK), although the Scandinavian countries remain, notwithstanding their higher than European average per capita footprints, within their territorial capacity; India, Pakistan, and Bangladesh exceed their territorial capacity by 0.1–0.2 hectares per capita. Assuming that such figures are broadly reliable, and even allowing that a nation has a sovereign right to benefit from all of its natural territorial endowment, then, it is evident that in the United States, Japan, and Europe, for instance, each person on average is additionally benefiting from the equivalent of more than two other persons' maximally sustainable ecological space entitlement.

Thus the second point is that a state's effective *command* of natural resources does not necessarily correlate positively to its territorial endowments of natural resources, and indeed the correlation can be negative; rather, where there is a positive correlation is between a state's capacity to command natural resources and the degree of development of its economy. Thus while countries at a similar level of economic development may have varying territorial deficits, according to their natural resource endowments, their command of natural resources as measured in absolute per capita ecological space utilization does not vary to any significant degree. Here the inequalities in ecological footprint per capita by nation track inequalities of economic development. For example, the figures are of the following orders of magnitude:[4] USA 9.5, Australia 7, Canada 8.5, countries of Western Europe vary but average at about 5, Japan about 4. In Latin American countries the range is between 1 and 3. In India and Pakistan it is 0.8 and in Bangladesh 0.5. In sub-Saharan Africa the range is between 0.6 and 1.2. Treating ecological footprints as a broad indicator of the global distribution of effective access to or command of environmental services as a whole, the inequalities revealed are dramatic but unsurprising.

It is this correlation that underpins the general thesis of 'ecological debt',[5] which was originally advanced by campaigners as a moral counterweight to the obligation of many poor countries to repay monetary debts to rich countries.[6] The lack of progress in getting debt relief led to the sharpening of the moral case by posing the question 'who owes whom?':

Industrialised countries prosecute highly indebted developing countries to pay off their foreign financial debts, at great cost to the millions who subsequently go without vital health and education services. But industrialised countries are themselves responsible for a much larger debt to the global community. Their reckless use of fossil fuels has helped create the spectre of climate change: a storm cloud that hangs over everyone's future. And it is poor people in poor countries that suffer first and worst from both extreme weather conditions related to climate change and from the struggle to clear unpayable, and often illegitimate, foreign debts. In many cases the payment of external debt causes further depletion of natural stocks and environmental degradation, because of the emphasis on and nature of the export sectors. (Martinez-Alier, Simms, and Rijnhout 2003)[7]

It may of course be asked how literally the idea of debt should be taken in this context, and how it might be quantified and attributed. These questions merit a much fuller discussion than I can enter into here. The question of this section, though, is only whether constitutional environmental rights in affluent states are likely to increase or reduce the inequalities described.

My third point relates directly to this question. Whatever the explanation for the correlation between economic wealth and disproportionate command of the earth's resources may be, the factors which are decisive in determining the extent of a state's command of natural resources and its capacity to exploit environmental services generally operate relatively independently of any right of its citizens to an adequate environment. While the precise causes of the massive disparities in command of resources may be a matter for debate between competing theories in the field of global political economy, none of the plausible candidates would place much explanatory weight on the specific effects of environmental rights of citizens in affluent countries. The causes of the existing inequalities are not a 'right to an adequate environment'—in the North any more than in the South—but of economic forces which that right, on key points of principle and practice, opposes. The impact of progressively constitutionalizing environmental rights in richer countries is not likely to be appreciably negative on poorer ones if the real drivers of global environmental degradation—and poverty—are the untrammelled exercise of property rights in natural resources.[8]

The fourth point, then, is that the right to an adequate environment, and what it also entails with regard to access to and control over natural resources, can be explicitly pitted, as a human right (and normative principle), against the system of rights which currently frame the processes of globalization and indeed foster, in the trenchant account of Vandana Shiva (2003), the exercise, especially by transnational corporations, of 'inhuman rights'. The right to an adequate environment thus cannot be invoked to justify continued domestic and foreign policies of rich countries which maintain that kind of pattern of distribution. The right to an adequate environment implies a right of access to a minimally adequate, if not equal, share of ecological space for each person. While it does not imply any objection to the industrious increasing, through technology and productive efficiency, the economic yield per unit of ecological space, it does imply that there can be no justification for some to make use of vastly greater quantities of ecological space when others are thereby left with insufficient even to meet their basic needs.

To sum up the answer to the question of this section, then, it can first be affirmed that since the right to an adequate environment implies principled opposition to the forces leading to the current environmental injustices, its normative thrust must be reckoned on balance to promise more good than harm to the interests of the worse off. To make good this promise it is obviously not sufficient that the right be given constitutional recognition in better off states. However, that recognition is not only unlikely to have seriously adverse effects on the worse off, it can actually play a necessary part in counteracting the adverse effects that are currently sanctioned by the existing international normative regime. For, as I suggested in the previous section, the influence of domestic recognition of the right on the development of international norms should not be underestimated. The constitutionalizing of the human right to an adequate environment by the most powerful states would provide important support for the generation of an international norm recognizing that right as a universal one. Certainly, a powerful state is unlikely to recognize the right as a principle in its international dealings unless it recognizes the right domestically.

Moreover, it is not just in formal legal terms that the domestic constitutionalizing of a right to an adequate environment can serve to further the ends of environmental justice globally. There is also the substantive point that giving constitutional prominence to the right serves to heighten awareness of environmental justice issues domestically. This heightened awareness, not only as officially recognized by the state, but as embodied in the values and practices of citizens and associations of 'civil society', can itself help foster the ethics of environmental justice more generally. The higher this awareness is domestically, the greater may be the perception of unjustified double standards globally which in turn can be a motivating force in civil society of affluent countries to press for greater environmental justice globally. It helps to foster the idea that human harm from environmental degradation is a human rights violation *wherever* it occurs. Certainly, the ethics and demands generated by the influential Environmental Justice movement within the United States, which was originally concerned primarily with the effects of 'environmental racism' particularly in the siting of hazardous industries, have furnished principles that are now appealed to by campaigners in many other, poorer, parts of the world.[9] This is hardly surprising, since once the criticism of socially discriminatory decisions within a domestic setting invokes the norm that decisions should in fact respect common humanity, and once that norm is recognized, there can be no boundary to its applicability.

I therefore conclude that the demands of justice—in principle and in practice—require extending environmental rights to the poor rather than denying them to citizens of affluent countries.

6.3 The value of constitutional environmental rights for poorer societies

In this final section I offer a very brief overview of the role played by constitutional environmental rights in less developed parts of the world to show: that the need for them in poorer countries is not nullified by the need for economic development; that poorer countries can draw benefit from the international environmental rights norms generated in other jurisdictions; and that environmental rights have in fact been effectively upheld by constitutional courts in poor countries.

6.3.1 The need for environmental rights is not nullified by imperatives of development

Environmental protection is sometimes spoken of as a luxury that the poor can ill afford. Yet in fact, for the poor, environmental issues can be a matter of survival or basic health and well-being conditions.

More often than not, environmental protection is crucial to the poor, who are more primary product and natural-resource dependent than the rich. Fishermen, loggers, peasants, hunters and gatherers—all are less able to escape environmental degradation than are the well off; moreover, all are better able to take advantage of labor-intensive nature-based opportunities than are the rich. The stake of the poor in environmental protection is fundamental.   (Herring 1999)

There is an intimate connection between environmental protection and food production which is critical for the poorest populations (Shelton 1992), as is the protection of water supplies

(McCaffrey 1992). Still, regarding the overall priorities of poorer states, some suggest that while it may be true that issues of environmental sustainability may prove important in the longer run, the pressures to develop economically in the shorter term militate against giving any priority to environmental protection. Yet, even if this may in some contexts and in some ways be true, it is not the whole story, and cannot simply be generalized as a principle justifying giving 'development' priority over environment. As was noted in the previous section, the poor are generally likely to be in more pressing need of environmental protection than the rich. Waiting to become rich enough to attend to environmental problems can be a seriously mistaken strategy.

The perception remains in some quarters that environmental protection is something that can and should be addressed only when a country is rich enough to do so, and that it is a 'low rate of return' activity. Yet the evidence is mounting that local environmental destruction can accelerate the poverty spiral not only for future generations, but even for today's population. It is obvious that countries which recklessly deplete their natural resources are destroying the basis of prosperity for future generations, but... as forests disappear and water is exhausted or polluted, it is the poor of today, especially children and women, who suffer most. (UNEP 2002: www.unep.org/aeo/234.htm)

Certainly there are tensions between the imperatives of environmental protection and economic development, but that is true not only for the poor. What is generally more true for the poor than for the rich is that they cannot afford to buy themselves freedom from environmental threats, and attempts at development under existing circumstances, with prevailing economic relations globally, appear unlikely to achieve the satisfaction of either imperative for the poor. The poor generally therefore have a particularly serious and pressing need for the protections promised by environmental rights (Trindade 1992).

Many of the world's very poorest countries are in Africa, and yet a significant number of African countries have a constitutional right to an adequate environment.[10] This fact alone does not necessarily mean the rights are always effective,[11] especially under existing circumstances, but it does mean that those states see it as being in their interest to have them, and thus serves to rebut that part of the criticism which suggests constitutional environmental rights are only aspired to by rich states. Part of the reason is that environmental protection is not conceived as a luxury but as an integral part of their most pressing concerns.

The 47 countries comprising sub-Saharan Africa depend more on their natural resource base for economic and social needs than any other region in the world. Two-thirds of sub-Saharan Africa's people live in rural areas and rely on agriculture and other natural resources for income. However, the environmental resource base of the region is shrinking rapidly. Environmental problems of sub-Saharan Africa include pollution of water supplies, massive deforestation, loss of soil and soil fertility, and a dramatic decline in biodiversity throughout the region. With increasing numbers of people migrating to urban centers in search of employment, sustainable development likely will become a priority for the protection of sub-Saharan Africa's complex and diverse environment. (http://greennature.com/article487.html)

Moreover, while parts of Africa have weak states and are plagued by a wide range of conflicts, these are frequently a result of environmental stress and scarcity (Mugabe and Tumushabe 2002). In most African countries there is struggle against socioeconomic and environmental problems on all fronts, and it is appropriate to see these as interrelated struggles rather than separate ones that involve trade-offs at the level of basic principle. Support for environmental rights is as important as for socioeconomic development more generally. The need for established internationally recognized norms is part of the process. For despite the prevalence of constitutional environmental rights in Africa, most of the countries have yet to interpret or apply them, and when a court considers an issue for the first time it will often look to cases from other countries.

Faced with compelling facts, a judge may wish to act but still be reluctant to issue a decision that risks being regarded as 'radical' or 'unprecedented'. The will and capacity of judges in particular African states to intervene on behalf of the environmental interests of their citizenry will be enhanced by an increased awareness of the decisions already taken by their counterparts in other national contexts, most particularly in other developing nations, where legal and political-economic conditions are comparable.

By applying and enforcing the environmental provisions contained in most national constitutions, judges across the world have enhanced recognition of the principle that enjoyment of decent environmental conditions is a fundamental human right. Invoking their decisions promises, therefore, to lend strength to the arm of judges and environmental advocates in Africa. The path has been cleared. It only remains to follow it. (Bruch and Coker 1999)

6.3.2 Illustrations of permeability in practice

Latin America is a region of less developed countries, which has been particularly progressive in relation to the right to a healthy environment. An express right to an adequate environment has been provided in the constitutions of most states in the region.[12] Fabra and Arnal cite cases referring to a wide range of applications of the right, which include protecting forests of indigenous peoples from logging, protecting villagers from adverse effects of industrial air pollution, protecting a national park, protecting mangroves from coastal shrimp farming industries, fisheries, and wildlife in a lagoon, protecting against using a cliff as a waste dump, and even the right to enjoy the ocean's view when impaired by the construction of a wall.

Fabra stresses how in order to strengthen arguments for the protection of the right to a healthy environment in their reasoning, judges in Latin America have relied heavily on international law: courts in Colombia, for instance, 'have taken decisions which point to model forms of implementing international law, using it as a direct legal source in their decisions to protect the right to a healthy environment' (Fabra 1996: 262). Finding legal support in even non-binding sources of international law such as the Ksentini Report, 'the Colombian courts have not only written

remarkable decisions in defence of the right to a healthy environment, but have also ordered concrete enforcement measures to
this end' (Fabra 1996: 262–3). In the conclusion of her study of
environmental rights in Ecuador, Fabra writes:

The positive influence of international law on national legal systems mate-
rializes in two ways: first, international legal mechanisms—particularly in
the field of human rights—provide alternative means for individuals to
seek redress of human rights and environmental violations when domestic
legal systems are ineffective. Secondly, the progressive development of
international law can facilitate positive changes in domestic law and
policy.   (Fabra 1996: 261–2)

The influence can work both ways. Domestic precedents can have
influence internationally—and not only domestic precedents
from affluent Western democracies.

   This process has become an increasingly dynamic one in recent
years. Ankersen reports that the character of the legal and judicial
systems in Latin America and the Caribbean has been undergoing
fundamental change.

Traditionally weak judiciaries are emboldened; precedent as a jurisprudential decision tool has become increasingly important; the apparatus of
administrative law has become more sophisticated and complex; increasingly sophisticated reporting systems and the 'globalization' of shared
jurisprudence through contemporary communication media have all contributed to the development of law in the region. (Ankersen 2003: 207)

He highlights in particular the importance of the Internet as
'a robust information dissemination tool whose significance in
fostering jurisprudential knowledge sharing cannot be under-
stated'. 'The post Rio convergence of environmental law and the
internet with democratic reform movements already under way in
the region has dramatically hastened the pace of innovation in
environmental law'. The relative ease with which decisions at all
judicial levels can be systematically reported, catalogued, and
shared means that although these decisions 'do not create

"precedent" in the way the common law tradition lawyers are accustomed to thinking, they are considered jurisprudence and, as such, have persuasive value, increasingly so'. Ankersen also observes that civil law judges must be aware that more lawyers are reading the opinions they are writing.

Something that is evident from the judgements cited by commentators is that there was a readiness of Latin American judges to refer, even prior to the express constitutionalizing of it, to a right to a healthy environment; this, plus the fact of the right's subsequent constitutionalization, and support for it, suggests the judiciary has been going very much with the grain of a sense of social and environmental justice that ordinary people feel to have been so widely betrayed in the region. Out of this same groundswell has emerged a dramatic expansion, in number and range, of environmental law organizations and networks in the region. Out of this proliferation a robust alliance of environmental public interest lawyers has emerged. Thus the core of environmental litigation in Latin America now, notes Fabra, consists of public interest actions, especially those formulated in human rights terms. These are also significant in the context of South Asia.

6.3.3 Poorer countries in the avant garde of environmental human rights jurisprudence

A further consideration that tends to counter the suggestion that environmental rights should be seen as a luxury to be pursued only by rich states is that some of the most interesting precedents for the effecting of such rights emanate from South and Southeast Asia. 'Probably more than any other jurisdiction on Earth, the Republic of India has fostered an extensive and innovative jurisprudence on environmental rights' (Anderson 1996b: 199); and perhaps the single most important case to date is from the Philippines.

In a report for the OHCHR-UNEP initiative on human rights and the environment, Jona Razzaque has examined the recent development of human rights and the environment in India, Bangladesh, and Pakistan. She notes that the nature of environmental and human rights problems is similar in all South Asian countries:

common concerns include water pollution (lack of control on the pollution of rivers, irresponsible construction of dams and barrages, lack of access to drinking water free from toxin or other contaminants, increased use of agro-chemicals/pesticides, storage and transportation of dangerous goods in package forms and pollution due to noxious liquid substances); degradation of marine and coastal resources (heavy metal contamination by industrial affluent, dumping of land based solid waste into the sea; heavy coastal construction, inland mining, poor land use practices, over fishing, destructive fishing techniques, shrimp cultivation); loss of coastal habitats and deforestation (substantial loss of mangrove forests, unplanned commercial fisheries); land based pollution (rapid industrialisation, mining, logging, firewood collection, livestock grazing, land degradation, hazardous waste, waste water disposal); water logging and salinity (rapid spread of irrigation, indiscriminate use of agro-chemicals, over exploitation of ground water); and air pollution (rapid and unplanned urbanisation, industrial pollution, increasing transport, domestic refuse, coal consumption, energy use pattern, fly-ash).   (Razzaque 2002: 3–4)

India, Pakistan, and Bangladesh do not provide express constitutional rights to an adequate environment but instead their judiciaries have used various existing constitutional rights to protect the environment. In particular, the right to life, a fundamental right, has been extended to include the right to a healthy environment in judgements of the courts.

Already in the 1985 case of *Kendra* the Indian Supreme Court had alluded to the 'right of people to live in [a] healthy environment with minimal disturbance of [the] ecological balance', but without however discussing the source of this right. In 1990, though, 'the link between environmental quality and the right to life was made explicit by a constitutional bench of the Supreme Court in *Charan Lal* v. *Union of India*, reviewing the constitutional validity of the Bhopal Act' (Anderson 1996b: 216). In 1991, the Indian Supreme Court interpreted the right to life guaranteed by Article 21 of the Constitution to include the right to a clean environment. In *Subash Kumar* v. *Bihar*, the Court observed that a fundamental right to life 'includes the right of enjoyment of pollution-free water and air for full enjoyment of life'. Anderson observes, 'in a country where the most serious costs of environmental damage fall upon impoverished and illiterate groups with limited access to the courts, the new environmental right is championed as a legal gateway to speedy and inexpensive legal remedy' (Anderson 1996b: 199).

The constitution of Bangladesh does not explicitly provide for the right to a healthy environment either in its directive principles or as a fundamental right. However, in the 1994 case of *Dr. M. Farooque* v. *Bangladesh*, the Supreme Court agreed with the argument of the petitioner that the constitutional 'right to life' extends to include the right to a safe and healthy environment. 'It encompasses within its ambit, the protection and preservation of environment, ecological balance free from pollution of air and water, sanitation without which life can hardly be enjoyed' (Chowdhury, J. in Razzaque 2002: 9). A similar willingness of courts to establish the right to a clean environment has also been demonstrated in Pakistan. In several cases the Pakistan judiciary 'firmly established a right to a healthy environment' (Razzaque 2002: 12).

It is significant to note that in most instances, courts have upheld environmental protection despite economic loss. '"Just like an industry which cannot pay minimum wages to its workers cannot exist," so tanneries must set up primary treatment plants to continue in operation' (*Mehta*, in Anderson 1996b: 220). Anderson acknowledges that a more difficult question arises where environmental protection conflicts not with the individual right to do business, but rather the collective or public interest in aggregate economic growth and development. He notes, though, that the need to strike a balance between economic growth and the protection of natural resources and the environment has been recognized by courts in a number of decisions (p. 220).

Undoubtedly questions of balancing growth with environmental protection are essentially political, but there are also good reasons why the
higher courts may fulfil this function: they are trusted as relatively neutral arbiters, they may draw upon expert committees for advice, and they
may be less hesitant to take difficult or unpopular decisions. If the courts
must balance, the conceptual system of rights may provide a useful tool,
since procedures for balancing other rights ... are well-established.
(p. 221)

What the illustrations from South Asia show, amongst other
things, is that there is a clear need and role for recognition of a
constitutional right to an adequate environment. If the activist
judiciaries of India and Pakistan have been able to infer such a
right from other constitutional materials, this shows its need and
relevance; but also, because it depends on activism, indirectly
suggests that an explicit right needs to be provided, especially in
states where judicial activism is not so readily accepted.

It is appropriate to close this brief overview of precedents with
the one which to date has the potentially most far-reaching
implications. The 1990 Philippine case of *Oposa Minors* has
attracted wide international attention and become a legal landmark regarding the concept of intergenerational responsibility.
This is a concept that has not been an explicit topic of the present
book, which has still needed to argue for environmental rights of
contemporaries, and yet some inspiration may be drawn from
finding that courts can sometimes do things in practice which in
theory, it is supposed, they cannot.

In March 1990, the lawyer Antonio Oposa, on behalf of his three
children and of fourty-one other children from all the geographic
regions of the country, filed a class suit representing their generation and generations yet unborn. The Government of the
Philippines was named defendant and the action sought to force
the cancellation of all the country's logging concessions. The complaint was based on the argument that the constitution guarantees
every person the right to a healthy and sound environment and
that the conduct of the defendant—that is, the practice of issuing
licences for rainforest exploitation in the Philippines—seriously
encroached upon the constitutional rights of the plaintiffs and, at

the same time, strongly interfered with the constitutional rights of succeeding generations not yet born.

The plaintiffs alleged that there were only 800,000 hectares left of virgin forests where commercial logging was taking place. They further alleged that the Government granted 92 timber license agreements covering an area of 3.9 million hectares, an act characterized as a grave abuse of discretion. At the rate of deforestation occurring in the country estimated at 120,000 hectares per year, the 800,000 hectares virgin forest reserve would be totally decimated in less than 10 years. Thus, there would be nothing left for the plaintiff-children to use, enjoy and benefit from when their time comes to be of age.   (Oposa 1997)

Upon motion of the Government, the trial court dismissed the case without hearing on the ground of, among others, lack of cause of action. It was in overturning this decision that the Supreme Court issued its remarkable ruling. The Supreme Court unanimously ruled *en banc* that the case indeed had a special and novel element in that the petitioners asserted that they represented their generation as well as generations yet unborn, yet it was willing to entertain the claim, finding 'no difficulty in ruling that they can, for themselves, for others in their generation and for the succeeding generations, file a class suit'.

The Court further stated, and significantly in the light of issues discussed in earlier chapters of this book:

While the right to a balanced and healthful ecology is to be found under the Declaration of Principles and State Policies and not under the Bill of Rights, it does not follow that it is less important than any of the civil and political rights enumerated in the latter.

In fact, the Court considered that the right 'belongs to a different category of rights altogether for it concerns nothing less than self-preservation and self-perpetuation...the advancement of which may even be said to predate all governments and constitutions' *Oposa et al.* v. *Factoran et al.* (224 SCRA 792 [1993]:804–5).

Antonio Oposa himself has himself written of the significance of this case:

it is the first case decided by the highest court of a country which discussed and implemented what had heretofore been a rhetorical call for responsibility to future generations for the world's natural resources. Furthermore, it brings to the fore—in the personal voice of our children— the imminent likelihood that our generation's wanton use of the earth's resources will inevitably adversely impact our children's generation and generations yet unborn.   (Oposa 1997)

6.4 Conclusion

A human right to an environment adequate for one's health and well-being is not a luxury. Moral consistency dictates it should apply equally to all. It will only apply to all if it is enforced, and, in a world still divided into states, it has to be enforced in the present epoch by states. That is why I have maintained in this book that the right ought to figure among the most fundamental commitments of a state as a fundamental right of the constitution. This will not be sufficient to guarantee effective enjoyment of the substance of the right for all people, but I believe that on balance the arguments show it would be wrong to deny that it is necessary.

Notes

1. The 1962 declaration referred to spells out some of these. David Held (2003) also summarizes some developments. For instance, a new concept expounded in 1967 as a means for rethinking the legal basis of the appropriation and use of resources was the 'common heritage of mankind' which was enshrined in the 1979 Convention on the Moon and Other Celestial Bodies and the 1982 Convention on the Law of the Sea:

    Further significant conventions were signed in the 1980s and 1990s to combat the risks flowing from degraded resources and other environmental dangers, including the international movement of hazardous wastes (the Basel Convention in 1989), air pollution involving the emission of CFCs (the Vienna and Montreal Protocols in 1985 and 1987), as well as a range of treaties regulating transboundary acid rain in Europe and North America. ...Principle 7 of the (Rio) Declaration demanded that states cooperate 'in a spirit of global partnership to conserve, protect and restore the health and integrity of the Earth's ecosystem'; and Principle 12 called for 'environmental measures addressing transboundary or global environmental problems' which should, 'as far as possible, be based on an international consensus' (1993: 4, 5). The results included conventions on biodiversity, climate change and greenhouse emissions, the rain forests, and the establishment of international arrangements for transferring technology and capital from the North to the South for environmental programs. (Held 2003: 171)

2. This is to capture a major 'North/South' fault line manifest, for example, at the 1992 Rio Conference.

3. The Basel Convention of 1989 prohibited the export of hazardous waste from rich countries except for recovery of raw materials or for recycling, but this exception provided a loophole through which 90 per cent of the waste continued to pass. It is estimated that the Organisation for Economic Cooperation and Development (OECD) countries exported 2,611,677 metric tons of hazardous wastes to non-OECD countries between 1989 and 1994 when agreement on a full ban was reached which would close the loophole at least 'in theory'. Martinez-Alier notes that although the Basel Convention has had a positive effect, the issue is far from over.

4. The figures cited are intended only as 'ballpark' ones, since there is a certain amount of variation between different published calculations referred to, and they are regularly modified. The orders of magnitude, though, are consistent between them. The following sources have been consulted: Venetoulis, Chazan, and Gaudet (2004); Wackernagel (1997); and subsequent updates of this report which are available at www.redefiningprogress.org.

5. How the (in-)justice of current allocations appears will depend to some extent on how one conceives of issues of global justice generally. Corresponding to the moral cosmopolitan outlook, justice would seem to require prima facie that each individual's footprint should be equal (if we adapt the position of, for example, Beitz 1979), or at least minimally adequate (e.g. Pogge 2002), regardless of where they live, which would entail some dramatic redistribution to counteract the current dramatic inequalities. A principled nationalist, by contrast, who would give priority to the sovereign right of each state over its own territorial resources, could amend that right so that it becomes a right to utilize resources equivalent to its own 'ecological capacity'—regardless of discrepancies between states. From the standpoint of

principled nationalism, then, justice would be satisfied if each state made a footprint that was equal to or less than its ecological capacity.

Issues can be raised for each of these general stances, but from an ethical standpoint, those affecting the nationalist position are most troubling. While it is not possible for me to explore these issues here, there is one observation I wish to make. This is that the idea of principled nationalism I have referred to would differ in its implications from those outlined in the nationalist perspective of David Miller (1999). A key reason he gives for opposing the general principle of global redistribution of natural resources is that if redistribution could be achieved it would be self-defeating by introducing a perverse incentive. If some pattern of just distribution of natural resources is to be maintained over time, he argues, then nations which are frugal and conservationist in their use of resources will constantly have to transfer resources to nations which are profligate in their use of them in order to maintain the required pattern. This argument is nullified, however, if we think of the 'pattern' in terms of equitable entitlements to ecological space. For then the profligate nation is seen to have drawn more heavily on the available ecological space than has the frugal nation, and thus disrupted the 'pattern' in such a way that any 'transfers' are due *from* the profligate nation, not to it. Thus when the issue is framed in terms of ecological space, the incentives work the 'right way'.

6. Since the beginning of the nineties, the concept of ecological debt has been promoted by in particular Latin American ngo's. Acción Ecológica (Ecuador) has played a key role in trying to define the concept and bringing together Southern action groups and ngo's. This led among other things in 2000 to the creation of the Southern Peoples' Ecological Debt Creditors Alliance. Friends of the Earth International decided in November 1999 to launch a campaign on ecological debt. The ecological debt was also incorporated in the demands of Jubilee 2000, the worldwide campaign for the cancellation of the financial debt.   (Centre for Sustainable Development 2004)

According to Martinez-Alier, writing with specific reference to Latin America, the relationship between the External Debt and Ecological Debt has two principal aspects. First is that exports are undervalued as their price does not include the various local and global social and environmental costs; second, the obligation to pay the External Debt and its interest leads to a depredation of the environment (and thus an increase in ecological debt). The idea of ecologically unequal trade is also unavoidable (see also Hornborg 2001 on this).

7. Certainly, the ecological debt is not easy to quantify, especially to the extent that it has arisen historically, for, as Martinez-Alier asks, 'How can we give monetary value to the devastating effects on the American and Oceanic populations of the European invasions, to the wars against the indigenous communities, to the cultural genocide, to the slavery or the resource looting produced since the XVI century?' (Martinez-Alier 2002: 179). Given that its point is to provide a moral reason for cancelling one debt rather than literally pressing for the payment of another, the precise calculation of ecological debt as such may be to some extent beside the point. The actual point is well articulated by Pogge: 'The better-off enjoy significant advantages in the use of a single natural resource base from whose benefits the worse-off are largely, and without compensation, excluded' (Pogge 2002: 202).

8. Hence, there is good reason to take 'uncompensated exclusion from the use of natural resources' (Pogge 2002: ch.8) together with other forms of environmental injustice. Hancock (2003), a work that came to my attention too late to include a discussion of in this book, argues for both of these as distinct rights.

9. For instance, the 'Environmental Justice Principles' developed originally at the 1991 People of Color Environmental Justice Leadership Summit in Washington, DC, were taken as the blueprint for the 'Bali Principles of Climate Justice'. The latter were developed in preparation for the 2003 Johannesburg Earth Summit by an international coalition of NGOs at the final preparatory negotiations for the Earth Summit in Bali in June 2002. (The NGOs included CorpWatch, Friends of the Earth International, Greenpeace International, Groundwork, Indigenous Environmental Network, Indigenous Information Network, National Alliance of People's Movements, National Fishworkers Forum, OilWatch Africa, OilWatch International, Southwest Network for Environmental and Economic Justice, Third World Network, and World Rainforest Movement.)

10. In a report which includes a survey and analysis of constitutional environmental provisions in fifty-three African states, Bruch Coker and VanArsdale (2000) found that at least thirty-two countries in Africa (approx. two-thirds) have some constitutional provisions ensuring the right to a healthy environment. They predict that the number is likely to increase. Most African constitutions that have been amended since 1992 generally have environmental provisions; the main exceptions being non-secular states. There are no distinctive differences in the content or context of the provisions around

the continent (which also has the regional agreement of the African Charter).

11. While in some African countries judicial review remains elusive, constitutionalism is changing this situation around Africa, as 'countries such as Niger increasingly allow citizens to invoke their constitutional rights in court' (Bruch, Coker, and VanArsdale 2000: 6). Bruch, Coker, and VanArsdale (2000) also note a gradual liberalization of standing for example in Tanzania, Kenya, Botswana, Nigeria, and Zimbabwe—the Supreme Court of the latter recognizing standing of a human rights organization to challenge the constitutionality of death sentences. The cost of bringing public interest cases is clearly a major issue given that the people most affected by environmental degradation tend to be the poorest and most marginalized. A number of African constitutions have sought to address the financial obstacles to access to justice (e.g. Guinea-Bissau, Madagascar, Mozambique, Malawi, and Namibia) (p. 55). Nevertheless, the authors expect that many governments will remain cautious about encouraging litigation, particularly since much of it would be directed at themselves (p. 56). There have been some precedents of applying the right in Africa: for instance, in the 1996 case of *Minister of Health and Welfare* v. *Woodcarb (Pty) Ltd,* a South African court 'held that the defendant's unlicensed emission illegally interfered with the neighbours' constitutional right to a healthy environment' (p. 16). Bruch and Coker believe, 'The process of opening courts to citizens to enforce their constitutional rights strengthens the judiciary, empowers civil society, and fosters an atmosphere of environmental accountability' (Bruch and Coker 1999: 1).

12. Ankersen (2003) gives: 'Argentina, Article 41, 1a parte, cap.2/; Brazil, Art. 5/, LXXIII; Chile, Article 19(8); Colombia, Article 79; Costa Rica, Article 50; Cuba, Article 27; Ecuador, Article 23, El Salvador, Article 117; Guatemala, Article 97; Guyana, Article 25, Chapter 2; Haiti, Title I Chapter 2, Article 52-1 & Articles 253-258; Honduras, Articles 145 & 172-3; Mexico, Title 1/, Chapter 1/, Artcle 4/, Paragraph 4/; Nicaragua, Article 60; Panama, Article 114 & 115; Paraguay, Tit 1d's, db's & g's, Chapter 1, Section 2, Artlicle 7&38; Peru, Article 2/Paragraph 22; Uruguay, Article 47; Venezuela, Article 127. In addition, in the English-speaking Caribbean, Jamaica has pending constitutional reforms that would confer the right. Bill Entitled An Act to Amend the Constitution of Jamaica to provide for a Charter of Rights and Freedoms and for Connected Matters, Chapter III 13.3(I).' The wordings of all the Latin

American constitutional environmental rights are to be found col-
lected at www.georgetown.edu/pdba/Comp/Ambiente/derecho.html.

Examples of the right to a healthy environment being upheld in
Chile, Argentina, Costa Rica, and Brazil are given in Bruch, Coker,
and VanArsdale (2000: 19–20).

Bibliography

Acevedo, Mariana T. (2000), 'The Intersection of Human Rights and Environmental Protection in the European Court of Human Rights', *New York University Environmental Law Journal*, 8(2): 437–96.

Aiken, William (1992), 'Human Rights in an Ecological Era', *Environmental Values*, 1(3): 191–203.

Alston, Philip (1984), 'Conjuring Up New Human Rights: A Proposal for Quality Control', *American Journal of International Law*, 78: 607–21.

—— (1999), 'A Framework for the Comparative Analysis of Bills of Rights', in Philip Alston (ed.), *Promoting Human Rights Through Bills of Rights: Comparative Perspectives*, Oxford: Oxford University Press.

Anderson, Michael R. (1996a), 'Human Rights Approaches to Environmental Protection: An Overview', in Alan E. Boyle and Michael R. Anderson (eds.), *Human Rights Approaches to Environmental Protection*, Oxford: Clarendon Press.

—— (1996b), 'Individual Rights to Environmental Protection in India', in Alan E. Boyle and Michael R. Anderson (eds.), *Human Rights Approaches to Environmental Protection*, Oxford: Clarendon Press.

Ankersen, Thomas T. (2003), 'Shared Knowledge, Shared Jurisprudence: Learning to Speak Environmental Law Creole (Criollo)', *Tulane Environmental Law Journal*, 16: 807–30.

Anton, Donald K. (1998), 'Comparative Constitutional Language for Environmental Amendments to the Australian Constitution', www. elaw.org/resources/text.asp?ID=1082.

Barry, Brian (1996), *Justice as Impartiality*, Oxford: Clarendon Press.

Batty, Helen and Gray, Tim (1996), 'Environmental Rights and National Sovereignty', in Simon Cancy, David George, and Peter Jones (eds.), *Natural Rights, International Obligations*, Boulder and Oxford: Westview Press.

Beitz, Charles (1979), *Political Theory and International Relations*, Princeton and Oxford: Princeton University Press.

—— (1994), 'Cosmopolitan Liberalism and the States System', in Chris Brown (ed.), *Political Restructuring in Europe: Ethical Perspectives*, London: Routledge.

Bellamy, Richard (1995), 'The Constitution of Europe: Rights or Democracy?', in Richard Bellamy, Vittorio Bufacchi, and Dario

Castiglione (eds.), *Democracy and Constitutional Culture in the Union of Europe*, London: Lothian Foundation Press.

Birnie, Patricia W. and Boyle, Alan E. (1992), *International Law and the Environment*, Oxford: Clarendon Press.

Bloch, Ernst (1961), *Naturrecht und menschliche Würde*, Frankfurt: Suhrkamp Verlag.

Boch, Christine (1999), 'The *Iroquois at the Kirchberg*, or, some Naïve Remarks on the Status and Relevance of Direct Effect', Harvard Jean Monnet Working Paper 6/99.

Börzel, Tanja A. (2002), 'Member State Responses to Europeanization', *Journal of Common Market Studies*, 40(2): 193–214.

Bowden, Paul (1995), 'Citizen Suits—Can We Afford Them and Do We Need Them Anyway?', in David Robinson and John Dunkley (eds.), *Public Interest Perspectives in Environmental Law*, London: Wiley Chancery.

Boyle, Alan (1996), 'The Role of International Human Rights Law in the Protection of the Environment', in Alan E. Boyle and Michael R. Anderson (eds.), *Human Rights Approaches to Environmental Protection*, Oxford: Clarendon Press.

—— and Anderson, Michael R. (eds.) (1996), *Human Rights Approaches to Environmental Protection*, Oxford: Clarendon Press.

Brubaker, Elizabeth (1995), *Property Rights in the Defence of Nature*, London and Toronto: Earthscan.

Bruch, Carl and Coker, Wole (1999), 'What's the Basis of Africa's Environmental Law?', *Innovation*, 6(2): 7–9.

—— Coker, Wole, and VanArsdale, Chris (2000), *Constitutional Environmental Law: Giving Force to Fundamental Principles in Africa*, Washington, DC: Environmental Law Institute.

Brandl, Ernst and Bungert, Hartwin (1992), 'Constitutional Entrenchment of Environmental Protection: A Comparative Analysis of Experiences Abroad', *Harvard Environmental Law Review*, 16(1): 1–100.

Callicott, J. Baird (1980), 'Animal Liberation: A Triangular Affair', *Environmental Ethics*, 2: 311–38.

Cambridge University Department of Land Economy (1999), 'Environmental Court Project Final Report', London: Department of the Environment, Transport and the Regions (former).

Cameron, James and MacKenzie, Ruth (1996), 'Access to Environmental Justice and Procedural Rights in International Institutions', in Alan E. Boyle and Michael R. Anderson (eds.), *Human Rights Approaches to Environmental Protection*, Oxford: Clarendon Press.

Caranta, Roberto (1993), 'Governmental Liability after Francovich', *Cambridge Law Journal*, 5: 272–97.

Centre for Sustainable Development (2004), 'Elaboration of the Concept of Ecological Debt', Research Project Description, Belgium: Ghent University, http://cdonet.ugent.be/english/ecological_debt.htm.

Churchill, R. R., (1996), 'Environmental Rights in Existing Human Rights Treaties', in Alan E. Boyle and Michael R. Anderson (eds.), *Human Rights Approaches to Environmental Protection*, Oxford: Clarendon Press.

Cranston, Maurice (1967a), 'Human Rights, Real and Supposed', in D. D. Raphael (ed.), *Political Theory and the Rights of Man*, Bloomington and London: Indiana University Press.

—— (1967b), 'Human Rights: a Reply to Professor Raphael', in D. D. Raphael (ed.), *Political Theory and the Rights of Man*, Bloomington and London: Indiana University Press.

Daniels, Norman (1975), 'Equal Liberty and Unequal Worth of Liberty', in Norman Daniels (ed.), *Reading Rawls*, Oxford: Blackwell.

Day, Martyn (1995), 'Shifting the Environmental Balance', in David Robinson and John Dunkley (eds.), *Public Interest Perspectives in Environmental Law*, London: Wiley Chancery.

—— (1998), *Environmental Action: A Citizen's Guide*, London, Chicago: Pluto Press.

Deimann, Sven and Dyssli, Bernard (1995), *Environmental Rights: Law, Litigation and Access to Justice*, London: Cameron May.

DeMerieux, Margaret (2001), 'Deriving Environmental Rights from the European Convention for the Protection of Human Rights and Fundamental Freedoms', *Oxford Journal of Legal Studies*, 21(3): 521–61.

Desgagné, Richard (1995), 'Integrating Environmental Values into the European Convention on Human Rights', *American Journal of International Law*, 89(2): 263–94.

de-Shalit, Avner (2000), *The Environment: Between Theory and Practice*, Oxford: Oxford University Press.

Dobson, Andrew (1996), 'Democratising Green Theory: Preconditions and Principles', in Brian Doherty and Marius de Geus (eds.), *Democracy and Green Political Thought*, London and New York: Routledge.

—— (1998), *Justice and the Environment*, Oxford: Oxford University Press.

—— (2000), *Green Political Thought*, 3rd edn., London and New York: Routledge.

—— (2003), *Citizenship and the Environment*, Oxford: Oxford University Press.

Douglas-Scott, S. (1996), 'Environmental Rights in the European Union—Participatory Democracy or Democratic Deficit?', in Alan E. Boyle and Michael R. Anderson (eds.), *Human Rights Approaches to Environmental Protection*, Oxford: Clarendon Press.

Du Bois, F. (1996), 'Social Justice and the Judicial Enforcement of Environmental Rights and Duties', in Alan E. Boyle and Michael R. Anderson (eds.), *Human Rights Approaches to Environmental Protection*, Oxford: Clarendon Press.

Eckersley, Robyn (1996), 'Greening Liberal Democracy: The Rights Discourse Revisited', in Brian Doherty and Marius de Geus (eds.), *Democracy and Green Political Thought*, London and New York: Routledge.

Epp, Charles R. (1998), *The Rights Revolution: Lawyers, Activists, and Supreme Courts in Comparative Perspective*, Chicago: University of Chicago Press.

Fabra Aguilar, Adriana (1994), 'Enforcing the Right to a Healthy Environment in Latin America', *Review of European Community and International Environmental Law (RECIEL)*, 3(4): 215–22.

Fabra, Adriana (1996), 'Indigenous Peoples, Environmental Degradation, and Human Rights: A Case Study', in Alan E. Boyle and Michael R. Anderson (eds.), *Human Rights Approaches to Environmental Protection*, Oxford: Clarendon Press.

—— and Arnal, Eva (2002), 'Review of Jurisprudence on Human Rights and the Environment in Latin America', Background Paper No. 6 for joint UNEP–OHCHR Expert Seminar on Human Rights and the Environment, 14–16 January, Geneva.

Fabre, Cecile (2000), *Social Rights under the Constitution: Government and the Decent Life*, Oxford: Clarendon Press.

Fernandez, Edesio (1996), 'Constitutional Environmental Rights in Brazil', in Alan E. Boyle and Michael R. Anderson (eds.), *Human Rights Approaches to Environmental Protection*, Oxford: Clarendon Press.

Fernandez, José L. (1993), 'State Constitutions, Environmental Rights Provisions, and the Doctrine of Self-Execution: A Political Question?', *Harvard Environmental Law Review*, 17(2): 333–88.

Fijalkowski, Agata and Fitzmaurice, Malgosia (eds.) (2000), *The Right of the Child to a Clean Environment*, Aldershot and Burlington, VT: Ashgate.

Fisher, Elizabeth (2001), 'Is the Precautionary Principle Justiciable?', *Journal of Environmental Law*, 13(3): 315–34.

—— (2003), 'Review of The Precautionary Principle in the Twentieth Century', *Journal of Environmental Law*, 15(1): 104–6.

Führ, Martin and Roller, Gerhard (eds.) (1991), *Participation and Litigation Rights of Environmental Associations in Europe*, Frankfurt-am-Main: Peter Lang.

Gewirth, Alan (1982), *Human Rights: Essays on Justification and Applications*, Chicago: Chicago University Press.

Glazewski, Jan (1996) 'Environmental Rights in the New South African Constitution', in Alan E. Boyle and Michael R. Anderson (eds.), *Human Rights Approaches to Environmental Protection*, Oxford: Clarendon Press.

Goodin, Robert (1992), *Green Political Theory*, Cambridge: Polity Press.

Gormley, W. Paul (1976), *Human Rights and Environment: The Need for International Cooperation*, Leyden: A. W. Sijthoff.

Gravelle, Ryan K. (1997), 'Enforcing the Elusive: Environmental Rights in East European Constitutions', *Virginia Environmental Law Review*, 16(4): 633–60.

Grosz, Stephen (1995), 'Access to Environmental Justice in Public Law', in David Robinson and John Dunkley (eds.), *Public Interest Perspectives in Environmental Law*, London: Wiley Chancery.

Habermas, Jürgen (1990), *Moral Consciousness and Communicative Action*, trans. Christian Lenhardt and Shierry Weber Nicholsen, Cambridge: Polity Press.

—— (1997), *Between Facts and Norms*, trans. William Rehg, Cambridge: Polity Press.

—— (1998), 'Remarks on Legitimation through Human Rights', *Philosophy and Social Criticism*, 23: 157–71.

Hancock, Jan (2003), *Environmental Human Rights: Power, Ethics and Law*, Aldershot and Burlington, VT: Ashgate.

Handl, Günther (1992), 'Human Rights and the Protection of the Environment: A Mildly Revisionist View', in Antonio Augusto Cançado Trindade (ed.), *Human Rights, Sustainable Development and the Environment*, San José de Costa Rica and Brasilia: Instituto Interamericano de Derechos Humanos.

Harding, Andrew (1995), 'Do Public Interest Environmental Law and the Common Law Have a Future Together?', in David Robinson and John Dunkley (eds.), *Public Interest Perspectives in Environmental Law*, London: Wiley Chancery.

Hart, H. L. A (1984), 'Are There Any Natural Rights?, in Jeremy Waldron (ed.), *Theories of Rights*, Oxford: Oxford University Press.

Hattingh, Johan and Attfield, Robin (2002), 'Ecological Sustainability in a Developing Country such as South Africa? A Philosophical and Ethical Inquiry', *International Journal of Human Rights*, 6(2): 65–92.

Hayward, Tim (1995), *Ecological Thought: An Introduction*, Cambridge: Polity Press.

—— (1998a), *Political Theory and Ecological Values*, Cambridge: Polity Press.

Hayward, Tim (1998b), 'Anthropocentrism', in Ruth Chadwick (ed.), *Encyclopedia of Applied Ethics*, Vol. 1, San Diego: Academic Press.

Held, David (2003), 'The Changing Structure of International Law: Sovereignty Transformed?' in David Held and Anthony McGrew (eds.), *The Global Transformations Reader: An Introduction too the Globalization Debate*, 2nd edn., Cambridge: Polity Press.

Herring, Ronald J. (1999), 'International Justice, Poverty and the Environment', Paper given at World Bank Conference, Johannesburg, www.worldbank.org/poverty/wdrpoverty/joburg/herring.pdf.

Hohfeld, Wesley N. (1918), *Fundamental Legal Conceptions*, New Haven: Yale University Press.

Holder, Jane (1996), 'Case Law Analysis. A Dead End for Direct Effect?: Prospects for Enforcement of European Community Environmental Law by Individuals. Comitato di Coordinamento per la Difesa della Cava and Others v Regione Lombardia and Others', *Journal of Environmental Law*, 8(2): 313–35.

Hornborg, Alf (2001), *The Power of the Machine: Global Inequalities of Economy, Technology, and Environment*, Walnut Creek, CA, Lanham, MD, and Oxford: AltaMira Press.

Howarth, David (2002), 'Muddying the Waters: Tort Law and the Environment from an English Perspective', *Washburn Law Journal*, 41: 469–513.

Howarth, William (2002), 'Environmental Human Rights and Parliamentary Democracy', *Journal of Environmental Law*, 14: 353–89.

Hunt, Murray (1998), *Using Human Rights Law in English Courts*, Oxford: Hart.

Jackman, Martha and Porter, Bruce (1999), 'Women's Substantive Equality and the Protection of Social and Economic Rights Under the *Canadian Human Rights Act*', Status of Women Canada Policy Research Fund Publication, www.swc-cfc.gc.ca/pubs/factsheets/200211_020510_7_e.html.

Jans, Jan (1996), 'Legal Protection in European Environmental Law: An Overview', in Han Somsen (ed.), *Protecting the European Environment: Enforcing EC Environmental Law*, London: Blackstone Press.

Jones, Peter (1994), *Rights*, Basingstoke: Macmillan.

Kiss, Alexandre (1992), 'Sustainable Development and Human Rights', in Antonio Augusto Cançado Trindade (ed.), *Human Rights, Sustainable Development and the Environment*, San José de Costa Rica and Brasilia: Instituto Interamericano de Derechos Humanos.

—— and Shelton, Dinah (1999), *International Law*, 2nd edn., Ardseley, NY: Transactional.

Krämer, Ludwig (1996), 'Direct Effect of EC Environmental Law', in Han Somsen (ed.), *Protecting the European Environment: Enforcing EC Environmental Law*, London: Blackstone Press.

Ksentini, Fatma (1994), *Final Report of the UN Sub-Commission on Human Rights and the Environment*, UN Doc.E/CN.4/Sub.2/1994/9.

Lau, Martin (1996), 'Islam and Judicial Activism', in Alan E. Boyle and Michael R. Anderson (eds.), *Human Rights Approaches to Environmental Protection*, Oxford: Clarendon Press.

Lefevere, Jürgen (1996), 'State Liability for Breaches of Community Law', *European Environmental Law Review*, 5: 237–42.

Light, Andrew and Katz, Eric (eds.) (1996), *Environmental Pragmatism*, London and New York: Routledge.

Lorenzen, Myriam (2002), Background Paper on the Project 'Environmental Human Rights', Amsterdam: ANPED, The Northern Alliance for Sustainability, www.anped.org.

Macrory, Richard (1996), 'Environmental Citizenship and the Law: Repairing the European Road', *Journal of Environmental Law*, 8(2): 219–35.

McCaffrey, Stephen C. (1992), 'Water, Human Rights and Sustainable Development', in Antonio Augusto Cançado Trindade (ed.), *Human Rights, Sustainable Development and the Environment*, San José de Costa Rica and Brasilia: Instituto Interamericano de Derechos Humanos.

Marchant, Gary E. (2003), 'From General Policy to Legal Rule: Aspirations and Limitations of the Precautionary Principle', *Environmental Health Perspectives* 111(14): 1799–803.

Marshall, T. H. (1950), *Citizenship and Social Class: And Other Essays*, Cambridge: Cambridge University Press.

Martin, Rex (1993), *A System of Rights*, Oxford: Clarendon Press.

Martinez-Alier, Joan (2002), *The Environmentalism of the Poor: A Study of Ecological Conflicts and Valuation*, Cheltenham and Northampton, MA: Edward Elgar.

—— Simms, Andrew and Rijnhout, Leida (2003), 'Poverty, Development and Ecological Debt', *Jubilee South Journal* www.deudaecologica.org/a_poverty.html.

Merrills, J. G. (1996), 'Environmental Protection and Human Rights: Conceptual Aspects', in Alan E. Boyle and Michael R. Anderson (eds.), *Human Rights Approaches to Environmental Protection*, Oxford: Clarendon Press.

Miller, Christopher (1995), 'Environmental Rights: European Fact or English Fiction?', *Journal of Law and Society*, 22(3): 374–97.

—— (1998), *Environmental Rights: Critical Perspectives*, London and New York: Routledge.

Miller, Christopher (1999), 'The European Convention on Human Rights: Another Weapon in the Environmentalist's Armoury', *Journal of Environmental Law*, 11(1): 157–76.

—— (2003), 'Environmental Rights in a Welfare State? A Comment on DeMerieux', *Oxford Journal of Legal Studies*, 23(1): 111–25.

Miller, David (1999), 'Justice and Global Inequality', in Andrew Hurrell and Ngaire Woods (eds.), *Inequality, Globalization, and World Politics*, Oxford: Oxford University Press.

Mugabe, John and Tumushabe Godber W. (2002), 'Ecological Roots of Conflict in Eastern and Central Africa: Towards a Regional Ombudsman', in Lyuba Zarsky (ed.), *Human Rights and the Environment: Conflicts and Norms in a Globalizing World*, London and Toronto: Earthscan.

Nickel, James W. (1983), 'The Human Right to a Safe Environment: Philosophical Perspectives on Its Scope and Justification', *Yale Journal of International Law*, 18: 281–95.

Norton, Bryan G. (1984), 'Environmental Ethics and Weak Anthropocentrism', *Environmental Ethics*, 6: 133–48.

—— (1991), *Toward Unity Among Environmentalists*, Oxford: Oxford University Press.

Odhiambo, Michael Ochieng (1998), 'Legal and Institutional Constraints to Public Interest Litigation as a Mechanism for the Enforcement of Environmental Rights and Duties in Kenya', Fifth International Network for Compliance and Enforcement (INECE) Conference, Vol. 2: 265–70, www.inece.org/5thvol2/odhiambo.pdf.

Olsen, Johan P. (2002), 'The Many Faces of Europeanization', *Journal of Common Market Studies*, 40(5): 921–52.

Oposa, Antonio (1997), 'The Power to Protect the Environment', www.oposa.com/oposa_family/environment2.htm.

Palerm, Juan R. (1999), 'Public Participation in Environmental Decision Making: Examining the Aarhus Convention', *Journal of Environmental Assessment Policy and Management*, 1(2): 229–44.

Pathak, R. S. (1992), 'The Human Rights System as a Conceptual Framework for Environmental Law', in Edith Brown Weiss (ed.), *Environmental Change and International Law: New Challenges and Directions*, Tokyo: United Nations University Press.

Pogge, Thomas (2002), *World Poverty and Human Rights: Cosmopolitan Responsibilities and Reforms*, Cambridge and Malden, MA: Polity/ Blackwell.

Popović, Neil A. F. (1996a), 'In Pursuit of Environmental Human Rights: Commentary on the Draft Declaration of Principles on Human Rights and the Environment', *Columbia Human Rights Law Review*, 27(3): 487–603.

—— (1996*b*), 'Pursuing Environmental Justice with International Human Rights and State Constitutions', *Stanford Environmental Law Journal*, 15: 338–74.

Raphael, D. D. (1967), 'Human Rights, Old and New', in D. D.Raphael (ed.), *Political Theory and the Rights of Man*, Bloomington and London: Indiana University Press.

Rawls, John (1972), *A Theory of Justice*, Oxford: Oxford University Press.

—— (1999), *The Law of Peoples*, Cambridge, MA and London: Harvard University Press.

Raz, Joseph (1986), *The Morality of Freedom*, Oxford: Clarendon Press.

Razzaque, Jona (2002), 'Human Rights and the Environment: The National Experience in South Asia and Africa', Background Paper No.4, Joint UNEP–OHCHR Expert Seminar on Human Rights and the Environment, Geneva.

Redclift, Michael and Sage, Colin (1999), 'Resources, Environmental Degradation, and Inequality', in Andrew Hurrell and Ngaire Woods (eds.), *Inequality, Globalization, and World Politics*, Oxford: Oxford University Press.

Redgwell, Catherine (1996), 'Life, the Universe and Everything: A Critique of Anthropocentric Rights', in Alan E. Boyle and Michael R. Anderson (eds.), *Human Rights Approaches to Environmental Protection*, Oxford: Clarendon Press.

Rest, Alfred (1997), 'Improved Environmental Protection through an Expanded Concept of Human Rights in Europe?', *Environmental Policy and Law*, 27(3): 213–16.

Roman, Andrew J. (1981), 'Locus Standi: A Cure in Search of a Disease?', in John Swaigen (ed.), *Environmental Rights in Canada*, Toronto: Butterworths.

Rosas, Allan (1995), 'State Sovereignty and Human Rights: Towards a Global Constitutional Project', *Political Studies*, 43: 61–78.

Ruhl, J. B. (1997), 'An Environmental Rights Amendment: Good Message, Bad Idea', *Natural Resources and Environment*, 11(3): 46–9.

Sachs, Aaron (1995), *Eco-Justice: Linking Human Rights and the Environment*, Washington, DC: Worldwatch Institute.

Sagoff, Mark (1988), *The Economy of the Earth*, Cambridge: Cambridge University Press.

—— (1998), 'Carrying Capacity and Ecological Economics', in David A. Crocker and Toby Linden (eds.), *Ethics of Consumption: The Good Life, Justice, and Global Citizenship*, Lanham, MD: Rowman and Littlefield.

Saward, Michael (1998), *The Terms of Democracy*, Cambridge: Polity Press.

Sax, Joseph L. (1990), 'The Search for Environmental Rights', *Journal of Land Use and Environmental Law*, 6: 93–105.

Scheinen, Martin (1994), 'Direct Applicability of Economic, Social and Cultural Rights: A Critique of the Doctrine of Self-Executing Treaties', in Krzysztof Drzewicki, Catarina Krause, and Allan Rosas (eds.), *Social Rights as Human Rights: A European Challenge*, Åbo: Åbo Akademi University.

Schneider, Mycle et al. (2001), *Possible Toxic Effects from the Nuclear Reprocessing Plants at Sellafield (UK) and Cap de la Hague (France)*, European Parliament: Scientific and Technical Options Assessment (STOA) Programme.

Schwartz, Herman (1992), 'In Defense of Aiming High: Why Social and Economic Rights Belong in the New Post-Communist Constitutions of Europe', *East European Constitutional Review*, 16: 13–16.

Shelton, Dinah (1992), 'Environmental Protection and the Right to Food', in Antonio Augusto Cançado Trindade (ed.), *Human Rights, Sustainable Development and the Environment*, San José de Costa Rica and Brasilia: Instituto Interamericano de Derechos Humanos.

—— (1993), 'Environmental Rights in the European Community', *Hastings International and Comparative Law Review*, 16: 557–82.

—— (2002), 'Human Rights, Health and Environmental Protection: Linkages in Law and Practice', *Health and Human Rights Working Paper Series No. 1*, World Health Organisation.

Shiva, Vandana (2003), 'Food Rights, Free Trade, and Fascism', in Matthew J. Gibney (ed.), *Globalizing Rights*, The Oxford Amnesty Lectures 1999, Oxford: Oxford University Press.

Shue, Henry (1980), *Basic Rights: Subsistence, Affluence, and US Foreign Policy*, Princeton: Princeton University Press.

—— (1988), 'Mediating Duties', *Ethics*, 98(4): 687–704.

Simms, Andrew (2001) 'Ecological Debt—Balancing the Environmental Budget and Compensating Developing Countries', World Summit on Sustainable Development Briefing Paper, International Institute for Environment and Development, London: www.iied.org.

Singh, Rabinder (1997), *The Future of Human Rights in the United Kingdom: Essays on Law and Practice*, Oxford: Hart.

Somsen, Han (1996), '*Francovich* and its Application to EC Environmental Law', in Han Somsen (ed.), *Protecting the European Environment: Enforcing EC Environmental Law*, London: Blackstone Press.

Soriano, Leonor Moral (2001), 'Environmental "Wrongs" and Environmental Rights: Challenging the Legal Reasoning of English Judges', *Journal of Environmental Law*, 13(3): 297–313.

Stein, Justice Paul (1995), 'A Specialist Environmental Court: An Australian Experience', in David Robinson and John Dunkley (eds.), *Public Interest Perspectives in Environmental Law*, London: Wiley Chancery.

Stevenson, C. P. (1983), 'A New Perspective on Environmental Rights after the Charter', *Osgoode Hall Law Journal*, 21(3): 390–421.

Sunstein, Cass R. (1993), 'Against Positive Rights', *East European Constitutional Review*, 2: 35–8.

Swaigen, John and Woods, Richard E. (1981), 'A Substantive Right to Environmental Quality', in John Swaigen (ed.), *Environmental Rights in Canada*, Toronto: Butterworths.

Thornton, Justine and Tromans, Stephen (1999), 'Human Rights and Environmental Wrongs: Incorporating the European Convention on Human Rights: Some Thoughts on the Consequences for UK Environmental Law', *Journal of Environmental Law*, 11(1): 35–56.

Trindade, Antonio Augusto Cançado (1992), 'The Contribution of International Human Rights Law to Environmental Protection, with Special Reference to Global Environmental Change', in Edith Brown Weiss (ed.), *Environmental Change and International Law: New Challenges and Directions*, Tokyo: United Nations University Press.

—— (ed.) (1992), *Human Rights, Sustainable Development and the Environment*, San José de Costa Rica and Brasilia: Instituto Interamericano de Derechos Humanos.

Tromans, Stephen (2001), 'Environmental Court Project: Final Report', *Journal of Environmental Law*, 13(3): 423–6.

Tucker, John C. (2000), 'Constitutional Codification of an Environmental Ethic', *Florida Law Review*, 52: 299–326.

UNEP (2002), *Africa Environment Outlook: Past, Present and Future Perspectives*, www.urep.org/aeo/index.htm

Upton, William (1998), 'The European Convention on Human Rights and Environmental Law', *Journal of Planning Law*, April: 315–20.

Venetoulis, Jason, Chazan, Dahlia, and Gaudet, Christopher (2004), *Ecological Footprint of Nations*, Redefining Progress: www.Redefining Progress.org.

Viljanen, Veli-Pekka (1994), 'Abstention or Involvement? The Nature of State Obligations Under Different Categories of Rights', in Krzysztof Drzewicki, Catarina Krause, and Allan Rosas (eds.), *Social Rights as Human Rights: A European Challenge*, Åbo: Åbo Akademi University.

Wackernagel, Mathis et al. (1997), *Ecological Footprints of Nations: How Much Nature do They Use? How Much Nature do They Have?*, Toronto: ICLEI.

Wackernagel, Mathis et al. and Rees, William (1996), *Our Ecological Footprint: Reducing Human Impact on the Earth*, Philadelphia: New Society.

Waldron, Jeremy (1993), 'A Rights-Based Critique of Constitutional Rights', *Oxford Journal of Legal Studies*, 13: 18–51.

Walzer, Michael (1980), 'The Moral Standing of States: A Response to Four Critics', *Philosophy and Public Affairs*, 9(3): 209–29.

—— (1985), *Spheres of Justice: A Defence of Pluralism and Equality*, Oxford: Blackwell.

Weber, Stefan (1991), 'Environmental Information and the European Convention on Human Rights', *Human Rights Law Journal*, 12(5): 177–185.

Weiss, Edith Brown (1992), *Environmental Change and International Law: New Challenges and Dimensions*, Tokyo: United Nations University Press.

World Commission on Environment and Development (WCED) (1987), *Our Common Future*, The Brundtland Report, Oxford: Oxford University Press.

Witzsch, Günther (1990), 'The Right to a Healthy and Decent Environment in New Lesotho Constitution?', *Lesotho Law Journal*, 6: 167–73.

—— (1992), *Lesotho Environment and Environmental Law*, Roma: Environmental Law Project.

Woolf, Lord (1992), 'Are the Judiciary Environmentally Myopic?', *Journal of Environmental Law*, 4(1): 1–14.

—— (1995), 'Preface', to David Robinson and John Dunkley (eds.), *Public Intrest Perspectives in Environmental Law*, London: Wiley Chancery.

Wynne, Brian (1994), 'Scientific Knowledge and the Global Environment', in Ted Benton and Michael Redclift (eds.), *Social Theory and the Global Environment*, London and New York: Routledge.

Index

THE ART OF MAKING DANCES